Doing a Research Project in English Studies

Doing a Research Project in English Studies is the essential guide to undertaking research and developing academic English literacy skills for students new to research. With a particular focus on the needs of students in contexts where English is used as a foreign or an additional language, this accessible textbook takes the reader through the research process in five main sections:

1 getting started (arriving at a topic, interacting with a supervisor);
2 finding bibliographic resources;
3 collecting data;
4 developing academic writing skills;
5 preparing for the oral defence.

Each chapter contains exercises; the answer key facilitates independent study throughout. Extracts from published research articles provide an invaluable illustration of the features of academic writing. This is a must-have resource for advanced undergraduate and postgraduate students embarking on a research project in English studies.

Louisa Buckingham is a Lecturer in Applied Language Studies and Linguistics at the University of Auckland. She has published on topics including academic writing, sociolinguistics, and English as a lingua franca.

Doing a Research Project in English Studies

A guide for students

Louisa Buckingham

LONDON AND NEW YORK

First published 2016
by Routledge
2 Park Square, Milton Park, Abingdon, Oxon OX14 4RN

and by Routledge
711 Third Avenue, New York, NY 10017

Routledge is an imprint of the Taylor & Francis Group, an informa business

British Library Cataloguing-in-Publication Data
A catalogue record for this book is available from the British Library

Library of Congress Cataloging-in-Publication Data
Buckingham, Louisa.
Doing a research project in English studies / by Louisa Buckingham.
pages cm
Includes bibliographical references and index.
1. English language—Rhetoric—Study and teaching (Higher) 2. Academic writing—Study and teaching (Higher) 3. English language—Study and teaching (Higher)—Foreign speakers. 4. Research—Study and teaching (Higher) 5. Report writing—Study and teaching (Higher). I. Title.
P301.5.A27B83 2016
808'.0420711—dc23 2015011495

ISBN: 978-1-138-84691-3 (hbk)
ISBN: 978-1-138-84693-7 (pbk)
ISBN: 978-131-572-085-2 (ebk)

Typeset in Goudy by
Keystroke, Station Road, Codsall, Wolverhampton

Contents

Preface

This textbook is intended for senior-year undergraduate students and Master's students with little research experience in contexts where English is a foreign language (EFL) or an additional language (EAL). It guides students and course instructors through the process of undertaking a research project in English studies (whether in English language, literature, translation or education) from the initial topic conceptualization stage through to the final presentation of the research project. For this initial research experience to be successful, students need to demonstrate an acceptable proficiency level in a wide variety of skills including conducting effective literature searches, communicating appropriately with an array of people, purposeful reading and, of course, writing.

An important objective of this book is to support the development of students' academic writing competence. This is often one of the chief challenges experienced by EFL/EAL students when embarking on their research project, as their undergraduate degree programme may have offered limited opportunity to develop advanced writing skills. While writing-related activities can be found throughout the textbook, Chapters 7 and 8 are dedicated to writing development. Chapter 3 focuses on the supervisor–student relationship in recognition that the successful completion of a research project also relies on the guidance and collaboration of an instructor. For many students, this may be the first time they experience this type of individual academic guidance and this section is intended to stimulate class discussion on issues that might arise in the course of supervision. Chapter 6 offers brief coverage of various data collection methods commonly employed by students at this level. This is because many university courses that instruct students on writing their research project also provide practical input on data collection methods. This textbook is not intended as an introduction to research methodology, however.

Many chapters include examples of students' writing, whether in the form of email communication or research writing. These examples are not entirely inventions; rather, they were modelled closely on students' work I have received over the years while teaching this type of course at different locations.

The first version of this textbook was written between semesters at the University of Nizwa (Oman) and selected material was piloted on senior-year undergraduate courses at this university and later also on the MA TEFL programme at Bilkent University (Turkey). While writing the book, I endeavoured to avoid unnecessary cultural references and idioms frequently used in English-language textbooks intended for use in native-speaker settings, as these contribute to making such texts needlessly difficult for EFL/EAL students to use independently and more challenging for instructors to use effectively in the classroom. As the textbook is envisaged for individual student use in the classroom and at home, I make frequent use of the second-person pronoun. In acknowledgement of the fact that students may undertake their first research project either as a senior-year undergraduate or at Master's level, depending on the structure of their degree programme, this book is intended for both target groups.

This textbook was largely written in a context in which access to quality academic journals was limited. Due to the prohibitive cost of accessing such material, many students and lecturers around the world are unable to consult such sources for study and research purposes and instead largely rely on open-source material. In recognition of such limitations, the approach in this book has been to summarize the main findings from selected studies in the boxes entitled 'Insights from the literature' included in most chapters. These enable users of this book to see how findings from published research have informed the exercises and recommendations included in each chapter. These boxes also provide instructors of mixed-ability classes with an opportunity to develop extension exercises related to these reading texts to challenge faster or more advanced students.

In addition, with generous permission from the respective authors, excerpts from published research articles have been included in many chapters to illustrate certain features of academic writing. While I acknowledge that research articles and undergraduate/Master's theses represent different writing genres, the two text types display many commonalities. As research articles often comprise the bulk of students' literature reviews, these excerpts also provide the opportunity to focus on developing strategic reading skills.

I thank Alice Chik (Macquarie University), Chi-Fen Emily Chen (National Kaohsiung First University of Science and Technology) and Lina Lee (University of New Hampshire) for granting me permission to reproduce excerpts from their published articles. I also thank John Morley (Manchester University) for permission to incorporate examples from his *Academic Phrasebank* collection and Mark Davies (Brigham Young University) for permission to use examples from the *Corpus of Contemporary American English.*

Finally, I gratefully acknowledge my debt to my colleagues on the Open Society Institute (OSI) Pre-Academic Summer School Programme. I have benefited much from their company and expertise over many a summer from Issyk-Kyl in Kyrgyzstan to Bilgi University in Istanbul and to Payap University in Chiang Mai; much of the material in this book was inspired by work done during these intensive summer programmes. I am grateful to the OSI Scholarship Department for supporting intellectual endeavours in Eastern Europe and Central Asia over the decades.

Acknowledgements

The publishers want to thank the copyright holders for letting them reproduce their work:

Chen, C.E. (2006). The development of e-mail literacy: From writing to peers to writing to authority figures. *Language Learning & Technology*, *10*(2), 35–55.

Chik, A. (2014). Digital gaming and language learning: Autonomy and community. *Language Learning & Technology*, *18*(2), 85–100.

Davies, M. (2008–). *Corpus of Contemporary American English: 450 million words, 1990–present*. Available at http://corpus.byu.edu/coca/.

Lee, L. (2011). Blogging: Promoting learner autonomy and intercultural competence through study abroad. *Language Learning & Technology*, *15*(3), 87–109.

Morley, J. (n.d.). *Academic Phrasebank*. The University of Manchester. Available at www.phrasebank.manchester.ac.uk/

Every effort has been made to contact copyright holders. If any have been inadvertently overlooked, the publishers will be pleased to make the necessary arrangements at the first opportunity.

1 Introduction

Whether you are embarking on your undergraduate senior-year research project or your Master's thesis, this research is both the final assessed work required for graduation and probably also the first piece of real research you have undertaken. In this sense, it represents both the successful completion of your degree and an initiation into conducting research. As your study will likely be assessed by a committee, this is also probably the first time that you have written for a wider audience than just your instructor. This book will guide you through the different stages of preparing your research project.

Each chapter covers a different topic related to the research process; most chapters include reading texts, together with examples, tips and exercises to check comprehension and allow you to apply what you learn. Some exercises encourage you to think about how our understanding of appropriate academic writing practice is culturally dependent. The answer key to these exercises is found at the back of the book together with the Appendices, which contain extra input related to some chapters. Exercises that are best done with a partner (or in a group) are labelled 'Discussion task'. There is no answer key to these tasks, as they are designed to elicit a variety of responses. Also, the appropriate answers for the questions posed here usually depend on your specific context; consider these tasks an opportunity to discuss the expectations or 'norms' in your setting. Most chapters include components entitled 'Insights from the literature'. These sections summarize research findings published by well-known authors in the field. Through these texts, you will become familiar with concepts and terms that relate to topics in this book. These summaries demonstrate that much of the information and advice contained in this book is based on research findings. By reading this brief summary of the literature and doing the accompanying Discussion task, you will gain an understanding of the choices available to you when composing texts and how conventions in academic writing in English have evolved. Throughout the book, the following icons signal each of these additional components:

 **Example**

 **Exercise**

 **Discussion task**

Throughout this book, you will read about how four students (Zareen, Zurab, Zeina and Zakia) approached different sections of their research project. While these students are not real people, their experiences are common to many students in contexts where English is used as an additional or foreign language. This icon will be used to indicate input from one of these students:

In addition, excerpts from three published research articles are included to illustrate particular features of academic texts, and to provide practice in reading authentic academic texts written for other scholars. By the end of this book, you will have a better understanding of how to read such texts strategically and use them to inform your own research. This icon is used to signal these texts:

The three texts used are the following:

- Chen, C.E. (2006). The development of e-mail literacy: From writing to peers to writing to authority figures. *Language Learning & Technology*, *10*(2), 35–55.
- Chik, A. (2014). Digital gaming and language learning: Autonomy and community. *Language Learning & Technology*, *18*(2), 85–100.
- Lee, L. (2011). Blogging: Promoting learner autonomy and intercultural competence through study abroad. *Language Learning & Technology*, *15*(3), 87–109.

Learning from your research project

Doing a research project:

- deepens your understanding of how we arrive at what we consider to be 'knowledge'.

- teaches you to distinguish between opinions and common ideas and what we think of as 'knowledge' or even 'facts'.
- helps you develop critical thinking skills. As you review information collected from books or from other people, you need to distinguish between information that seems reliable, objective or factual, and information that is based on opinion and is likely to be subjective.
- teaches you to plan your work and organize your time. A research project involves a series of steps that have to be undertaken within a determined period of time. This is an opportunity to develop time management and planning skills at the start of your professional career.
- teaches you how to investigate a topic and locate relevant information using the library and electronic resources, such as the websites of institutions, organizations or newspapers. This involves the ability to sift through and organize coherently large amounts of information.
- helps to develop your objective reasoning skills. In most cases, your research project will contain one or more claims about what you believe to be true and these should be supported by convincing argumentation or evidence.
- broadens your understanding of the beliefs and practices of people in your community and extended social context. If you use methods such as interviews, questionnaires or observations to collect data, you will gain experience in interacting with people beyond your usual social circle.
- enables you to engage with a topic in greater depth. After graduating, you may not have the opportunity to learn again in this methodical, structured manner with the guidance of a supervisor, and you are unlikely to have access to so many interesting books and journals!

All of the aforementioned skills are useful in professional contexts. They are all 'multi-purpose', transferable skills that will build your confidence in your ability to compile and analyse information and work with a variety of people in different social contexts. Above all, the experience of doing an original piece of research will give you confidence in your ability to investigate a topic, develop an informed point of view and convince other people of your ideas.

If, after finishing your research project, you feel that you enjoyed this experience, consider enrolling on a research-oriented higher degree such as a Master's or a PhD. Your supervisor or department should be able to provide advice on this.

The stepping stones of your research project

Undertaking research, whether a small- or a large-scale project, entails carrying out multiple activities; some occur simultaneously, some separately. The list below is intended to help you visualize the process, although your own sequence of activities may be a little different. Think of this as just a guide. Although arranged in list form for the sake of convenience, the research process is not linear and does not comprise discrete moves. For instance, the literature search is an ongoing process that usually continues right up until the end of the research project; you will likely be drafting different sections of your work at different points of the research process, and the need to revise and redraft is constant.

1. Choose a topic.
2. Contact your assigned supervisor.
3. Obtain authorization from your department to research your chosen topic.
4. Begin your literature search.
5. Read as much as possible and take notes while reading.
6. Plan your project.
7. Develop your data collection instrument (if you intend to collect data).
8. Begin your data collection.
9. Make notes of what you might write in each section of your project.
10. Start drafting your project.
11. Revise your work.
12. Consult the Writing Centre for feedback on your writing (if your university has one).
13. Send each chapter to your supervisor for comments and corrections.
14. Ensure the formatting of your project is in accordance with university requirements.
15. Ensure the list of references is complete.
16. Submit the completed project to your supervisor for a final revision.
17. Receive approval from your supervisor that you are ready to present your work.
18. Prepare copies of the final version and submit them to the department.
19. Prepare a brief oral presentation on your project (if this is a requirement at your university).

Discussion task 1.1

Your research project from start to finish

Looking at the list above, discuss with a partner the activities you expect to undertake. (Add any activities you think are missing.) Note down the numbers in the approximate order in which you will do the activities, indicating which could be done simultaneously. Consider how much time you will need for each activity.

2 The preliminaries
Getting started

Choosing a topic

For many students, the process of choosing a topic is fraught with anxiety and indecision. In some contexts, rather than expecting students to arrive at a topic individually, the department provides a list of potential topics. Where a choice is available, issues influencing the decision will include the student's areas of interest and anticipated career path, as well as previous experience of learning and teaching languages. At undergraduate level, many students have not yet formed a clear idea of their specific academic interests or where they can expect to work after graduation and this can hinder the process of arriving at a topic. In such cases, the following prompts may be helpful. As indicated below, it is helpful to inform one's thinking from a variety of sources and reflect critically on the information one gathers. This will be particularly helpful during the process of narrowing the research topic and formulating a research question (or questions).

Your university studies

Look at the course material and lecture notes from the subjects included in your degree programme. Consider the following:

- What did you enjoy doing? What did you find interesting?
- What did you find difficult? What did you dislike studying?
- What study-related problems did your fellow students experience during their studies?
- What topics or issues might be particularly relevant to your future career?

Your school years

Think back to your school years. What issues or problems do you remember related to teaching, learning and communication in the school context? These may be specific to teachers and the teaching process, fellow students, learning materials, the curriculum or the involvement of parents. They might be shared across different schools and the broader teaching and learning community in your country or region, or alternatively they may be the product of specific localized conditions.

Your work experience

Some students may already have professional language teaching or translation experience, whether from full-time or casual part-time work. Such experience can provide valuable insights into language-related issues that arise in work-related contexts, some of which may invite research. If you have work experience, reflect on issues that arose during your interaction with learners, colleagues, texts and didactic materials.

The world around you

Consider how English is used in the business world around you; English is often used in shops, advertising and in the media. This is not a neutral phenomenon, as the use of a particular language or dialect in professional and social contexts may give rise to certain tensions. To gain an understanding of how different people may experience the use of different languages or dialects in their social and professional environment, both printed texts and personal informants are invaluable sources of information.

Non-academic texts such as magazines, newspapers or institutional websites are often an important source of information about topics of current concern or importance in society. Taking notes of recurring topics or issues, different points of view and examples is a good way of tracking public discussions and framing of topics in the public arena. For instance, you may identify certain tensions relating to language instruction or language use within particular contexts that invite further exploration.

Digital texts often represent a less formal text type but they are also an important medium for the use of English. Consider the use of English on the Internet and in telecommunications within your cultural context. English commonly appears in emails and text messages, and on social networking sites. What could you investigate about language use in these texts?

Texts are not the only sources of information; social contacts, whether family or acquaintances, can help stimulate your thinking. For instance, talk to people in your family who are teachers or who work in institutions where foreign languages are used (such as businesses or banks) and enquire into their experience and views on the position and use of particular languages or dialects.

In addition to what people do with language, how people perceive language and speakers of language is a further domain of study. This may, for instance, lead you to consider perceptions of the presence of English in academic or professional contexts, perceptions of linguistic ability, or questions related to perceptions of particular social or regional dialects.

The university library

Browsing the bookshelves in the sections for English language, linguistics, translation and education can be an effective way to gather ideas. While your university likely has an electronic catalogue, leafing through the physical books in specific subject areas can provide insights into commonly addressed topics and may help to generate ideas for further work. Once you identify topics that appear relevant to your context or interests, search for other books on the same general theme.

> **Tip 2.1**
>
> **What research is *not***
>
> - Your research project is *not* a personal essay about your opinions and ideas.
> - It is *not* a summary of information you find in books and articles.
> - It is *not* a collection of long quotes or paragraphs you have copied from different sources from the Internet.

Narrowing your topic

The topic you initially choose may be very broad. It is quite normal to start with a general topic and then go through a process of narrowing or refining it to arrive at a research question (or questions) or topic with a specific focus. Typically this will involve narrowing it to a particular group of people, level and location or context. For example, you won't investigate 'English language learners', but rather learners (male or female) in a particular year of study on a particular degree programme in a particular department (or school). If you are thinking about investigating learners' understanding or use of a particular aspect of English (whether a syntactic structure or vocabulary) or skill, you will likely focus on a particular context of use, such as a specific text type or communicative context.

If majoring in literature, you can narrow your topic by limiting your study to a particular theme, period, author or work. You might examine the characters, the depiction of places or people, or perhaps metaphors that appear in the work(s) you select. Alternatively, you could compare the works by two authors, or novels from different periods. In addition to studying the content of the literary work, you might consider investigating issues related to the production, reception and translation of the work. For instance, you might investigate how the author's personal beliefs, whether religious, philosophical or political, are represented in his/her work, how the work of another author influenced the style of writing of your chosen author, or the sociopolitical reasons why a particular author or work was popular at a given time. Sometimes a particular novel becomes successful long after the author is dead; alternatively, the novel is more popular in translation in a foreign country than it ever was in the original in the author's own country – you might ask yourself why. For this type of project, you will do library work; that is, the information you need for your project will be found in reference texts in the library and online.

If your project is in the area of translation, you might compare language use in a particular text type (for example, advertising texts, product descriptions or medical texts) in each of the two languages you study. As terminology in particular specialized fields, such as law, may lack a one-to-one correspondence in the source and target language, you might choose to investigate this lack of congruence and enquire into how translators have approached the translation of specialized texts. Alternatively, you might examine how students in a particular year of study translate certain linguistic features into the target language. Translation majors with an interest in literature might investigate how particular cultural concepts have been conveyed in the translated work of a particular author.

An additional consideration when formulating a research topic concerns access to the information or data needed to help you answer your research questions. A research topic that seeks to prove or disprove an idea or claim may be based on a hypothesis. This is a narrowly focused claim, something you believe to be true based, for example, on observations of your environment combined with insights acquired from academic literature. To test your hypothesis, that is, to determine whether convincing evidence exists to support your claim, you will probably collect and analyse data. Thus, before deciding to undertake this type of study, you need to ensure you are able to compile (and analyse) the required data.

Examples 2.1 to 2.4, illustrating how students arrived at their research topic, may help you develop your own ideas. Read these descriptions before doing Exercise 2.1.

Example 2.1

English education

Zareen noticed that female and male university students in her country seemed to approach their studies differently; she also noticed that within her English education degree programme, girls usually achieved higher grades than boys. She looked at the statistics on education and literacy provided by UNESCO[1] on the Internet. These showed that in her country more girls completed primary, secondary and tertiary education than boys.

This led to her interest in exploring the *general topic* of gender and achievement in language studies at university. After talking to people and reading introductory literature on gender and educational achievement, she decided that students' grades were related to their attitude towards their studies. This prompted her to formulate a more *specific topic*: What attitudes do male and female students in their third and fourth years in the Department of Foreign Languages have towards their studies?

As 'attitudes' was still a very fairly general concept, she talked to teachers and the parents of her friends about the reasons why girls were more successful and sought information on motivation and achievement in introductory textbooks in the library. As a result, she identified two main factors linked to motivation and achievement that she considered likely to be most relevant to her cultural context: social pressure and job prospects.

Following this, Zareen's main hypothesis was that female students on her study programme were more successful than male students because they invested more effort in their studies than male students, as evidenced by their behaviour. Her second, related, hypothesis was that girls felt more social pressure to achieve than boys (i.e. their families had higher expectations of them). Her third hypothesis was that more female students than male students believed that their achievement at university would strongly influence their ability to find a job related to their studies upon graduating.

To test her hypotheses, Zareen looked at students' behaviour (class attendance, completion of homework, hours of study a week), their results (their level of achievement), and their beliefs and their family's beliefs about the importance of success at university and the likelihood of finding a suitable job upon graduating. She used a questionnaire to collect data on these related topics. These data provided her with evidence that could be used to test her claim.

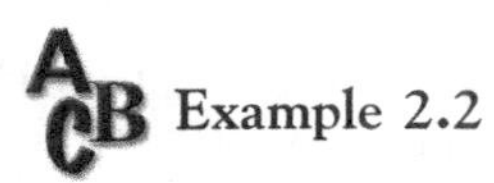

Example 2.2

Applied linguistics

During his studies, Zurab noticed that he found it easier to speak to the instructor in person than to write an email. He asked his friends about their experience of writing emails to instructors and discovered that most students were uncomfortable writing such emails and were convinced they did not do it well. This suggested that investigating the *general topic* of how students write emails to their teachers might be worthwhile. When he looked at his friends' emails, he found many different types, so he decided to narrow his focus to a *specific topic* by only looking at examples where a student makes a request. This seemed difficult to do in a foreign language, as many students claimed they felt shy about making a request and unsure of the appropriate language to use. As his *research question*, Zurab proposed to investigate how students express politeness when they formulate requests to teachers by email.

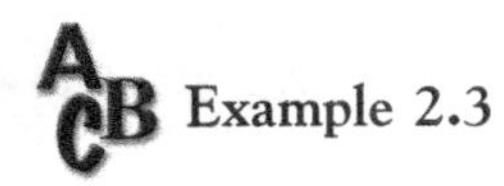

Example 2.3

Translation

Zeina was interested in the *general topic* of how students translated polysemous words when translating from the second language (L2) into the first language (L1). She was aware that students often select the incorrect meaning of the word for the given context, resulting in an incorrect translation. After talking to her peers and her lecturers, she was able to narrow her focus to the *specific topic* of translation students' awareness of the polysemous nature of words in English and their ability to translate them into their L1. After narrowing her topic, she was able to formulate a hypothesis: students who demonstrate an awareness of the different denotations of a particular word in the L2 will be more likely to translate it appropriately into the L1.

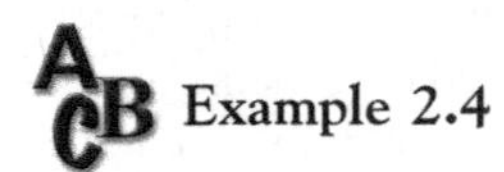

Example 2.4

Literature

As her *general topic*, Zakia wanted to examine differences in the depiction of women in literary works from a particular period in two different cultural contexts. Her preliminary idea was that the particular social roles assigned to women in novels produced in different cultural contexts reflect different notions of what is socially acceptable for each gender in the respective contemporary sociocultural context. After consulting academic literature on how gender is performed in different social and cultural contexts, she narrowed her focus to a *specific topic*. She decided to compare the depiction of the social roles of middle-class women in an early twentieth-century novel by a British author with a novel by an Egyptian author from the same period.

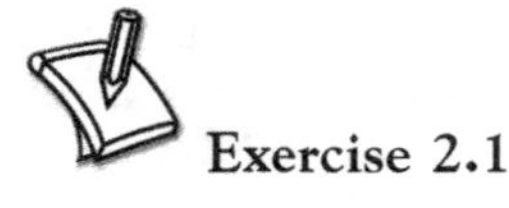

Exercise 2.1

Narrowing your topic

1 Write down your topic in general terms. Start narrowing your topic by adding more precise information. This could be information about the group of people or author you intend to study, the place (or institution) where your informants are located, a particular approach to teaching, a particular text type or subject area, or a concept or theory from literary studies. Don't limit yourself to only one specific focus, but consider alternatives. Noting these down can help you keep an open mind about different possibilities at this early stage.
2 Compare the different ways you have found to focus on your topic with your neighbour. Focusing on one example, discuss how you could develop it into a specific research question.

Drafting a research project proposal

Most universities require students to submit a research proposal before they begin their research project. This proposal is an official form that will be reviewed and signed by your supervisor. This form is like an agreement between you, your supervisor and the department on how you will proceed. This section guides you through the information you will probably need to provide:

Project title: The title needs to be fairly short. It should give the reader an accurate idea of what your project will be about – think of key words that should be in the title. Ideally, titles should also catch the reader's attention. This is the preliminary title, as you might think of a more appropriate one later.

Topic summary/Abstract: In your brief summary about your proposed project, begin with a general statement about the topic, indicate succinctly why further research is warranted, and state what you hope to discover. Briefly explain how you will undertake this proposed study, such as the type of data or texts you intend to use. Indicate why this topic is considered to be of interest and describe its broader relevance to the field.

Research question(s): What is the main question you propose to answer in your research? (There may be more than one question.) The research question(s) should be quite specific and answerable by using the methods or the approach you describe below.

Background/Rationale/Problem statement: Provide the context and motivation for your study so the rationale for investigating this topic is clear. It may be that you chose the topic after noticing some related issue or concern in your social or educational context, or in the media. If you have chosen a literary topic, think of the relevance it may have to your understanding of a society or culture at a particular period, or other literary works.

Approach/Methods: When working at postgraduate level, you will need to identify the approach you intend to take in your research. This means situating your work in a theoretical or conceptual framework, and identifying an appropriate research method. A Master's degree programme will include a course specifically on research methods. At the level of an undergraduate research project, it will probably be sufficient to explain the rationale behind your intended approach to the texts you will study, or to the collection and analysis of your data. You also need to describe how you will conduct the study and identify the different stages involved.

Objectives: Formulating objectives involves identifying specific steps that contribute to your overall research goal. These intermediary steps, or sub-stages, may be tasks you need to complete or the responses to questions that contribute to answering your main research question(s). They may also involve steps in conducting your research, such as how you collect and analyse data. Typical verbs used when formulating objectives include 'identify', 'compare', 'examine', 'investigate' etc.

For example, Zurab's objectives were the following:

- to compile a collection of at least 50 emails written in English by students in the Department of English to their lecturers containing a request;
- to identify the types of requests that students make in emails written in English to their lecturers;
- to examine the linguistic features of students' 'request emails' that convey politeness;
- to identify linguistic features that students under- or over-use or inappropriately use when expressing politeness in English; and
- to identify features used to express politeness in students' L2 emails that reveal influence from the students' L1.

Exercise 2.2

Your project proposal

Use the section headings Title, Summary, Research question(s), Background, Methods and Objectives to draft a preliminary project proposal for your research topic. As you are unlikely to have all the information required, at this stage your proposal can just reflect what you could potentially do.

Alternatively, select one topic from Examples 2.1 to 2.4. Draft a project proposal for this topic. To complete each section, imagine how you would approach this topic.

The organization of your project

During your initial meetings with your supervisor, it is useful to have a plan of how you intend to structure your project. In addition to helping to focus the discussion, it may also function as a type of informal agreement between you and your supervisor regarding how your study will be structured. This plan will also help you organize your writing and keep focused on the particular points you need to address in the section you are working on.

Your plan could follow the model in Example 2.5. The title of each section is fairly standard and the sections should be numbered. In the 'Content' column, use key words or short phrases to identify the topics you anticipate covering. Remember, this is just to help you (and your supervisor) visualize your project and organize the information; it will also serve as a checklist of topics you need to cover in each section. In the 'References' column, note any bibliographic sources that could be relevant to each section. Noting down important bibliographic references will remind you (and your supervisor) of what you need to read (or look for) and will alert you to any lack of bibliographic sources in particular sections.

ABC Example 2.5

Your plan

Section	*Title of section*	*Content*	*References*
Front matter	Table of contents Dedication Acknowledgements Abstract		
1	Introduction	Background Definitions Significance of the study Research question(s)	
2	Literature Review	Topics to be covered in the Literature Review	
3	Methods	A description of the approach taken to investigate your topic The steps involved in gathering data	
4	Results	A description of the findings (often presented using graphs, tables and/or examples)	
4.1	Discussion/Analysis of Results (may also be a separate chapter)	A discussion of findings relevant to the research question(s) An analysis of results as they relate to the literature	
4.2	Recommendations (optional; may also appear after the Conclusion)	Specific, realistic actions that arise from the findings	
5	Conclusion	A summary of the main points from the study relevant to the research question(s) Significance of the findings Shortcomings Opportunities for further research	
No number	Appendices	Documents relevant to the data collection process (e.g. letters to institutions to request permission, questionnaires, tests etc.)	

(Continued)

(Continued)

Section	Title of section	Content	References
No number	References	An alphabetical list of all works cited Do not number this list Use the citation style recommended by your department (e.g. APA or MLA)	
No number	University documents (these documents will vary depending on the institution)	Statement of authorship (if required) Photocopy of your approved research proposal	

Exercise 2.3

Creating a plan

Create a plan for your research project similar to the one in Example 2.5. Include sufficient detail in the Content and References columns to ensure that both you and your supervisor are clear on what you will do, how you will do it and what bibliographic sources you will use.

Note

1 United Nations Educational, Scientific and Cultural Organization, available at http://en.unesco.org.

3 Working with your supervisor

Initiating the student–supervisor relationship

Institutions differ regarding the assignment of supervisors; some institutions allocate supervisors, whereas others allow students a choice. If you do have a choice, it is preferable to find a supervisor who is actually interested in your topic, rather than just choosing an instructor you personally like. To find out about your instructors' academic interests, think about the courses they teach and read about their research interests and publications on the university website. Bear in mind that some instructors already have students under their supervision and may not be able to accept another.

During your first meetings, it may be advisable to ask about your supervisor's expectations regarding the supervisory relationship. Supervisors each have their own personal style and tend to operate a bit differently. You will gradually discover how your supervisor prefers to work, but it might help to ask a few direct questions early on.

These are the sorts of things you might talk about:

- How often should you have meetings?
- Will your supervisor want to see hard (paper) or soft (electronic) copies of the drafts of your work?
- How much time does your supervisor usually need to look through a draft chapter?
- Will your supervisor be available for consultation during holiday periods?
- How should you contact him/her?
- Can your supervisor recommend or lend you articles or books suitable for your Literature Review?
- Can your supervisor lend or show you examples of (good) projects from previous students to help you understand how to organize your work?
- How much feedback will your supervisor give you on language use?

Arrive prepared for each meeting with your supervisor. Make a list of topics you want to talk about, the questions you have and the material you want to show your supervisor. By doing this, you are likely to feel more confident about the meeting and you will be less likely to forget particular questions you want to raise.

Students usually feel more satisfied with the outcome of a meeting if they were clear about their objectives or purpose before they went in. You may decide to keep the list of topics visible during the meeting and take notes of your supervisor's advice and responses. Having your 'agenda' will also help you steer the discussion towards the issues you want to discuss. You will only have a certain amount of time, and you need to ensure you focus on the really important issues early on. Sometimes your supervisor might digress and begin talking about something that is not relevant to your project, or the meeting may be interrupted by a telephone call. Having an agenda to hand might give you the courage to say, for instance, 'I have two more questions I wanted to ask', and thereby keep your supervisor's attention on your needs.

Bring your recent work to the meeting. This work may be related to a reading text (an article or book chapter), the draft of a chapter or the description of a data collection instrument, for instance. If your supervisor had previously told you to make certain changes to your work (for example, to the organization or to your use of language), this is the opportunity to show you have tried to incorporate or respond to your supervisor's suggestions, even if you are uncertain whether you have done so correctly.

Try not to be disheartened if your supervisor's comments seem critical; although you may feel discouraged, this feedback is intended to help to improve your work. Not only is your supervisor guiding you towards sharpening your critical reading and writing skills, but he/she also understands the standards of work expected of students by the department. To keep things in perspective, imagine how you would feel if your supervisor gave no substantive comments on your work and told you everything 'seemed fine'.

Before leaving the meeting, make sure you have a clear understanding of what your supervisor wants you to do next. If you are not clear, ask your supervisor to suggest to you what your next step(s) should be. The meeting is wasted if you leave not knowing this. You might also end by asking whether it would be convenient to meet again within a certain timeframe (e.g. a few weeks or a month). Having a date to work towards can be very motivating.

Exercise 3.1

Working with your supervisor

1 Think of three people in the department who you think would be good as a supervisor for your project. Why did you choose these names?
2 Write a list of things you would like your supervisor to do for you during the period that you work together.
3 Now write a list of things you believe your supervisor will expect you to do.

Compare what you have written with your neighbour. Talk about the expectations you have for yourselves and your supervisors.

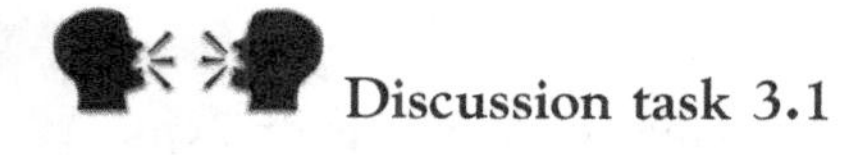

Discussion task 3.1

Communication with your supervisor

With a partner, discuss possible answers to each of the scenarios below:

1 You finish a chapter of your research project and you email it to your supervisor. A week passes and you don't hear back from her. What should you do?
2 You finish a chapter of your research project and you email it to your supervisor. The next day you go to her office and ask her if she has read your chapter. She seems quite irritated when you ask this. Why?
3 You finish a chapter of your research project and you email it to your supervisor. Three days later you realize you hadn't sent the latest draft. You email your supervisor with the latest draft telling her to ignore the previous one. In her reply, she seems quite irritated. Why? What could you have done?

Writing emails to your supervisor

Many supervisors prefer that you use email to arrange meetings and to send in drafts of your work. Although you may have written many emails to family and friends, this may be the first time that you have ever sent an email to a university instructor. Like many students, you may feel unsure about how to write the email appropriately and how to express what you want to say in English. Issues connected with differences in social status and authority (i.e. student versus university lecturer), culture and language often mean that students find writing emails to supervisors challenging. Nevertheless, knowing how to write such emails is important for your relationship with your supervisor. If you don't express yourself appropriately, you might come across as being a bit rude or your supervisor may simply not understand what you want to communicate. This section provides guidance on maintaining effective email communication with your supervisor.

Expected levels of formality in written communication vary considerably from culture to culture, and they also vary between individuals. Within one department there may be lecturers who prefer that students address them with their title, while others may prefer that students use their first name. You may find that your initial emails to your supervisor are more formal, but that they become more informal as the communication exchange progresses. When you exchange a number of emails about the same general topic within a short period of time, it is quite normal that emails become briefer and may not include all the components listed below; for instance, they may comprise just a message of one or two lines without greetings or names. It is advisable, however, to take the cue with regard to formality and politeness from your supervisor.

The components of your email

An email usually consists of a number of different components or steps. As mentioned earlier, not every email includes all components, but when initiating email communication with your supervisor, it is a good idea to include an opening (usually with a greeting), the main message and a closing, as described below.

Greeting: You can begin your email with a greeting such as 'Dear . . .', 'Hello' or 'Good morning', followed by your supervisor's name. While in English-speaking countries it is usual to use the person's surname after a title (Dr/Mr/Mrs/Ms), in other countries it may be usual to use the person's first name. If you are uncertain about the appropriate title or which name to use, the safest move is simply to ask your supervisor or, alternatively, check with the department's administrative staff. A comma may sometimes, but not always, appear after the person's name.

Following this, it would be helpful to tell your supervisor who you are and remind your supervisor of the title of your topic, particularly if you have not been in touch recently. All instructors receive many emails each day and, as undergraduate courses tend to be quite large, they may not know or remember who you are from seeing your email address.

Main message: This is the most difficult part of the email to write, as it depends on what you want to say. If you need your supervisor to undertake some action, you may feel unsure of how to formulate the request appropriately. The following are some examples of formulations you can use in your emails. Of course, variations are possible; these are just examples that may help you create your own. Some examples are more formal than others.

1 You are sending a draft for your supervisor to check.

> Please find attached my draft of Chapter 1.
>
> I have finished revising the draft of Chapter 1. I have attached it to this email.

2 You want your supervisor to check your work.

> Could you please have a look at my draft of Chapter 1 and get back to me?

3 You urgently want your supervisor to check your work. In this case, it would be appropriate to indicate why you want him/her to check your work as soon as possible; 'because I want to finish it soon' would not be considered an appropriate reason.

> If it were possible to have a look at my work soon, I would be very grateful. I need to make a trip to Salalah at the end of the month, and I would like to finish this chapter before then.

4 Your supervisor sent you some bibliographic material in a previous email and you need to acknowledge that you received it.

> Thank you for sending me those articles about my topic.

5 You want to ask your supervisor whether some bibliographic material you found is a suitable academic source for your project.

> I found this article on the Internet and I think it would be useful for my project. Could you please take a quick look and tell me whether it would be a suitable source?

6 You want to ask your supervisor if you could make a change to the topic or the approach used in your research. In this case, it would be a good idea to give a reason why you would like to undertake this change so your supervisor can better understand your intentions.

> I was wondering if I could change my topic from [previous topic title] to [new topic title].
>
> I would like to change my topic to . . .
>
> I would like to ask you if I could change my topic to . . .
>
> I want to do this because . . .

7 You don't understand a comment your supervisor made on your work.

> I am not sure what you meant by [issue] in your comments. Could you please explain this to me again?
>
> I could also come to your office if that would suit you.
>
> If you would like me to visit your office, I could come by any time next week.

8 You sent an email to your supervisor; one week later you still have not received a reply.

> I sent you my draft chapter by email last week. I have not received a reply, so I just wanted to check with you whether you could look at it sometime soon. I am attaching it again here for convenience's sake.
>
> I sent you my draft chapter by email last week. As I have not received a reply from you, I just wanted to check whether you received it. If you could look at my work sometime over the next week, I would be very grateful.

9 You want to make an appointment with your supervisor.

> I would like to come to your office to talk about [topic of conversation]. Are you by any chance available sometime this week? [or] Are you available on Wednesday at 2pm?

Closing: Before ending your email, you might like to thank your supervisor for any help he/she has given or is about to give. One of the following expressions might be useful (other phrases are also possible):

> Thank you; Thank you for your help; Thank you in advance for your assistance; Thank you again for the materials; Thank you for your suggestions.

A closing greeting often appears before the writer's name. In your initial emails, it is advisable to include your full name. Some students also include their student number or course code. Students frequently forget to include their name when ending emails, perhaps because they assume lecturers know who they are from the email address or from previous emails. If you do tend to forget, consider creating an automated 'sign-off' that includes your name and contact details. The following expressions are commonly used to end emails (other phrases are also possible):

> Best; Best wishes; Best regards.

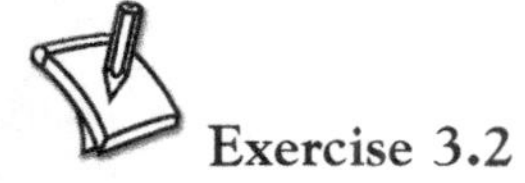

Exercise 3.2

Looking critically at emails

Look at the examples listed below of emails sent by students to their supervisor. In each email, some components could be improved. With the help of the information above on composing emails, rewrite each of the seven emails below:

Example 1

Hello Dr;

I am Zlata.

My title research is about initiating and sustaining elementary students' motivation toward learning EFL

But, I would like to change my topic to another. Can I ? I saw motivation is too general and has alot of issues.

Example 2

Good morning Dr,

This is the final draft of my project proposal.

Example 3

Hello Dr. Luisa

Thanks for books that sent to me and I send you the changes in the Introduction

Example 4

Dear Dr.

Regarding my project, I had shock when I saw your replay.

Also you wrote about plagiarism whereas I put all information with it's sources.

I need you help to tell me what can I do now.

regards, Zoran

Example 5

Good morning Dr. Louisa

This is the last draft of chapter 1&2, I hope you check it as fast as possible to present it next week.

Thanks Zofia

Example 6

Good afternoon Dr. Buckingham

Could you please tell me when you finish to check my project.

Thanks Zeki

Example 7

Dear Dr. Louisa

Hello. How are you?. I sent for u an email but you didnt answer till now. please replay for me. thank you. Zurab

Exercise 3.3

Writing emails to your supervisor

Below are two situations you may experience while doing your research project. For each situation, write an appropriate email. Use the suggested phrases in the previous section to help you.

Situation 1

You want a meeting with your supervisor.

You want your supervisor to look at your work before the meeting; you attach the chapter.

You want to change the number of participants you will use for your data collection.

Situation 2

You have to change the day of the meeting.

You need a copy of an article about your topic that your supervisor told you about.

Longer emails

While doing your project, you are likely to write emails asking a series of questions or explaining a series of issues. This could make your email quite long and complex. It may help to plan your email. Think carefully about the questions you want to ask and the issues you want to explain. It might help to organize the information by separating the topics into different paragraphs, or by using bullet points or numbering to organize the information (sometimes paragraph formatting is lost when sending an email). This will also make it much easier for your supervisor to read and respond to your queries. If you want to talk about a number of different topics, consider including a brief topic heading next to the number.

If your supervisor responds to your email but does not answer your questions, it might be that he/she did not identify your questions. Your supervisor is more likely to address your needs if you ask your questions directly (e.g. 'Are 50 respondents enough for my survey?') rather than indirectly, or by implying you would like feedback from your supervisor (e.g. 'I'm not sure if I will have enough respondents; maybe I will only get 50'). Avoid burying your questions within other issues; state your questions very clearly at the beginning or end of a paragraph, or simply separated from other issues by using the 'enter' key on your keyboard or by numbering them.

Exercise 3.4

Clarity in long emails

This exercise shows a long email from a student. The supervisor finds it hard to identify what exactly the student wants to communicate, whether a response is needed to specific questions and whether the supervisor should clarify the student's doubts. Reorganize the layout of the email so that it is easier for the supervisor to understand, and reformulate the parts of the message that you think could be expressed more clearly.

> Dear Louisa,
>
> Owing to some impracticalities of implementing a study on code-switching, I had to change my topic. My new topic is a study on how teachers use questions in class with their students. I want to compare how teachers do this in Turkish and how they do it in English. So I thought I should use Turkish teachers and foreigner teachers, but maybe I can use just Turkish teachers who teach in Turkish language and English language. I don't know. I've started doing research and writing the background to the topic. There aren't any studies looking at questions in Turkish but other countries have done studies on questions in English. I also believe this new topic will be much more of use to my home institution and will be appreciated more by

our school head and by my colleagues, since it can be used later to look at teacher talk in the classroom and teachers assessing students.

At Akbulut Technical University we have lecturers teaching in Turkish and English. The classes in Turkish are for degrees like law and Turkish literature but some courses just have some lectures in Turkish like politics and economics. So I can focus on teachers in departments or for particular courses, I am not sure. So, what I wish to do is to conduct a quantitative study on the types of questions teachers use in each language. Because I think that teachers maybe change their style of interacting with students in the classroom depending on the language they use. During the study, I'll first make a list of the types of questions that teachers use in the classroom (I know an article about this for English but I don't know one for Turkish). After that, I'll design an observation sheet to use in the classroom. I'll compare the differences between the two groups by analyzing the results from my observations. Maybe I'll make interviews with the instructors. Hopefully. . . I believe it will be a worthy study and tell us how teachers use different languages in their teaching if I can complete it successfully.

I hope you like my new topic, because I liked it a lot :) I want to go on with this topic, if it's approved. Have a nice holiday . . .

Yours sincerely . . .
Zeki

Email etiquette

There are few hard rules about email etiquette as so much variation in style exists in this mode of communication. Nevertheless, you should be careful about using informal language or addressing your supervisor in a familiar tone, unless he/she gives you the cue that this is acceptable. Such cues could be the form of address (e.g. 'Hi', 'Hey', 'Dear student'), the way he/she ends the email (or 'signs off') and the presence of informal words, phrases or symbols such as emoticons (e.g. ☺). Your supervisor is unlikely to use shortcuts typical for mobile phone text messaging in emails to students. Student emails containing text-speak (e.g. 'R U in UR office?') are usually received with irritation by instructors.

Although we usually write emails quickly and we may need to respond to several emails at once, spelling and grammar still matter. We all sometimes make minor mistakes in our emails (and you will probably find some in your supervisor's emails if you look hard enough). Proofread your email before sending it. When you communicate with your lecturers by email, the language you use indirectly provides information about how seriously you take the course and how much you value their time and advice. If you send your supervisor a message that shows pretty good control of spelling and grammar, you are also giving them a positive message about your attitude and ability.

Exercise 3.5

Appropriate style in emails

1 In some countries, the level of formality between lecturers and students can be quite different from lecturer to lecturer. Look at the two emails below sent by lecturers (Lisa and Louisa) to students (Examples 1 and 2). What differences in formality do you find?

2 Now look at the replies from students (Examples 3 to 6). The four students use different levels of formality:
   a In your view, which students' emails would likely be acceptable to lecturers who prefer greater formality in their email communication with students?
   b Which would likely be acceptable to lecturers who are comfortable with less formality in their email communication with students?
   c Are there any examples that both types of lecturer might find inappropriate?

Lecturers' emails

From: professor@uni.ac
To: students@uni.ac
Date: 1 March 2013
Subject: book – Monday

Example 1

Hi everyone,
Just a quick reminder – bring your textbook to class on Monday. We need to do some of the exercises to help you with exam prep.
Hope you all have a great weekend.
See you on Monday,
Lisa

Example 2

Dear students,
Please bring your textbook to the ENG245 lecture on Monday.
Best regards,
Louisa Buckingham

Students' replies

From: students@uni.ac
To: professor@uni.ac
Date: 3 March 2013
Subject: Re: book – Monday

Example 3

i got the book from u but i borrowed it to my friend and now i dont hve it ☹. Can u send me a handout of the exercises so i can do thm in class? thx

Example 4

hi!
how are you?
I am not feeling very well so i am not coming to class on Monday. Can u please put the answers to the exercises in the book on the course website?
From Zeki

Example 5

Dear Lisa
I am your student in ENG245. I missed the class last week and I don't know what exercises we should do for exam preparation. I will come to class on Monday but can you also tell me which exercises from the book before?
See you, Zlata

Example 6

Dear Dr. Louisa
I hope you are well.
I got a low mark for the assignment and I want to know how I can improve my grade in the exam. Will these exercises in the book also be in the exam?
Can I come to your office hour?
Thank you, Zurab
ENG245
Student no. 4567974394

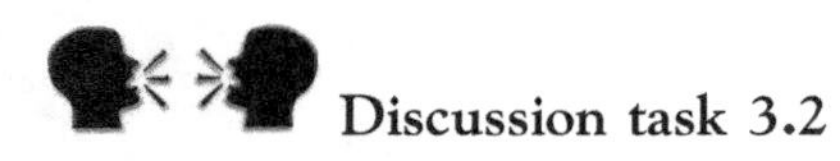

Discussion task 3.2

Formality and cultural differences

Discuss the following questions in small groups:

1 What differences have you noticed between the appropriate level of formality and the organization of a message in emails between lecturers and students in your L1 cultural context and in some English-language cultural contexts?
2 What difficulties might students from your country experience when writing an email in English to request something from a visiting lecturer they don't know well?

Insights from the literature 3.1

Emailing your instructors

University life is replete with exchanges between university staff and students. We are constantly doing things with language – formulating requests, and providing logistical information, clarifications, confirmations or excuses – and so much of this happens not orally, but through email. Email has become an essential mode of communication between lecturers and their students, and most universities provide students with an email address to encourage them to use this channel to communicate with university administration and academic staff. While e-communication is an integral part of university life, students may nevertheless feel uncertain about writing emails to their lecturers due to differences in status. Such insecurities are likely to be compounded by the perceived challenge of writing such an email in English for students for whom English is not their first language. In studies describing EFL (English as a foreign language) and ESL (English as a second language) contexts, Biesenbach-Lucas (2007), Chen (2006) and Economidou-Kogetsidis (2011) point out that students are usually not taught email etiquette, lack models and usually do not receive feedback on the linguistic choices they make in their emails, even when a student's language use is perceived as inappropriate. Unsurprisingly, students may thus cause irritation by failing to make appropriate stylistic choices congruent with the level of imposition of their request when communicating with their lecturers. The degree of formality in lecturers' interactions with students may differ, which may contribute to students' uncertainty regarding what might be considered a suitable way to address their lecturer via email and formulate a request.

The ability to appropriately formulate requests via email to one's lecturers involves socio-pragmatic awareness and skill; students need to judge their relationship with academic staff, evaluate the degree of imposition they bring about through their request and display an awareness of discourse choices that shape hierarchical social relations in a particular cultural context (Chen, 2006; Economidou-Kogetsidis, 2011). Such discourse choices include forms of address, topics that may be raised (beyond academic affairs) and the use of words or phrases to soften or mitigate the degree of imposition of a request.

As email is an asynchronous medium of communication, students have time to formulate and revise their message, a luxury not available in real-time, face-to-face communication. Notwithstanding, textual features typical of instant messaging increasingly appear to influence students' style of writing emails (Economidou-Kogetsidis, 2011; Stephens, Houser & Cowan, 2009). Thus, features such as emoticons, abbreviations, orthographic and grammatical errors, the absence of salutation in the opening and closing position of the message, and even the omission of the sender's name increasingly feature in email messages.

Lecturers may perceive inappropriate discourse choices as irritating, discourteous or even disrespectful, as students may seem to address them as a peer rather than acknowledge their asymmetrical status, or appear to give them little choice in whether they comply with a student's request (Biesenbach-Lucas, 2007; Economidou-Kogetsidis, 2011). According to research in a US university context, the following features (in order of gravity) were considered by lecturers to be particularly irritating: unclear requests, disorganized messages, addressing the lecturer inappropriately, spelling errors, omitting the sender's name, the use of shortcuts (e.g. 'RU' for 'are you'), omitting any form of address, omitting the subject line and overly long emails (Stephens, Houser & Cowan, 2009).

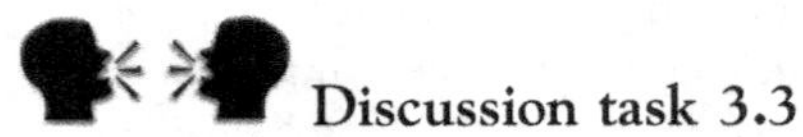

Discussion task 3.3

Communication with your instructors

Discuss the following questions in small groups:

1 Do you find it easier to communicate with your supervisor (or your instructors) in person or through email?
2 If you use your phone to send text messages, to what extent do you think that features of instant text messaging have influenced how you write emails?
3 If you were a university instructor in your country, how formal would you like your students to be in their emails to you? Discuss your reasons for your answer.
4 Which of the following would you find irritating in a student email if you were a university lecturer?

unclear requests	disorganized messages
addressing the lecturer inappropriately	spelling errors
omitting the sender's name	the use of shortcuts (e.g. those typical in texting)
omitting any form of address	
overly long emails	omitting the subject line

4 Finding literature

One of the most challenging and time-consuming stages of any research project involves gaining a deeper understanding of the topic through locating and reading a wide variety of relevant books and articles. In the first two chapters of your project, you need to demonstrate how your work is situated within a body of knowledge. While you may have consulted academic literature for previous university assignments during your Bachelor's degree, your research project will involve a more systematic review of literature related to your topic; your university may even stipulate that you include a certain minimum number of academic sources in your Literature Review. At this point, you probably aren't familiar with the relevant literature. This part of doing research is usually an ongoing task in the sense that you will reread selected works during the writing stage and search for related items when you notice a gap in your review of the literature. This section focuses on how and where to look for appropriate academic literature for your project.

What are academic sources?

For your project, you must as far as possible use authoritative sources. These will usually be *academic*, meaning that they are articles published in journals or books whose authors are usually affiliated to a university. When we say the author is an *authority*, this means that the work produced by this person has been critically reviewed by peers also knowledgeable about the field of study, and these have endorsed the work. The author may have published a number of pieces on the same general topic area, demonstrating a depth and breadth of knowledge about the field, and a development in his/her grasp of the issues. The author's work is open to public criticism or praise from other academics. This *peer review* is an important part of the quality control of academic work. Information you come across on private or institutional websites doesn't undergo this process. Of course, not all authors are authorities in their field. You will begin to recognize the names of authors who have published important studies on your topic as your reading progresses. If you find an author has written an article in a good journal or published a book with a good publishing company, or if you find other authors cite the person's work, it probably means that you can consider this author an authority on your topic for the purposes of your project.

Tip 4.1

A cautionary word

Identifying literature for your research project is *not* finding and copying information from personal websites, Wikipedia, blogs or any other of the thousands of non-academic websites that exist on the Internet.

Keywords

To find relevant information from books, journals, electronic databases or the Internet, you need to think of *keywords* that will guide your search. In this section, we will talk about how our four students employed keywords for their respective literature searches.

To find literature on students' attitudes towards their studies and levels of achievement, *Zareen* used the following keywords: 'gender', resources 'student achievement', 'university grades', 'attitudes' and 'study habits'. She usually combined two of these terms – for example, she typed in 'gender' and 'student achievement' – or even three terms: 'gender', 'attitudes' and 'student achievement'. Between each keyword she typed 'and'.

Zurab needed academic sources on students' emails in an L2. He decided to keep his search broad at the beginning and also look for sources on students' emails in their L1. He did a keyword search using the terms 'emails' and 'students', and then he included other keywords such as 'requests', 'second language' and 'politeness'.

Zeina searched for information about polysemous words and translation. Her keywords were 'polysemous words' and 'translation'; later she also added 'Arabic'. She also wanted to find information about the use of dictionaries and about typical errors so she added these two keywords ('dictionary' and 'error') to her searches.

Zakia's research was on the depiction of women in literature; she used keywords such as '20th century literature' and 'gender roles', but she also searched for 'gender roles' and 'Arab literature' or 'British literature' and varied her searches by adding the names of particular British and Arab authors.

In each case, these students experimented with different terms and with different combinations of terms. They did multiple searches and each time they arrived at different results; some searches were productive, others less so. This process helped them develop a sense of good search terms or keyword combinations for their needs.

Tip 4.2

A keyword search

To find literature for your research project using keywords, do *not* write a sentence (or a question) in the search field.

To search using keywords, identify the most important terms that are used to talk about your topic (e.g. 'colonialism', 'motivation', 'simultaneous interpretation' . . .) together with words that are important to describe a particular aspect of your topic (e.g. type of institution, the level of students, gender, nationality, language . . .).

Tip 4.3

Narrowing your bibliographic search

Did your search give you hundreds or thousands of results? Try narrowing your search. Use 'and' to combine search terms.

Search for a phrase by connecting the words with the underscore '_' (e.g. 'polysemous_words and English').

Use 'or' to combine terms (e.g. 'primary or secondary school').

Exercise 4.1

Keywords

1 An effective search usually means combining a keyword 'term' with a keyword descriptor. Try the following two searches using www.scholar.google.com. Replace the word 'Arabic' with your L1. Compare the results from each search. Which search produced more useful results?
   a simultaneous interpretation AND university students AND English AND Arabic;
   b simultaneous interpretation AND Arabic.
2 Write down five or six different keywords for your research topic. Which ones do you think would be good combinations for your bibliographic searches? Compare your list and your combinations with those of your neighbour. Now do a search with your keywords using www.scholar.google.com. Which combination gave you more results? Which combination gave you the most useful results?

Where to look for literature

The Internet

As seen in Exercise 4.1, a useful Internet site to find previous research on your topic is Google Scholar (www.scholar.google.com). Insert your keywords (or keyword combinations) into the search field to find bibliographic material relevant to your topic. Not all information in the search results will be useful; you need to skim read the short description of each result. As you may have hundreds (or even thousands) of results, it would probably be sufficient to skim through the first two or three pages of results. When you use Google Scholar, a 'PDF' symbol appears to the right of some results. This tells you that the document is freely accessible and can be downloaded onto your computer. If your university library does not subscribe to quality academic journals, these open-access publications can be useful.

While the Internet is a tremendous resource, it is important to remember that there is no quality control of the information you find. Google Scholar contains academic-type documents (such as articles and conference papers), but the quality can vary enormously. If the publisher is a quality academic journal or an official organization (national or international), the document may well be useful for your research project. If you are not sure whether the document or information you have found is appropriate, ask your supervisor.

When you download a document from the Internet, note down the site (the URL) where you found it (i.e. copy the site information from your browser and paste this into a Word document). This information should appear in your list of references, usually accompanied by the date when the site was accessed (e.g. 'Accessed on 10 January 2013'). This is included because some documents may disappear from the site or they may be altered in some way (information may be added or deleted). Including the date when the document was accessed informs your reader that at that particular time (e.g. 10 January 2013), the information you refer to was accessible on that site.

Exercise 4.2

Evaluating Internet sites

1 Go to the following Internet sites. Can they be used as authoritative sources for your research project? Give reasons for your answer.
   a www.mingoville.com
   b www.tefl-tips.com
   c www.readingmatrix.com
   d http://llt.msu.edu
   e http://iteslj.org
   f www.awej.org

2. After accessing these sites, go back and look at the URLs. Do the URLs provide any clues as to whether the site might be useful for academic purposes?
3. Find two other websites, one appropriate and one inappropriate as a reference for academic research. Explain how you judged their suitability.

Tip 4.4

Evaluating the appropriateness of websites

How can you tell if an Internet site would be considered an authoritative source of information for your project?

1. Look at the URL. You should be able to tell whether it is an institution or a private website.
2. Is the site that of a private institution? If so, the information on the site is probably for promotional purposes and not suitable for academic work.
3. Is this site a private website? The information on private websites cannot usually be considered to be objective or 'academic'. They are not usually suitable as background reading on your topic and should not be used for your Literature Review.
4. Is the site that of a national (or international) institution? Websites of national institutions often have useful documents available. These may be studies that were done in the country by researchers working for the institution or academics based at a university. If the studies were funded by an institution or by the government, the information they present may not be impartial, but on occasion they may be the only source available for some information.
5. Is the site that of a university? Sometimes universities have documents (or links to documents) that are accessible from their website. These are usually authored by an academic who is an authority on the topic. Sometimes these documents have been published in a journal with open access. Such documents may be useful for your work and can be considered suitable for your background reading and Literature Review.
6. Is the site that of a journal? Some journals are open access, others are not. If it is open access, this means that you can read and download the articles from the website without having to pay. You will find many journals have an open-access policy. While the quality of some open-access journals can be quite high, this is not always the case. If you are not sure, check with your supervisor whether it would be appropriate to use a particular article downloaded from an open-access journal. Articles in subscription journals can only be downloaded if the university provides access or by paying.

Exercise 4.3

Wikipedia

1 What do you know about Wikipedia? If you have used this resource during your studies, what sort of information did you search for? How did you use this information from Wikipedia for your course or assignment?
2 Look at the list of references of some articles or books you located for your topic. Did any of these authors cite Wikipedia in their references?
3 Go to the Wikipedia site in English. Enter one of your keywords for your topic. Read the results. What have you learned about your topic by reading this information? How useful is this information to you? (You can do the same search using the Wikipedia site in your L1 or in a different language to compare the results.) Now read the information again more carefully. In what way does the information that appears on this Wikipedia page differ from what you may read in a book or journal article?
4 For academic work, when might Wikipedia be useful? When should we not use Wikipedia?

The library

Familiarize yourself with the selection of books in the relevant section of your university library, whether this is applied linguistics, translation, literature or education. Using the catalogue will help you discover what the library holds. You might find it most useful to search the catalogue using keywords in the 'subject' field (just one keyword – not combinations), or you can search using the author's surname or the title of the book if you know them. The librarians are trained to help you search for material and they can show you how to use the catalogue.

In addition, just browsing the library shelves can be very rewarding and will likely lead to the discovery of items that your catalogue searches did not reveal. Check the contents page and the index of promising-looking books for terms pertinent to your study. Frequently, a book may contain relevant information about your topic even if the book title did not signal this. Try to browse the shelves at least once a week while you are planning your study. Although you may not be aware of your progress, by the end of this period you will likely be much more familiar with the literature on your topic.

Exercise 4.4

Using the university library catalogue

1 Enter the university library catalogue. Start a search. Enter 'motivation' in the search field 'subject'. Which results seem to be relevant to a research project about language learning?

2 Now put 'language teaching' in the search field 'subject'. Which results seem to be relevant to a research project about language learning?
3 Enter 'Dörnyei' in the search field 'author'. How many books does the library hold by this author? What does this author write about?

Electronic bibliographic resources

Universities often have subscriptions to academic journals and books in electronic form. If this is the case at your university, take some time to browse these important academic resources. Try searching in journals using keywords, searching for specific authors or simply browsing through different volumes to see what has been published over the years. If you get too many results with your keyword searches, narrow the search by using a more precise term or joining two terms with 'and'. If you use material from these electronic sources in your research project, cite the authors' works just as you do for hardcopy journals and books.

Exercise 4.5

Searching in electronic journals

If your university has subscriptions to electronic journals, try the following exercises:

1a Find the journal *TESOL Quarterly*. What sort of topics can you read about in this journal?
1b Find the journal *Language and Society*. You can guess the topics you can read about in this journal from the title, but does this journal have an article that talks about your country or region? Do a search to see what results you get.
1c Find another journal related to applied linguistics (or translation or literary studies) that you can access through your library. What topics can you read about? Has it published something related to your topic?
2 Look at the keywords that appear under each Abstract in Exercise 5.2 (p. 42). Do a search in these journals using these keywords. What do you find?
3 Look again at the topics and keywords of Zareen's, Zurab's, Zeina's and Zakia's projects (see the section on 'Keywords' earlier in this chapter, p. 30). Choose one topic and look for articles that seem to be relevant in these journals.
4 Using the electronic journals you have accessed, do a search using the keywords you identified for your study. Remember to narrow your search if you get too many results.

Recording bibliographic information

As you begin to find academic sources for your work, make a habit of noting down the relevant bibliographic information. Don't wait until you start to write up your list of references; by that time you will have forgotten where you found material and you most likely won't have all the details you need to include for each item. While it is usually possible to check incomplete bibliographic references by searching for the item on the Internet, it is still advisable to record the complete reference at the start. This is the information you will need to record:

Author or editor: Some articles or books may have more than one author; you need to record all names. Some books may be edited volumes. This means that the book contains chapters by different authors; the editor is the person responsible for assembling and revising the whole work, but he/she may also have authored one (or more) of the chapters. If you use a chapter from such a book, you must note both the name of the editor and the author. If you are using a document from the Internet, it may not necessarily be clear who the author is. Look for the name of the institution. Use this in place of the author's name. If the document has no author and there is no name of an institution, this is probably a sign that it is not an appropriate bibliographic reference for your research.

Title: Some articles or books may have a long title. Note down the complete title. If it is an edited work, you need the title of the book and the title of the chapter(s) you use. Most documents you use from the Internet will also have a title. Again, if there is none, this is probably a sign that it is not an appropriate bibliographic reference for your research.

Year, publishing company, page numbers; volume and issue number: The year of publication is provided on almost all published material. If it is a book, convention requires that you also record the city where it was published; this is usually printed on one of the first pages of the book (ask your supervisor or a librarian if you can't find it). For chapters from an edited volume, the page numbers of the chapter are needed. For a journal article, record the page numbers of the complete article, together with the journal's volume number and issue number (if they exist).

For more information on how to record bibliographic information, see Appendix 5.

5 Reading

Reading strategically

Reading for your research project begins before you start to write and it may well continue after you think you have finished writing. It is normal to spend more time reading (and searching for texts) than actually writing. In light of the high reading load involved in a research project and the challenge of reading academic texts, it is advisable to consider how best to approach this important part of your study. This chapter will describe useful strategies for reading academic publications.

You shouldn't read everything you locate about your topic; rather, you need to recognize the more important authors or texts. Browsing the bookshelves in the library and the electronic resources can help you recognize 'central works' and 'central authors'. After selecting what to read, identify the sections that relate to your topic within the book or the article. Being selective in one's reading and prioritizing reading tasks help prevent the reading load from becoming overwhelming. If your reading load seems infinite, this is a sign that you need to be more strategic.

Preparing the Literature Review section will require a longer literature search and more intensive reading than any other chapter of your project, but this reading should also inform other chapters of your study. For instance, you will read to better understand the rationale for investigating your topic and to inform the formulation of your research question(s) (the Introduction section), for guidance in the design of your data collection instruments (the Methods section) and to identify how other authors explain their findings and relate them to the literature and the implications they draw (the Discussion and Conclusion sections).

Academic reading

Reading academic material is very different from reading other text types such as fiction, newspaper texts or Internet sites. Academic texts tend to be much more challenging and students often struggle to read texts for their courses or research. This is because such texts may:

- use formal or very specific words that you may not see or hear in everyday language;

- use terminology typical for the field of study;
- use many complex noun phrases;
- use long sentences (with multiple dependent clauses);
- talk about abstract concepts with few (or no) concrete examples;
- be very 'dense', with a lot of information and few (or no) illustrations, diagrams or section headings;
- have sentences containing lists of references to other authors;
- discuss the work of other authors that you have not read.

Because of this, students may find it difficult to extract meaning from the texts they read. Decoding a single sentence may involve so much effort that students lose sight of the broader idea or the main points expressed throughout a paragraph.

It is probably best to start reading general, introductory texts about your research topic. Our students Zareen, Zurab, Zeina and Zakia, for instance, will read broadly on their topics to gain a general understanding of the issues involved and frequently used terminology. This is how their specific topics are related to broader areas of study:

- Zareen's topic is related to motivation, gender and education.
- Zurab's topic is related to language learning, writing skills, technology and communication, and pragmatics.
- Zeina's topic is related to semantics, contrastive analysis and translation.
- Zakia's topic is related to gender roles, gender stereotypes and cultural studies.

The library is likely to have general or introductory textbooks on these subject areas. Often you will also find an introductory chapter about your general topic in an edited volume on applied linguistics, translation, literary studies or education. You can locate such chapters by browsing the shelves, looking for introductory texts and reading the contents pages of promising-looking texts. If your library has a good online catalogue, you can also browse the library at home, but the information provided online can be quite limited.

The language used in general or introductory textbooks is often easier than the language of academic journal articles. These books are often written specifically for students and they don't assume considerable prior knowledge about the subject area. Terms may be clearly explained and a glossary of terms may even be included at the back. Also, citations of other authors are often less frequent in a book (or book chapter), whereas you might find the multiple author citations in journal articles distracting.

Academics write journal articles for their peers and they are an important channel by which academics participate in a global discourse community within their discipline. As they are not written specifically for students, the language used is likely to be more specialized and prior knowledge of the topic is usually assumed. An author may only explain a term when he/she wishes to clarify how it is used in that particular study, which may differ from how other authors use the term. In a journal article, an author must cite other authors, particularly in some sections of the article such as the Introduction or the Literature Review (or Background). Not all disciplines require the same quantity of author citations, however; typically, fewer author citations appear in literary studies than in education and linguistics. The language used in journal articles may also be denser – that is, with more terminology, long noun phrases and quite complex sentences. One reason for this is the strict word limit imposed on journal articles, which means that authors need to formulate ideas very concisely.

Reading a journal article

The organization of information in a journal article is very structured. It is common to find section headings throughout the article; these may also be numbered. As these section headings signal where particular information is located, reading the entire article from beginning to end may not be necessary in the first instance. It may be enough to read several sections in detail, before using the reading strategies of skimming and scanning to identify pertinent information from the other sections.

Even when reading the entire article, it is not necessary to read each section in the given order in which it appears. While approaches to reading vary depending on the text and individual preferences, the approach described here is one possibility. The *Abstract* (if one exists) is the logical starting point. This is a selective, focused overview of what the study was about and the methods and type of data used, and may include a brief indication of the results. As such, it allows the reader to quickly pinpoint information such as where the study was done, who the participants were, how data were collected and what theoretical approach was used. Its purpose is to allow readers to evaluate whether the topic of the article is relevant to their needs and whether they should read further. If the article appears useful, two other important sections to look at early on are the *Introduction* and the *Conclusion*.

The *Introduction* will tell you how the author has contextualized or framed the study, and how it relates to other published work; it will likely also include the research question(s). This background information can help you develop a sense of the broader issues relevant to your topic. The following questions are intended to help you reflect on the structure of a journal article Introduction. Using an article relevant to your topic, underline the relevant information or write key words in the margin in response to these questions:

- What do we already know about this general area of study? What have previous studies uncovered? What is generally known about this topic?
- What was (were) the main question(s) that the author wanted to answer? (What was (were) the research question(s)?)
- What was the motivation for the study? (Why did the author do the study?)

The *Conclusion*, of course, will usually tell you more about what the author actually did in the study and how the results were interpreted, but it might also provide suggestions for new research questions. It might surprise you to learn that readers often don't read this final section last; the reason is simple – if we know how the 'story' ends, we may find it easier to read through the middle sections! Some Conclusions may be very short and they may not contain useful information about the main findings; in this case, you may have to look at the previous section, the Discussion (if there is one), or the last few paragraphs of the Results section where the author may summarize the main findings.

After reading these previous sections, turn to the *Methods* and *Results* sections to learn more about how the study was conducted and details of the results. These two sections can often be quite technical and you may encounter unfamiliar terminology. To help you navigate these sections, try to locate the important points such as the following (again, try underlining this key information):

- Where was the study done?
- What sorts of data were used in the study?
- If data were collected from people (participants), who were they (number, nationality, L1, age)?
- If texts were used, how were they chosen? What type of text? How many?
- What did the participants have to do?
- How was their performance evaluated?
- If texts were analysed, how was this analysis done?
- What were the results?
- Did these results provide a clear answer to the research question(s)?

In the field of literary studies, the Methods and Results sections may be absent or not clearly signposted, as studies in this discipline are often shaped around a discussion of ideas rather than data. The Results section may also be followed by a *Discussion* section. In their attempt to interpret the findings, authors will endeavour to address questions such as the following:

- How should we understand these results? What do they mean in terms of teaching/language learning/literature/translation practice?
- How do these results relate to the findings of previous studies?
- How can we apply this new understanding to the practice of teaching and learning languages/to our understanding of literature/to the practice of translating?
- Do these findings leave any questions unanswered?
- Do the findings lead to more questions?

The *Literature Review* (this section may have an alternative title such as *Background*) contains a description of what previous studies have found and, perhaps, how the studies were conducted; often the author will try to show that previous work on this topic was insufficient or limited in some respect.

By demonstrating that questions remain unanswered, or the topic is not clearly understood, the author is then able to claim that the topic warrants further research. This allows the author to justify the current study and present it as worthwhile and useful. By reading the overview of previous research, you will likely learn about other articles or books relevant to your research project. Indeed, examining author citations in the literature we read is an important way to identify additional bibliographic resources. Sections such as the Introduction and the Literature Review in particular provide opportunities to broaden one's understanding of key terms and to identify standard phrases commonly used when describing features of the study. Some of these terms or phrases may be useful in your study (see, for example, Tip 5.1, p. 50).

Exercise 5.1

Looking at journal articles

Find two articles from different journals relevant to your topic. Compare how the content is organized.

1. What similarities and differences do you notice? (For example, are there sections with sub-headings? If so, are the names of the sections the same? Are they numbered?)
2. Can you predict what the article will discuss in each section?
3. In terms of organization, which article do you find easier to follow? Why?

Exercise 5.2

Reading an Abstract

Below are three Abstracts taken from published articles. Identify the following information in each. Note that, in some cases, the information may be given across multiple sentences; alternatively, one sentence may serve multiple purposes. Finally, not all information will be present in every Abstract:

- the research question(s) or topic;
- reference to a theory or an approach used in the study;
- motivation for the study;
- background information relevant to the study;
- information about how the author did the study;
- an indication of the findings;
- an indication of how the results were analysed;

- an indication of how the findings could be interpreted (i.e. do they confirm or disconfirm previous findings?);
- an indication of the study's implications and recommendations.

1 Chik, A. (2014). Digital gaming and language learning: Autonomy and community. *Language Learning & Technology*, 18(2), 85–100.

Abstract

The relationship between digital game play and second language (L2) learning is a particularly tricky issue in East Asia. Though there is an emerging presence of Chinese online games, many more young people are playing the English- or Japanese-language versions of the most popular commercial off-the-shelf (COTS) video games. In other words, most Chinese gamers are playing L2 digital games in their leisure time. Informed by research on out-of-class L2 learning, this paper discusses findings from an exploratory study investigating L2 gaming and learning practices in young people's everyday lives. Drawing on rich data from gaming sessions, stimulated recall, focus group discussion, individual interviews and online discussion forums, this paper argues that gamers exercise autonomy by managing their gameplay both as leisure and learning practices in different dimensions (location, formality, locus of control, pedagogy and trajectory). At the same time, gameplay-as-learning practices are supported by wider communities of digital gamers who take on roles as language teachers and advisers. The paper discusses the research and pedagogical implications for L2 gaming and learning.

Keywords: Learner Autonomy, Second Language Acquisition, Computer-Assisted Language Learning.

2 Chen, C.E. (2006). The development of e-mail literacy: From writing to peers to writing to authority figures. *Language Learning & Technology*, 10(2), 35–55.

Abstract

Though e-mail has become a common interpersonal communication medium, it does not mean that this medium is used without difficulty. While people can write e-mails to peers in any manner they like, writing e-mails to authority figures requires higher pragmatic competence and critical language awareness of how discourse shapes and reflects power asymmetry in an institutional context. For L2 learners, the challenge of composing this type of e-mail can be greater due not only to their limited linguistic ability but also their unfamiliarity with the target culture's norms and values. To provide a deeper understanding of how an L2 learner develops e-mail literacy in the target language environment, this paper presents a longitudinal case study of a Taiwanese graduate student's e-mail practice in English during her studies at a U.S. university for two and a half years.

Using a critical discourse analysis approach, the study reveals the complexity of an L2 learner's evolving e-mail practice and struggle for appropriateness, particularly in her e-mail communication with professors. Her development of e-mail literacy is discussed in relation to her evolving understanding of the e-mail medium, changing performance of student identity, increasing knowledge of student–professor interaction and realization of culture-specific politeness.

[No keywords provided.]

3 Lee, L. (2011). Blogging: Promoting learner autonomy and intercultural competence through study abroad. *Language Learning & Technology, 15*(3), 87–109.

Abstract
The current study explores closely how using the combined modalities of asynchronous computer-mediated communication (CMC) via blogs and face-to-face (FTF) interaction through ethnographic interviews with native speakers (L1s) supports autonomous learning as the result of reflective and social processes. The study involves 16 American undergraduate students who participated in blogs to develop their intercultural competence over the course of one-semester study abroad. The results show that blogs afforded students the opportunity to work independently (e.g., content creation) and reflect upon cross-cultural issues. Critical reflection, however, relied on the teacher's guidance and feedback, as most of the students were cognitively challenged by not being able to clearly articulate different points of view. It is likely that students were not accustomed to reflecting. The findings also indicate that task type fostered autonomy in different ways. While free topics gave students more control of their own learning, teacher-assigned topics required them to critically think about the readings. Lack of access to the Internet at the host institution and family also contributed to a limited level of social interaction. The study concludes that well-designed tasks, effective metacognitive and cognitive skills, and access to the Internet are essential to maximize the potentials of blogs for learner autonomy and intercultural communication.

Keywords: Computer-Assisted Language Learning, Learner Autonomy, Task-Based Instruction.

Reading a book

It would not be usual to read the academic books we consult for research purposes in the manner we read a novel. That is, we do not usually start at the beginning and read through page by page until we get to the end. It is important to develop effective reading strategies for approaching books, otherwise you may find them difficult and demotivating. Scan the *contents page* and the *index* for information relevant to your topic (use your keywords). Before reading the sections or *chapters* that appear relevant, check the layout and structure of the chapter. This awareness will help guide your reading of this section. Most chapters will have a title (some chapters begin with a chapter summary or *Abstract*) and section headings may be used within the chapter. If so, leaf through the chapter identifying the headings and skim read the first few sentences of each subsection. After obtaining a general idea of what the chapter covers, it will be easier to locate relevant sections. Try to identify the general idea that the author wants to express, any important *terms* and their *definitions* that are used and useful examples that help you follow the discussion. If the chapter includes separate *Introduction*, *Discussion* and *Conclusion* sections, it can be helpful to skim read these sections before reading the entire chapter closely.

Note-taking while reading

While reading large amounts of material, keeping track of important information you encounter becomes critical. It is advisable to print the texts that require close reading, as this means that you can underline important sections and write notes to yourself in the margin. This helps you locate specific information more easily when you start drafting your work. Your notes in the margin should capture the key idea or important information in just a few words; if you write any more than one or two phrases, you will find yourself submerged in detail again. Ideally, your notes in the margin should prompt you to recall the idea discussed in this section of the text.

Exercise 5.3

Note-taking

Read this excerpt from the Literature Review section of Chen's (2006, p. 37) article on students' use of email. Zurab has taken notes of the main ideas. Read through the text. Add any additional notes in the margin of Paragraph 1. Complete the note-taking for Paragraph 3 by jotting down the main ideas in the margin.

> This type of e-mail practice [e-mail communication with professors] has received increasing attention from researchers and educators because they found that the e-mails that L2 learners write often contain some inappropriate language use and may even produce a negative impact on their studies. Probably the earliest study on L2 learners' e-mail communication with professors was conducted by Hartford and Bardovi-Harlig (1996).

Results from previous studies – 4 points

They compared how international graduate students and U.S. graduate students made requests to professors via e-mail and reported four important findings: (a) international students used fewer mitigating forms in their request e-mails that produced a negative impact; (b) they used institutional explanations less frequently for their requests; (c) they mentioned their personal needs and time frames more often for their requests; and (d) they acknowledged imposition on the faculty members less often than U.S. students. The authors concluded that the L2 students' use of these discourse forms and strategies reflected an overestimation on the part of the student of the faculty member's level of obligation to comply with their requests and that they seemed not to recognize the different status that the student and the professor assumed in the academic context. This study points out crucial pragmatic problems in L2 students' request e-mails sent to professors, yet it does not explain why they used these socioculturally inappropriate discourse strategies.

Status differences important

Subsequent studies on student-to-professor e-mail communication have similar findings. Biesenbach-Lucas and Weasenforth (2000) found that L2 students used fewer modal constructions and hedged expressions in their e-mails than did U.S. students; instead, their e-mails often contained inappropriate pleading for help from the professor. In addition, L2 students employed negotiation moves less frequently and solicited professor responses less explicitly, which indicated that they lacked effective negotiation skills, which might hinder them from achieving their communicative goals. Examining the same e-mail data, Biesenbach-Lucas (2005) further pointed out that L2 students demonstrated less initiative and weaker capability in using e-mail to interact with professors than did American students, particularly in providing progress reports, negotiating project topics, requesting professor responses, and offering potential response points for the professor. Both studies attributed the deviation of L2 students' language use in e-mail to their adoption of an inappropriate cultural model that might be acceptable within their native cultural experiences but is not acceptable within the U.S. academic culture. Furthermore, Biesenbach-Lucas (2005) speculated that some L2 students' limited experience with the e-mail medium in their home countries might also make their e-mail use ineffective or problematic. Hence, she suggests that L2 students need to learn appropriate ways of both interacting with professors and using this medium.

Previous findings – lacked spec. pragmatic skills

Understanding complex nouns

Specialized academic texts often contain a lot of complex noun phrases – that is, noun phrases with a number of elements, whether noun + noun, adjective + noun, or noun + prepositional phrase. Two different noun phrases may also be combined with a connector such as 'and'. The use of complex noun phrases increases the information density of the text and, if you are not very familiar with this text type, decoding it can be challenging. If you find yourself reading a sentence several times, trying to understand the meaning, it might be due to the complexity of the noun phrases. To 'unpack' such noun phrases, it is useful to identify the main or the *head* noun; the other elements of the phrase serve to define or specify this noun.

Exercise 5.4

Complex nouns

1 Here is a list of complex noun phrases from Chen's (2006) article on the use of email by students. In the first three examples, the head noun has been underlined for you. Identify the head nouns in the remaining examples.
   - a e-mail <u>interaction</u>
   - b U.S. <u>professors</u>
   - c request <u>strategies</u>
   - d request e-mails
   - e request acts
   - f lexico-syntactic mitigating forms
   - g lexico-syntactic modifications
   - h pre-request support moves
   - i Chinese-speaking students

2 Try 'unpacking' these noun phrases. For instance:
   - a lexico-syntactic modifications = modifications to the lexico-syntax
   - b e-mail interaction =
   - c request strategies =

3 In the paragraph below, the noun phrases have been 'unpacked'. The text is now longer, less concise and unidiomatic. Replace the underlined sections with the appropriate complex noun phrase. Try to avoid looking back at the previous exercises as you do this!

   With a focus on Chinese-speaking students' <u>interaction through e-mail</u> with <u>professors from the U.S.</u>, both Chang and Hsu (1998) and Chen (2001) found that the <u>strategies to make requests</u> that Chinese students used in e-mails differed from what U.S. students did. U.S. students tended to structure their e-mails making requests in a direct sequence placing the act of requesting at the beginning of the message, but their linguistic forms of the request act were more indirect involving more lexico-syntactic forms with a mitigating function. In contrast, students from China tended to structure their request e-mails in an indirect sequence using many pre-request moves with a supporting function and placing the request act at the end, while their linguistic forms of the request act were more direct with fewer modifications to the lexico-syntax. These findings are consistent with studies on Chinese speakers' oral and written requests (Kirkpatrick, 1991, 1993; Nash, 1983; Zhang, 1995a, 1995b), which indicates that students who speak Chinese probably transfer the request strategies that they normally use in Chinese to the English request e-mails written to professors.

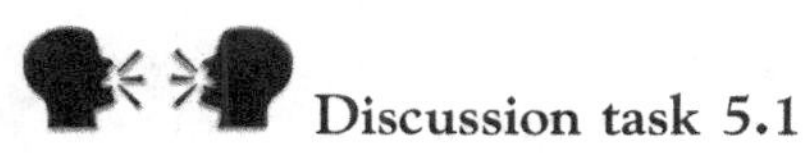

Discussion task 5.1

Complex noun phrases

1 Write down five complex noun phrases that you have seen used in academic texts in English. 'Unpack' each phrase as you did in Exercise 5.4. In small groups, look at the extended versions. In each case, can you identify what the original complex noun phrase was?
2 Does your L1 use this type of complex noun phrase in academic discourse? If so, note down three complex noun phrases in your L1. In small groups, discuss how you would express each concept in English.
3 Insights from the literature 5.1 describes the development of the use of complex noun phrases. Which type of complex noun phrase do you find most challenging to understand in reading texts? Which do you find most difficult to produce?

Insights from the literature 5.1

Complexity in academic texts

Complex noun phrases have become an increasingly frequent feature of written academic discourse over the last century; similarly, compared to early examples of written academic discourse, the variety of structures displayed by these constructions has become much more varied (Biber & Gray, 2011). In their study of the development of complex noun phrases from around the seventeenth century until today, Biber and Gray (2011) point out that the range of early examples of this construction was quite limited; typically they were either place nouns (e.g. '*Greenwich* Park', '*farm* house', '*ground* floor') or concrete/tangible nouns (e.g. '*chamomile* tea', '*coffee* house', '*corn* field'). The frequency of use and the types of constructions increased in the nineteenth and twentieth centuries. Complex noun phrases began to include types of institutions (e.g. '*school* proposal', '*union* member'), states or conditions (e.g. '*cancer* cells', '*maternity* hospital') and intangible nouns (e.g. '*class* examination', '*weather* bureau'). Nominalized verbs also appeared as premodifiers (e.g. '*extradition* treaty', '*government* officials', '*research* fund', '*trade* legislation', '*transport* union', '*enrolment* date'). Late in the twentieth century, complex noun phrases comprising three (or more) nouns became widespread (e.g. '*oil tanker* driver', '*justice department* official') (Biber & Gray, 2011, p. 238). The authors conclude that while such constructions have become commonplace in writing, particularly in academic and journalistic writing genres, they remain infrequent in spoken communication. Biber and Gray (2010) demonstrate how academic discourse displays a much more compressed style compared to spoken language on account of frequent complex noun phrases. Such constructions compress meaning into a few words by attaching pre- and post-modifiers to the head noun. Such modifiers may be another noun (e.g. '*hair* style'), a nominalized verb (e.g. '*participant* perspective'), an adjective (e.g. '*social* science') or a prepositional phrase (e.g. 'pattern *of behaviour*'). It is not unusual to find multiple modifiers in one noun phrase. As the authors contend, the meaning expressed by these complex constructions may not be obvious to readers unfamiliar with the topic or unused to written academic discourse. Although phrases may have the same structure, the meanings they express may be quite different. For instance, in the following examples of complex noun phrases comprising a head noun and a prepositional phrase post-modifier, the meaning relationship between these two components (i.e. the head noun and the modifier) may be quite different: 'houses *in the suburbs*' (houses located in the suburbs); 'a decrease *in consumer consumption*' (consumer consumption decreased); 'houses *on the market*' (houses that have been offered for sale). Biber and Gray (2010) point out that this compact writing style in genres such as academic discourse helps writers pack a lot of information into limited space. This information is largely predictable for readers knowledgeable about the subject matter, and the condensed style allows readers to scan material quickly and extract information. However, for novice readers without specialist knowledge in a particular academic field, such noun phrases can be difficult to decipher.

As the structure of complex noun phrases can be quite unpredictable, learning how to correctly formulate complex noun phrases commonly used in a particular discipline is part of acquiring specialized written discourse competence. As literacy skills become more sophisticated, writers – whether native or non-native users of English – tend towards increasing complexity and variety in their use of noun phrases. In their comparison of how two groups of non-native English-speaking students use noun phrases, Parkinson and Musgrave (2014) show that the use of attributive adjectives as noun modifiers (e.g. '*experimental* research') appears to develop early as these are used by both the lower- and the higher-proficiency groups; in contrast, only the higher-proficiency learners appear confident in using participle adjectives as noun modifiers (e.g. '*driving* lesson') and this group also makes greater use of nouns as pre-modifiers (e.g. '*university* exam'). In other cases, however, little or no difference could be found between the two groups' use of complex noun phrases, such as in the case of noun phrases modified by a prepositional phrase beginning with 'of' (e.g. 'construction *of knowledge*'); similarly, little difference was found between the use of relative clauses by the two groups (e.g. 'students *who failed the exam*'). Nevertheless, despite their prevalence in formal academic writing, complex noun phrases are often neglected in pedagogical grammar books or academic writing guides (Biber & Gray, 2010).

From reading to writing: critically engaging with the literature

After reading a number of academic sources, you will start to become familiar with the specialized terms being used and the array of ideas discussed in relation to your topic. In your own Literature Review, it will be important to read a number of key studies relevant to your topic and demonstrate that you understand the main issues discussed in these works. A stronger Literature Review will also show an awareness of the disagreements or controversies that exist, in recognition of the fact that authors don't always agree with each other. This awareness of the various perspectives discussed will help you develop your own views. Perhaps you also find ideas or views that you disagree with or that have limitations; for example, they do not seem applicable to the context of your country or your L1. Building your awareness of alternative viewpoints and interpretations and considering your own position in relation to these is part of 'critically engaging with the literature'. Such engagement will help you situate your own work within the existing literature.

Showing limitations, disagreeing or extending previous claims

Being able to indicate limitations in previous research is evidence of critical engagement with the literature. Of course, you will need to provide support or evidence for your ideas or beliefs. For instance, if you believe that claims or findings are not entirely relevant or applicable in your own cultural context, you need to demonstrate convincingly why your social, educational or linguistic context differs from the context in which the author's research is situated. If you disagree with a claim made by an author, think carefully about how to express this. Citing an authoritative source that supports your view or that provides counterevidence to the claim adds credibility and authority to your position. In the absence of a suitable reference to support your view, your counterview may sound like a personal opinion.

It is quite possible that you cannot find a published source for some important information. In this case, you might also consult a reputable academic who would be considered to be authoritative on that particular matter. Instead of citing a book or an article to support your claim, you will cite this person's name, followed by 'personal communication' in brackets. This shows that you consulted an authoritative source orally or via email. Only do this if you are sure you cannot find the necessary information in reputable books or articles, or to supplement information you have already found in published material.

You may also critically engage with the literature by demonstrating that a topic, a phenomenon or a concept described in a study can be applied to contexts in your own country. You may also wish to show that a claim is only partially true or relevant in your own cultural context, and that limitations to its applicability exist.

Tip 5.1

Phrases to help formulate a critical stance

The following phrases may help you formulate your views as you interact critically with the literature. These phrases are part of the *Academic Phrasebank* (Morley, n.d.).

Introducing questions, problems or limitations

'A weakness with this argument, however, is that . . .'

'One of the limitations with this explanation is that it does not account for . . .'

'One problem with this explanation is that . . .'

'However, this method of analysis has a number of limitations.'

'Another problem with this approach is that it fails to take X into account.'

Referring to previous work

'Researchers have not treated X in much detail.'

'Previous studies of X have not dealt with . . .'

'Most studies in the field of X have only focused on . . .'

'The research to date has tended to focus on X rather than Y.'

Incorporating criticisms from other writers

'Many scholars now argue that this approach has had only limited success.'

'Jones (2003), for example, argues that . . .'

'Jones (2003) has also questioned why . . .'

'However, Jones (2003) points out that . . .'

Insights from the literature 5.2

The reading–writing nexus

For many students, the Literature Review may be the most challenging section of their research project. It involves multiple steps and skills. In addition to the technical skill of learning to use online databases for an effective and efficient literature search, strategic thinking skills are equally important, as students need to identify what to search for, prioritize what they read and, within this material, identify references to additional relevant sources. During the literature search, students also need to note down the results of their explorations and reading in order to form an idea of how material relates to the research question(s). New understandings from the literature might lead to a reformulation of the research question(s), which in turn might prompt the student to steer the literature search in a different direction.

Research into how postgraduate students undertake reading in preparation for and while writing their Literature Review has shown that reading and writing are not decompartmentalized stages of research. Rather, at this level of study, the reading, literature search and writing processes are interlinked. Based on her interview data with postgraduate students from the humanities, Kwan (2009, p. 188) claims that 'that "key" literature does not exist "cut-and-dried"'; that is, it would be unusual for students to base their research solely on a list of sources they receive from their supervisor. Rather, knowledge about what to read and how to use the material in one's research typically evolves through discovery and knowledge formation processes that entail a nexus of searching, reading and writing. Nevertheless, the majority of Kwan's informants acknowledged their supervisors' initial guidance in identifying (and providing) central references for their work. Such contributions could be in the form of lists of recommended readings or the indication of central names and works related to the topic or methodological approach. Supervisors or mentors were also helpful in making sense of the sometimes overwhelming number of hits that students received from their online bibliographic searches.

Kwan's informants also noted how, through interacting with their supervisor while undertaking their Literature Review, they might learn about a different theoretical paradigm or methodological approach that changed to some degree the orientation of the research. Some students admitted that their supervisors had not been forthcoming in their initial search for literature, and that they had found greater support through engaging with the academic community of students and lecturers in their institution or through electronic communication with academics and students elsewhere. Kwan (2009) concludes that the process of identifying relevant authors and literature, and reading for the purpose of thesis writing, is often a very social undertaking, during which time the student may interact with a range of individuals.

Kwan's (2008) informants appeared to do most of the actual reading while they were simultaneously involved in actually writing the Literature Review. While the initial reading of sources served to help students create a rough outline of the structure of their Literature Review and start to write, students would often pause the writing process to return to read the literature intensively. This helped students clarify their ideas, overcome gaps in their knowledge and generate references to cite to support claims or ideas expressed. The process of reading while writing led some students to critically re-evaluate and rewrite sections they had already written. Some supervisors also identified inconsistencies or gaps in students' writing that required the students to consult the literature and redraft the section.

Emerging from the conversations between Kwan (2008, 2009) and her informants is an image of literature searches, reading and attempts to write the Literature Review section occurring in stops and starts at various stages of the research process. New discoveries led to a revision of previously written paragraphs or even a revision of the methods used, and newly uncovered sources led to the search for and reading of additional, related sources, often taking the student in a different direction. Kwan (2009, pp. 188–9) advises against the idea of a Literature Review resulting from a 'neat and tidy' or 'closed' list of references that is passed from supervisor to student; rather, she underscores the need for students to view the process of finding and engaging with literature as very much a social process that benefits from interacting with academics on-site and elsewhere.

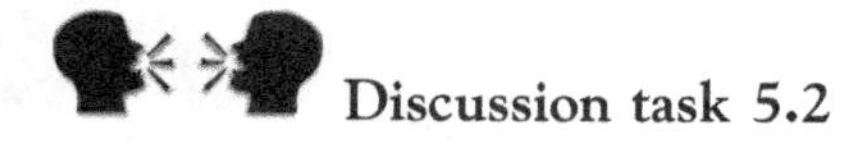

Discussion task 5.2

The reading–writing nexus

Before doing this task, read Insights from the literature 5.2.

1. Think of a time when you conducted a literature search for an essay or a research paper you wrote for a university course *or* reflect on how you have conducted your literature search and begun reading for your research project. Share with your partner what you learned about the connection between reading, writing and your literature search during this process.
2. In light of your experience, what particularly rang true for you in the discussion on reading and writing in Insights from the literature 5.2? After reading this box, identify one thing you intend to try in future.

6 Collecting data

Most student research projects in English language studies involve the collection and analysis of data. Indeed, for students interested in topics related to applied linguistics, translation or education, the data component will likely be central to the study. A library-based study involving the analysis of a literary text might be more usual for students of literature, however. Before launching into collecting data, you need to consider which data collection method would be best suited to elicit the information required to answer the research question(s). Subsequently, attention needs to be given to the data collection instrument, the location, the informants (or respondents), the timing and obtaining permission to collect data from your selected informants.

Access and ethical issues

For data collected in an educational institution, a letter of introduction from the university requesting access to classes or teachers will usually be required. Your supervisor or the head of department should be able to assist with this. Similarly, to interview or email a public official such as a representative of the Ministry of Education, a letter from your supervisor or the department is needed to explain in general terms the purpose and the sort of information required. These logistical steps need to be taken well ahead of the actual data collection, as time is required to establish the right contacts and secure access.

Gaining access to people and institutions for data collection purposes requires initiating a relationship based on a degree of trust. In the course of your data collection, informants may share personal experiences and views, or you might be given access to privileged information. It is important that this trust is respected. In most cases, the identity of the participants in your study should not be revealed. To ensure individuals remain anonymous, you can give them a simple code name; this could be a number (e.g. 'Teacher 1', 'Teacher 2' etc.) or a pseudonym. It is usual to provide study participants with a statement in writing informing them that their participation is voluntary, that the data will be treated in a confidential manner, that their identities will not be revealed and that they may withdraw from the study whenever they wish. The exact content of such a statement depends on the study. Usually, this statement is signed and dated by each participant to confirm they received it and agree to participate under these conditions.

Your institution may have an office or committee that oversees ethical issues related to research conducted at your university. If so, there is likely to be an established procedure to obtain approval to conduct research involving people. While these procedures differ greatly from institution to institution, they usually require the researcher (in this case, the student) to provide a detailed description of his/her proposed interaction with participants and an explanation of how the data from participants will be used. As obtaining approval can be quite time-consuming, this formality should be built into your research timeline.

Choosing your participants

The choice of participants for your study is vital, as the data you elicit, or the information you compile, will depend to a large extent on who you ask. Your research question(s) should guide your selection of participants or informants. Once it is clear who your target group is, consider what the ideal number of informants might be. A larger participant group (or data set) does not necessarily mean a higher-quality research project or more reliable findings. The appropriate number of respondents depends on your research question(s) and your data collection instrument. For instance, it is very unlikely that you will undertake interviews with 100 students, but it is very easy to use a questionnaire with this number.

Discussion task 6.1

Thinking about participants

Look again at the description of Zareen's, Zurab's and Zeina's projects in Examples 2.1–2.3 (pp. 8–10). In pairs, discuss the following questions:

1. How many students should Zareen use in her study? How might she locate these students in order to administer the questionnaire? What sort of information would she need to tell her participants with regard to their participation?
2. Whose emails should Zurab study (i.e. which group of students)? How many emails should he collect? How should he collect them? What sort of information would he need to tell his participants with regard to their participation?
3. How many students should Zeina use in her study? How might Zeina locate these students in order to administer her test? What sort of information would she need to tell her participants with regard to their participation?

In your group discussion, you may have mentioned some of the following information:

- *Zareen* compiled data from female and male students staying in the university hostels. She aimed for a total of 100 participants: 50 males and 50 females. She informed her potential participants by hanging information sheets about her study on the notice board of each hostel, by distributing leaflets and by making an announcement to students in the dining hall at a time when most students arrive for a meal. She informed students (in the written texts and orally) that their participation was voluntary and their identities would not be revealed. She also told them how much time they would need to complete the questionnaire.

- *Zurab* decided to study how English majors write emails. He chose to include students in their third year of study. At the beginning of the semester, he went to the 300-level lectures and asked for volunteers. There were a total of 38 students at this level. He requested that students in each class send emails to him that they sent to their teachers during the semester (using the cc function); he gave all the volunteers this request and his email address in writing. He distributed this information in writing and included a paragraph in the text assuring students that their participation was voluntary, that their identities would not be revealed and that their emails would only be gathered for the purposes of the study and would not be forwarded to anyone else. At the end of the semester, he had managed to collect around 35 emails from 14 different students.
- *Zeina* developed a short test involving the translation of sentences containing polysemous words from English into Arabic. She administered this test to all students enrolled on a 300-level course in translation in one semester. A total of 35 students were enrolled, but she only managed to get 31 students to complete the test (19 girls and 12 boys). The week before giving the test, she visited the class and distributed information in writing about the purpose of the test and assured students that their participation was voluntary and that their identities would not be revealed.

Zareen had a sample of 100 students from a total population of 625 English major students. *Zurab* managed to include 14 students from a total of 38 in his study and *Zeina*'s sample comprised 31 students. As you can see, Zeina's sample was more representative of the total population than Zareen's and Zurab's.

The three students used different sampling methods:

- *Zareen* used a variety of techniques to get her sample. By targeting students accommodated in the hostel, she potentially had convenient access to large numbers of students. She also identified an event (the evening meal) as being an opportune moment to inform as many students as possible about her study in person. She then requested volunteers from those present at this 'event'.
- Similar to Zareen, *Zurab* first selected one group of students, and then he requested volunteers.
- *Zeina*'s sample group (i.e. translation majors in their final year of study) was selected because this was a convenient way of locating a suitable number of informants with the required profile.

Tip 6.1 provides more information on selecting or locating participants for your study.

Tip 6.1

Sampling strategies

Below are a few examples of approaches to locate participants for your study. Some studies use a combination of approaches.

Probability sampling:

- *Random sampling*: You select the participants randomly (e.g. select a location, such as a busy pedestrian zone, and distribute the questionnaire to passers-by). Note that this is not entirely random, as the sample still reflects the characteristics of the population that might visit the chosen location. Collecting data at different locations could mitigate this.
- *Systematic sampling*: You select every second or every tenth person, for instance (having the class attendance list would help in identifying these).
- *Stratified sampling*: You select randomly within a specific group.
- *Cluster sampling*: You select clusters within a population (e.g. select one student's name from the attendance list and then select five more students sitting closest to this person in the class).

Non-probability sampling:

- *Convenience sampling*: You select the participants who are most convenient.
- *Voluntary sampling*: The participants volunteer (self-select).
- *Purposive sampling*: You choose only the participants who you think will be most interesting or most relevant to your study (e.g. limit the sample to students who have a TOEFL score above 550 or who have spent time in the UK).
- *Snowball sampling*: You increase your sample by asking your initial participants (identified by one of the above methods) to identify other people whom would be suitable (e.g. select all students from one class and then ask them each to nominate another two students from a different class whom they think match the required profile).
- *Event sampling*: You use people who attend a particular event as your participants (e.g. people attending the Student Council meeting).

Data collection instruments

Questionnaires

Questionnaires are good for collecting specific information about large numbers of people. They are usually used to elicit short answers about a number of different topics; these often include some biographical information (age, gender, major, L1, length of time in a particular job etc.) and topics relating to a person's opinions or habits. They are less well suited to gathering information about people's beliefs and experiences, as answers to such questions are more difficult to anticipate in a selection of set responses to a closed question, and difficult to capture in a one- or two-sentence answer to an open question. Nevertheless, questionnaires can still be used for this purpose.

This section describes different ways of formulating questions for use in questionnaires and interviews. Any question can be formulated in different ways and it is quite normal to change the wording of a question several times at the preparation and trial stages of a questionnaire. How a question is formulated can affect the type of answer elicited, both in terms of the length and the content of the response. You might change the formulation of a question, for example, because you realize that it doesn't elicit the type of information you need, or because respondents don't easily understand the question.

Anonymity in questionnaire design

In most cases, it is unlikely that you will need to identify each person who completes your questionnaire; in fact, your respondents may be more open and truthful in their answers if the questionnaire is anonymous. This means not requesting the person's name, student ID number, date of birth or any other information that may later help to identify them. The anonymity of the questionnaire can also be compromised by juxtaposing certain biographical data in your description of participants. For example, revealing a participant's age, gender and place of origin increases the likelihood that the person can later be identified. Some information, such as age, may be considered private. Unless it is essential to have precise biographical information, age may be elicited in the form of the person's age group rather than exact age (e.g. 'Circle the correct answer: You are 20–30; 31–40; 41–50; above 50').

Although the completed questionnaires may be anonymous, you still need to treat them confidentially and not show completed questionnaires to others. This information has been shared with you under certain conditions and these conditions need to be respected, even after the study has finished.

Question types: closed and open questions

Closed questions limit the range of answers a respondent can give. Usually, the possible answers are provided for the respondent to choose from. The purpose of closed questions is usually to elicit information where the response is 'Yes' or 'No' or a category such as gender or nationality. You can also elicit opinions by providing answers in the form of a scale. Closed questions allow you to calculate your results relatively easily. The disadvantage of this question type is that the pre-set responses may not actually reflect the views or experience of the respondent, who may feel forced to give a particular answer. This can be avoided to some extent by providing an 'opt-out' option (e.g. 'Don't know') or by giving the respondents the chance to write their own answer by inserting an 'other' option.

Open questions do just that; they don't limit the range of possible answers the respondent can give and answers for such questions are not predictable either in length or content. Open questions begin with 'Why', 'How', 'What do you think' etc., and they are often used to find out about people's beliefs or the reasons for their actions. It is usually advisable to place open questions towards the end of the questionnaire. If they appear at the beginning, some respondents might not complete the questionnaire because it looks like too much work. Also, if they appear at the end, respondents will have had time to reflect on the general topic as they work through the short-answer questions, and they might have thought of something extra to add by the time they reach the end.

The data elicited from open questions are harder to describe in your Results chapter and difficult to quantify. The usual approach is to code for the content of the responses. This involves reading through the responses several times to identify themes. This procedure is described in more detail in the section on coding interview data in Chapter 7 (p. 102). Answers from open questions can also be more difficult to work with for the simple reason that someone's handwriting may be hard to decipher, or responses don't make sense or don't actually answer the question.

Some researchers use open questions in an initial questionnaire to gather information about the general area. This initial survey of ideas, opinions and experiences enables the researcher to identity the topics or categories that should be used in the questionnaire for the real data collection in the study. This information can also guide the researcher in providing possible answers to closed questions that reflect how respondents are likely to respond to a given question.

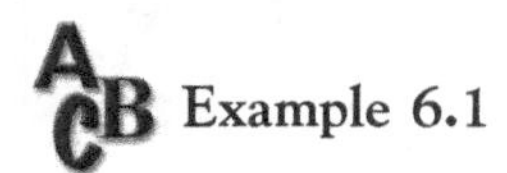

Example 6.1

Question types

Here are some examples of closed and open questions that Zareen used in her questionnaire to elicit data on student achievement and gender:

1 Your gender: Male Female

2 Have you ever failed a course during your degree programme? Yes No

2a If you answered 'Yes' to Question 2, why do you think you failed the course(s)?

3 Do you think you are capable of getting a higher GPA in the next semester? Yes No Don't know

3a If you answered 'Yes' to Question 3, what do you think you need to do to raise your GPA?

Formulating questionnaire items

It can be surprisingly challenging to formulate a question so it is unambiguous and easily understandable and elicits the required information. Some examples of poorly phrased questions are as follows. First, the wording of a question can lead the respondent to give a particular answer, because it becomes very hard to disagree with what is said. As a particular response is predictable (i.e. respondents might feel forced to agree with it), the answer isn't actually very informative. For instance:

> Do you think teachers should give equal attention to female and male students in the classroom?

Second, questions that make certain assumptions (e.g. that the respondent has had a particular experience or shares a particular opinion) should also be avoided. For instance:

> What did you find difficult about using the online chat function during the course?
> Give three reasons why knowing a foreign language will be important for your career.

The first question here assumes that all students experienced difficulty. A student who did not find anything difficult might mention something simply in order to give an answer. The second example assumes that all respondents are learning a language for professional reasons, but not everyone learns a language for this reason, and not all language learners have careers. Finally, keep the language used in your question simple. This is not the place to use terminology, uncommon or formal sounding words.

Questions that seem straightforward can be quite ambiguous in practice. For instance:

> How many people are there in your family?
> How many languages do you know?

In the first example, the concept of 'family' is very ambiguous. Does this include grandparents or an aunt who is living in your house? Think carefully about the information you need, and ask specific questions (e.g. 'How many siblings do you have?'). In the second example, it is not clear what it means to 'know' a language. For example, if you completed a beginner-level French course, do you 'know' French? When asking about competency in languages or about computer skills, for instance, it is more informative if respondents rate their ability (e.g. beginner, intermediate, advanced). In the case of languages, you can also ask about each of the four skills (speaking, writing, reading, listening).

Exercise 6.1

Closed questions in questionnaires

Below are examples of items from Zareen's questionnaire. For each question, think of a potential problem with how the question and answers are formulated.

Please circle the correct answer:

1 I attend my classes.
 a Always b Regularly
 c Sometimes d I am often absent
2 I have failed a course before.
 a Yes b No
3 When my teacher gives me study notes and holds a special revision class, I usually get a higher grade in the exam.
 a Yes b No

When Zareen piloted her questionnaire (see the section on piloting in this chapter, p. 74), she realized that these questions were confusing. For Question 1, students had different ideas of what 'regularly', 'sometimes' and 'often' meant. Also, the difference between 'I sometimes attend classes' and 'I am often absent' was not clear. For Question 2, students were not clear whether they were meant to answer with respect to their Bachelor degree studies or include their time in the Foundation Institute[1]; also, Zareen realized she needed more information from the students who had failed a course. For Question 3, respondents told Zareen that their teacher gave them a revision class, but didn't give them study notes. Zareen realized students were confused about how to answer because she was asking two different things in the one question. She decided to change the questions to the following:

1 During the Fall semester 2012, you:
 a were never absent in any class.
 b missed no more than 5 classes in total.
 c missed between 6 and 10 classes.
 d were absent for more than 10 classes.
2 Since beginning your Bachelor degree, how many courses have you failed?
 a None b One c Two d Three e Four or more
3 What does your teacher do to help you prepare for exams? (Tick the ones that apply to you.)
 a He/she gives us revision notes.
 b He/she holds a revision class.
 c He/she tells us the topics that will be in the exam.
 d He/she gives us a practice (or 'mock') exam.

e Other ______________________

f My teacher doesn't do anything to help us prepare.

4 Which things from Question 3 were most effective in helping you prepare for an exam? Put your answers in order of preference (1 = most useful).

1

2

3

If you have a closed question with a yes/no answer, it may be appropriate to add a 'Don't know' option. This allows respondents to 'opt out' rather than be forced to provide an answer that doesn't actually represent their view. For instance, your respondents might feel obliged to answer 'Yes' or 'No' when they actually are not sure; alternatively, they may avoid answering altogether. Depending on the question, this third option could also be 'No opinion', 'Undecided' or 'Neutral'. Similarly, for a multiple-choice question, it might be appropriate to provide an 'Other' option with a space for the answer. For this type of question, provide what you believe are the three or four most likely answers and allow the informant to insert an alternative answer at the end:

1 Is it important for your future career to get high grades at university?

a Yes b No c I don't know

2 What is the best place for you to study?

a At home b At the student hostel

c In the university library d Other (please write the place) ______

For most items in her questionnaire, Zareen used a *Likert scale*. This means that the respondent could choose the most appropriate answer from a scale of closely related items. Usually, questionnaires have five items on the scale. Example 6.2 uses a typical Likert scale to capture degrees of agreement or disagreement. You could use a similar scale for a different concept. For example, you want students' feedback on learning materials you have developed, and you decide to ask how useful they found the different resources. You might use a five-point Likert scale like this: 'Very useful'; 'Quite useful'; 'Neutral'; 'Not very useful'; 'Not useful at all'. In both this example and the one below, the 'neutral' option is in the middle. Survey respondents have a tendency to choose a middle option on a scale, so you could try moving this option to the left or the right on your scale to try to counter this.

A second type of scale requires respondents to indicate where they perceive themselves to be on a scale. Typically, scales of 1 to 11, 1 to 7, or even 1 to 5 are used. The left and right sides of the scale are polar opposites (see Example 6.3). The higher number (i.e. 11) signals agreement (or a positive response), and the lower number (i.e. 1) disagreement (or a negative response). If you have a list of items, respondents may tend to choose a similar response for each item on the list. To counter this, you could reverse the position of the positive and negative responses (i.e. put '1 = Strongly disagree' on the right and '11 = Strongly agree' on the left). To obtain the overall results for this type of scale, calculate the median rating for each item using the data from all respondents.

Example 6.2

Zareen's questionnaire

	Strongly agree	*Agree*	*Neutral*	*Disagree*	*Strongly disagree*
1 I have trouble following lectures.					
2 I understand how my teachers calculate my grades for my courses.					
3 I like to study for assessments with other students.					
4 I typically complete course assignments before their deadline.					
5 I am good at studying independently.					
6 I compete with other students to get a good grade.					
7 Getting a high grade is important for me.					
8 When I see other students' high grades, I feel motivated to try harder.					
9 My family expects me to get high grades.					
10 My lecturers should give me good grades because I (or my family) pay fees to attend this university.					
11 Learning a lot is more important than getting very high grades.					
12 I typically wait until the night before the exam to study.					
13 It is important for me to be among the top five students in my class.					

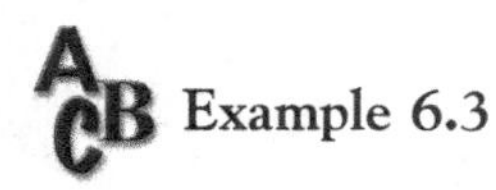

Example 6.3

Response scales

1 I have trouble following lectures in the English department.
1 = Strongly disagree 11 = Strongly agree

1	2	3	4	5	6	7	8	9	10	11

2 It is difficult for me to understand exams when the instructions are in English.
1 = Strongly disagree 11 = Strongly agree

1	2	3	4	5	6	7	8	9	10	11

Questionnaire length, presentation and organization

The order of items in your questionnaire needs some thought. As a general rule, begin with the easier questions that require short answers, and leave open questions and questions that are potentially sensitive until the end. Also, it is usually advisable to ask more general questions before specific questions. General questions allow the respondent to start reflecting on the topic and they contextualize the more specific questions. Think of this as allowing your respondents time to 'warm up'.

The overall number of items included and the time required to complete the questionnaire are important considerations. If a questionnaire seems too long or too much work, respondents may not complete it. You can check whether the length is acceptable during the piloting stage.

Finally, consider the visual impact of your questionnaire. Ensure it looks both serious and interesting. If it looks messy or unappealing, you may find it hard to get a response or your respondents may not take it very seriously. Considerations such as font size, typeface choice, layout and correct language use are important, and you should ensure there is enough space provided for answers to open questions.

Your questionnaire should ideally be in the respondents' L1. This way you can be more confident that your participants have understood the questions and that their responses really reflect their views. In the appendix of your project, however, you may need to provide versions of the questionnaires in the L1 and in English (ideally, one of these should be a completed version so the reader can see an example of a respondent's answers). Ensure you get someone with advanced bilingual competence to check your translation.

At the top of the questionnaire, include a short message to the participants, briefly describing your study in general terms and, if necessary, giving instructions on how to complete the questionnaire. Example 6.4 shows the brief introduction that Zareen provided on her questionnaire (it was translated into the respondents' L1).

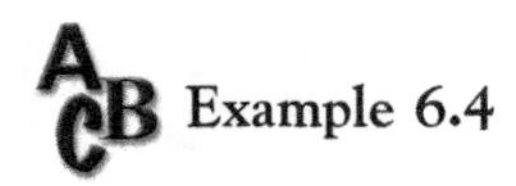

Example 6.4

Zareen's, questionnaire introduction

Dear Students,

I am a senior student in the English Section. I am doing my graduation project on the differences in attitudes towards university study and the levels of achievement of female and male students in the Department of Foreign Languages at the University. I would appreciate it if you could complete this brief questionnaire. The questionnaire is anonymous and your answers will be treated confidentially.

Please respond to the following statements by ticking or circling the most appropriate answer.

Thank you in advance for your cooperation.

Administering your questionnaire

The questionnaire can be delivered in either electronic or paper form, depending on who the respondents are, where they are located and what type of data you wish to collect. If the respondents are your peers, a paper questionnaire can be distributed in class. If the respondents are at different locations, consider sending your questionnaire in electronic form. If you have many closed questions, an electronic questionnaire may be preferable as some tools for creating questionnaires automatically calculate results. For instance, questionnaires can be easily created using the 'Form' option on Google Drive if you have a Gmail account. The website link to the questionnaire is then sent to respondents. There are other options available on the Internet worth exploring, such as Survey Monkey.

How the email accompanying the questionnaire is formulated will affect whether people respond. Ideally, you will have first made contact with the person before sending the questionnaire. If not, the person may just delete the email. If the response rate is low, send a carefully formulated reminder email. Such emails can be tricky to formulate as you need to achieve the right balance of assertiveness and deference; that is, the email both instructs the recipient to undertake the task, but also acknowledges the imposition involved and the recipient's freedom of action.

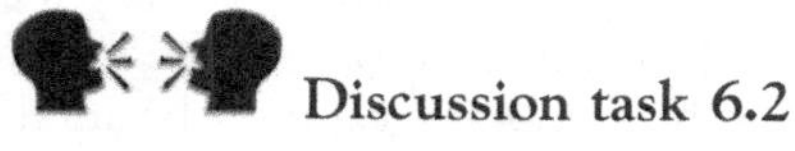

Discussion task 6.2

Composing a reminder email

The following examples are reminder emails sent by students to encourage a higher response rate to their questionnaire. The second example was more successful in this endeavour. Read the two examples below and discuss in small groups the questions that follow.

Example 1

Dear

Could you please update me regarding the questionnaire?

please note that I am running out of time and your fast response is highly appreciated. Moreover I have a shortage of 120 responses from faculty members, Your cooperation will help me move to the next step because I want to graduate soon

looking forward to hearing from you as soon as possible. . . .

Thanx ☺

Example 2

Dear colleague,

We would like to kindly draw your attention once again to our short survey about the importance of foreign languages in professional life. We have received over 50 responses thus far and the average time for completion is under 5 minutes. Please help us reach over 100! ☺

We would like to again ensure you that your answers will be anonymous and aggregated at the presentation of results.

Thank you for your assistance in this endeavour!

Sincerely,
Tomas

1. Why was Example 2 more successful? What advice would you give to the student who wrote Example 1?
2. Discuss the pros and cons of each example with respect to your own cultural context. Together, formulate a reminder email in English to recipients you don't personally know that would be appropriate in your cultural context.

Interviews

Collecting data through an interview rather than a questionnaire provides the opportunity to explore a topic in conversation with the interviewee; it is likely you don't know exactly how the conversation will develop and what topics will be raised. This unknown quality is one of the exciting things about interviews. Just how controlled the interview is, however, depends on the type of questions posed and the opportunities given to the interviewee to expand on information or to digress.

Before arranging your interviews, consider how you will capture the interviewee's answers. If a recording device is to be used, interviewees should be informed of your intention to record them. When people know they are being recorded, they may be more careful about how they express themselves. If the presence of a recording device appears to discourage the interviewee from giving a candid answer to a particular question, consider offering to turn off the recording device for that part of the interview and noting down the answer by hand. Note-taking during the whole interview may be impractical, as it is not easy to transcribe fast enough to capture the responses fully and accurately.

Confidentiality and respectful conduct

Before the interview, inform the interviewee that all information he/she shares with you during the interview will be treated anonymously and in confidence. Some researchers put a statement to this effect in writing and ask the interviewee to sign it. For your undergraduate project, this may not be required, as your research is still at a very introductory level, but it will likely be necessary for research at postgraduate level.

After the interview, it is good practice to send your transcript of the interview to the interviewee. This post-interview contact also allows you to ask for clarification if you found something unclear when transcribing or translating responses. While no answer may be forthcoming, the interviewee will have had the opportunity to correct any information that does not accurately reflect his/her viewpoint. The interviewee may even ask you to delete some information; it is quite normal that in the course of the conversation the interviewee may mention something that, in hindsight, he/she does not wish to share with other people. The interviewee should have the opportunity to 'take back' anything that was said if it later seems inappropriate. This respectful gesture demonstrates your serious approach to the person's input.

When using interview data in the Results chapter of your project, you can omit certain information that might identify the person or that could be too sensitive or unreliable (i.e. the interviewee might criticize the school or colleagues in a very subjective manner). Alternatively, you may also choose to get in touch with the interviewee again and check whether this response accurately reflects the person's views. Participants may be assigned a different name (or a number) in the Results chapter. You might also choose not to name the institution explicitly; for instance, could write 'the Foundation Institute at a private university in [name of country]' or 'a high school in [name of city]'. However, it may be necessary to name the institution where data were collected so the committee evaluating your project knows exactly where the study was undertaken.

Interview types

Interviews may be structured, semi-structured or unstructured. In a structured interview, the interviewer asks the same set of questions in the same order for each participant. Typical examples of structured interviews are marketing surveys or public-opinion polls. The interviewer may call at people's homes or telephone them and will run through a pre-established set of questions. No follow-up questions are posed. The semi-structured interview enables the researcher to elicit richer, more descriptive data. It is a more flexible approach, as the exact order of the questions and the formulation of each question may vary depending on the circumstances. The interviewer uses a set of questions or topics as a guide and may also ask additional follow-up questions. The final option is an unstructured interview. Here the interviewer does not arrive with a pre-established list of questions, but rather allows the questions to evolve naturally out of the conversation. To conduct unstructured interviews successfully, the interviewer needs to be very skilled to ensure that the conversation is still directed towards the topics or themes he/she wishes to discuss. They also tend to be more time-consuming and the data are less reliable as you may not actually ask every participant the same questions. You will likely undertake a structured or a semi-structured interview for your study; these are easier to do if you have less experience and more appropriate for the type of topics that undergraduate students investigate.

Carefully consider the questions you want to include in your interview protocol or guide (the list of questions). Choose your questions wisely; not only is your interviewee likely to have limited time, but also if the conversation continues too long, fatigue, irritation or disinterest may start to affect the quality of information elicited. The order of questions is also important. For an interview to be successful, you need to gain the trust of the interviewee. Avoid asking questions that require the respondent to reveal personal or potentially sensitive information early in the interview. It often helps to allow the interviewee time to 'warm up' a little by asking general questions before focusing on something specific. This allows the interviewee time to recollect different experiences and knowledge related to the topic. In some cases, however, specific questions at the beginning of an interview are necessary.

Open questions are very common in interviews. For each closed question posed, consider whether following up with an open question would be appropriate. It is easier to respond nimbly during the interview if you have considered this beforehand. For instance, if you ask 'Have you ever failed a course at university?', it would make sense to pose an open question to follow up (e.g. 'In your opinion, why didn't you get high enough grades to pass?').

Some questions may require greater self-disclosure than one might normally feel comfortable with. If this is the case, the interviewee may simply avoid giving a candid answer. To encourage a truthful answer, interviewers sometimes present the topic as though it were widespread, or they ask the interviewee to report about 'other people' before reporting about themselves. For instance, rather than ask directly 'Have you ever failed a course at university?' (a potentially embarrassing question), one could ask one of the following:

- 'Do you know students in your year who failed a course?'
- 'I've heard that some students failed a few courses in their final year. Do you know people who failed?'
- 'Many people fail a course at some point during their studies; have you ever had this experience?'

Tip 6.2

Interviews

For an interview to go well, and to facilitate continued contact with the interviewee after the meeting, it is important you make an initial positive impression and establish rapport with your interviewee. The following suggestions may help you achieve this:

- Begin the interview by briefly introducing your research topic and objectives. Consider bringing a brief outline on paper (with your name and contact details) in case your interviewee would like to keep the main details as a reference.

- Have a letter of introduction ready from your department or university. The interviewee may wish to see evidence concerning who you are and why you requested an interview. While this information may have been sent in advance by email, it is advisable to have a copy available on the day.
- Dress appropriately for the context; arrive on time; be clear about how much time you need for the interview; don't extend the interview beyond this time unless the interviewee agrees.
- Begin by thanking the interviewee for receiving you and end by thanking him/her for taking the time to talk to you. Ask whether you might contact him/her again by email in case you need to ask a follow-up question.

Discussion task 6.3

Technical problems during interviews

Together with a partner, read the following statements. For each one, identify what occurred during or after the interview that prompted this remark or exclamation. What is the message you can take away from each one?

During the interview

1 'I thought it was recording . . .'
2 'Does that flashing light mean "record" or "pause"?'
3 'I'm going use my phone to record you. Oops! Looks like it needs recharging!'
4 'Gee, the batteries must have run out. Can I ask you the last ten questions again?'
5 'I need a power outlet for my recorder . . . Oh, you don't have one in this room?'

After the interview

1 'Where are my notes from the rest of the questions for this person?'
2 'I don't know who this person is . . . When did I write these notes?'
3 'I thought that truck going past was loud!'
4 'I can't decipher my own writing. I wonder what her answer was?'
5 'I can barely hear his voice. I guess the recorder wasn't close enough.'
6 'I forgot to ask two important questions!'
7 'I can't believe it . . . I recorded over my last interview!'

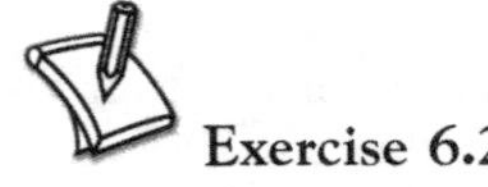

Exercise 6.2

Preparing for an interview

A number of tasks are involved in preparing for an interview. Put the following into the order in which you think you would do them:

1 Decide how you will capture the responses during the interview. Will you take notes? Record them? If so, what will you use to record?
2 Decide on potential follow-up questions you might ask.
3 Draft the questions you want to ask (or themes you want to talk about). Are the questions clear? Do they elicit the information you want to elicit?
4 Think about the order of your questions. Do you allow the interviewee to 'warm up' at the beginning?
5 Think about the first few sentences you will say as you sit down with your interviewee. What are you going to say that will build confidence and encourage a friendly, open exchange?
6 Test how long it takes (on average) to go through all the questions by doing a mock interview with one of your peers (give the person a role to act out to make it more realistic).

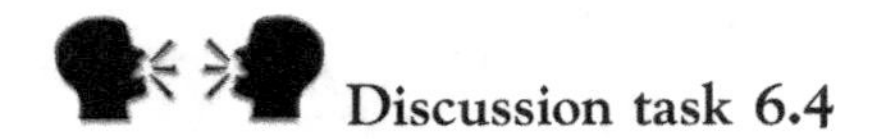

Discussion task 6.4

Planning an interview

For this task, you will interview a peer about his/her experience of one of the following topics:

- preparing for exams during school and university years;
- learning how to write a successful essay for school and university (in your L1 and in English); or
- coping with the heavy reading load during university studies.

1 Together with a partner, draft the list of questions you will ask about the topic you have chosen.
2 Read Insights from the literature 6.1 and note useful suggestions regarding question types and the interview procedure. Make any changes you wish to the list of questions you have drafted.
3 Interview your partner. Exchange interviewer/interviewee roles.
4 After you have experienced both roles, exchange views on how you found being the interviewer and the interviewee. Try to offer your partner suggestions for improving his/her interviewing technique. Were any questions less

successful at eliciting information? If so, what changes could you make to them?

Insights from the literature 6.1

Developing your interview skills

The success of an interview depends on the usefulness of the 'talk' that the interviewer is able to generate during the exchange. Getting the interviewee to speak openly about topics relevant to your research project is quite a skill. It takes a lot of practice and reflection to develop one's interviewing ability, and at this point you are likely to be just starting to develop these skills. Whereas in an everyday conversation we usually speak in quite general or vague terms, useful interview data is rich in detail. Richards (2003, p. 53) advises interviewees to 'seek the particular' in the sense that it is important to steer interviewees towards providing more specific information than they would usually do in conversation. In doing so, the interviewer runs the risk of making the interview seem like an interrogation. To counter this, the interviewer needs to use a variety of question types, open and closed, which invite the interviewee to describe an event or situation in general terms, adding impressions or opinions, and then focus on specific aspects as required at particular points of the exchange. Knowing when to prompt the interviewee to focus on the specifics requires good listening skills, a sense of timing, and sensitivity with regard to the dynamics of the interaction. The challenge of listening attentively and listening over a sustained period shouldn't be underestimated (Richards, 2003). While listening, the interviewer should signal his/her attention through verbal and non-verbal responses such as 'Hmm', 'Yes', 'Aha' or using nodding and eye contact as non-verbal cues where appropriate. As Richards (2003) points out, it is important not to constrain the interviewee to a rigid agenda of questions and topics, but rather to allow space for the interviewee to touch upon topics or mention details that appear important to him/her.

Although novice interviewers are usually advised to avoid or minimize the use of closed questions as they generate short responses (often just 'Yes' or 'No'), Roulston (2011) notes that closed questions can help to shift the focus to specific issues or factual information, and they can be an important way of checking understanding of previous talk. Richards (2003) maintains that a variety of different question types helps provide the right focus at different points of the exchange. The five question types he identifies are: opening; check and reflect; follow-up; probe; structuring. As he notes, it is useful to begin interviews by using an *open question* that encourages an extended response. The phrasing of such questions might be 'Tell me about . . .' or 'Talk me through . . .', for instance. Questions to *check understanding* of what has been said might be formulated by paraphrasing what the interviewee just said; in response, the interviewee may provide clarification or additional details. *Follow-up questions* are used to elicit additional information about something the interviewee might say. Sometimes it might be enough to simply show interest (e.g. by saying 'Really?', or by asking a 'wh- question'), but in other cases the interviewer may have to ask explicitly for more information. Similar to follow-up questions, *probing questions* are used to gain a better understanding of an event or topic by asking for more detail. Wh- questions usually serve this purpose but, again, questions phrased as 'Can you tell me more about . . .' may also be suitable. Finally, *structuring questions* allow the interviewer to transition between different stages of the interview, for example, to return to an earlier topic (e.g. 'Coming back to the topic of . . .') or to move ahead to a different topic (e.g. 'Moving now to the topic of . . ., could you tell me about . . .'). Interview skills can only develop through practice and reflection; one approach to support this development is to record trial interviews, listen critically to the exchanges and consider how alternative ways of phrasing questions might affect the evolution of the interviews.

Observations

If your topic is related to the teaching–learning process or the use of language in the workplace, it may be appropriate to collect data through observations of the classroom or the workplace; this may be in addition to data you collect through interviews or questionnaires. Observations can provide valuable insight into real-life practice; what people say they do and what they actually do in practice may be quite different!

The researcher may take a non-participatory or participatory role during the observation. As a non-participant, you don't take part in any activities and the goal is to be as unobtrusive as possible. You will probably have a checklist of things you are looking for and you will be taking detailed notes during your observation. As a participant, you take an active part in the usual activities undertaken at this location. For example, in a classroom context, you may contribute as a student, or you may choose to team-teach the lesson with the class teacher. This gives you the perspective of what is happening in the interaction as someone involved in the process. Most students take a non-participatory role in their research, as this is easier for novice researchers.

There are two approaches to observations: unstructured or structured (or planned). The former approach involves the researcher undertaking observations without a preconceived plan of what to focus on; in this case, the researcher needs to take notes on everything that is happening. Later, the researcher looks through the data to find patterns. Alternatively, during a structured or planned observation, the researcher has a clear framework of what he/she is intending to observe, usually in the form of a worksheet with a list of topics.

The focus may be on how often something happens, how certain statements or questions are formulated, who is involved, where people stand in relation to one another, the sequence of certain events or exchanges, or reactions to certain prompts. As your project is small-scale and undertaken over a limited period of time, it is very likely you will take the latter approach. Before entering the classroom, you need to think carefully about what you need to focus on, how you will record your observations, and what additional things you might look out for.

Collecting data through observations requires careful planning, as well as time and energy to carry them out effectively. They may be much more time-consuming than questionnaires, for instance. As an observer, the researcher does not control the process, and has to be present for quite a long time (or on many different occasions). How long observations should be or how many observations are needed will depend on the context and the topic, but it is important that you do not limit yourself to just a couple of observations. First, the phenomenon you are studying simply may not occur during the period of time you are present. Second, your presence will inevitably have an effect on the people you came to observe, which means that the data collected may not reflect what normally happens in that particular setting. To mitigate this effect, the teacher and students need to become accustomed to your presence. As a guideline, observations should continue until reaching saturation point; that is, the point when the data seem repetitive and nothing new is observed.

To minimize your impact, sit in a corner or at the back of the room where you have a good view of the activities, but out of the direct vision of the people you are observing. Over a period of several observation sessions, they may start forgetting there is a visitor in the room, which is what you are aiming for. This is not a realistic goal in all contexts, however. For instance, in gender-segregated contexts (e.g. a girls' or a boys' school), it will be difficult for a female researcher to collect data in an all-male environment (and vice versa), as the researcher will never have an 'invisible' presence in the room. In this case, it might be worthwhile asking a sibling or peer to assist with your data collection. This would require careful training of the assistant to ensure the person collects data in the manner you would. If you decide to do this, it might help to undertake several trial observations together and compare your data.

Exercise 6.3

Creating a data collection instrument for observations

1 Consider this research topic chosen by a student majoring in English education:

> Zeki wants to study Turkish–English bilingual instructors' use of the L1 and the L2 in university lectures. He will collect data from observations.

Create a data collection instrument for Zeki to use in his observations. Consider the following: what is Zeki looking for exactly? How should he record his observations?

2 If you are at an institution where some lectures are offered in English, you could try the following task. Use the worksheet you have created and collect data from a couple of lectures given in English by native speakers of your L1 in different departments. How effective was your observation worksheet? What changes would you make to it?

Piloting your data collection instrument

Once you have designed your questionnaire, test or observation worksheet or you have decided on your interview questions, it is important to test how your data collection instrument actually works in practice – that is, whether your respondents understand the instructions and whether the answers they give provide you with the type of data you aim to collect. This is not a minor detail; your whole study rests on of the effectiveness of your data collection. Trialling (or piloting) your data collection instrument can help test its effectiveness and it allows you to make changes to the choice and formulation of questions before launching into your data collection. It is not usually possible to collect data from the same sample group twice because you made a mistake the first time! When piloting the data collection instrument, do a trial run with a group that has similar characteristics to your target group. If you are unable to pilot your data collection instrument with a similar group, you could trial it with people able to provide constructive, objective feedback on its effectiveness. If these respondents complete the task you give them (i.e. they understand your instructions and the questions), and their answers are representative of the type of information you wanted to elicit, your data collection instrument was successful. It is quite usual, however, to make changes to your instrument in light of the experience of trialling it. Typically, questionnaire items may need to be reformulated, reordered, added or deleted. If you did Exercise 6.3, you probably discovered that the initial experience of observing a class helped you make adjustments to the observation worksheet.

Focus-group discussions

A focus group is a gathering of people brought together by the researcher for the specific purpose of discussing topics related to an area of research. The researcher has the role of the facilitator of the discussion, although if the discussion starts to move off track, the researcher's role may become more of a moderator. The point of a focus group is to elicit people's views in relation to a topic and to examine how people make sense of certain situations and experiences through talk. For instance, the focus group might help you understand why people in your work environment or community believe changes need to be made to their education system, or how the need to use English in the work environment may affect people's performance at work.

Focus groups are not suitable for all types of studies. For example, if you want to compare the views of different groups of people, if you need the same information from a range of people or if you need to observe actual behaviour, you should use one of the previous data collection methods (questionnaires, interviews or observations). A focus-group discussion is not a suitable method to compile data on whether people agree or disagree with a particular idea or phenomenon. A focus group is a public setting and, just as in any other interaction, people may not necessarily disclose their true opinion. Participants may choose not to voice an opinion if it is not in harmony with those expressed by other group members. Alternatively, participants may publicly agree with an idea, but disagree in private.

Focus groups may be used in addition to other data collection methods. For instance, after compiling data about your topic through questionnaires, you could present the focus-group participants with a selection of the results for them to discuss. This might help you understand the reasons underlying the views and opinions expressed in your data. Alternatively, this method may be used at the initial phase before you collect data through questionnaires or interviews to provide you with an insight into the range of views and experiences a group of people has in relation to your topic. This can help you select the topics to include in your data collection instrument. The data generated through focus groups are not quantifiable or generalizable; that is, you shouldn't present your findings numerically and you shouldn't generalize the findings from your small focus-group discussion to a larger population.

The typical group size of a focus group is around six. Larger groups offer fewer opportunities for individuals to participate; however, if you have too few participants, the range of views and experiences within the group will likely be narrower. Participants may all know one another, or may be strangers. It is advisable to avoid including people of very different social or professional status, as these hierarchies may influence how openly participants speak during the discussion. The discussion may last around 60–90 minutes depending on the group. If the discussion continues too long, participants may start leaving, which will inevitably change the discussion dynamics.

The usefulness of a focus-group discussion depends on how well the researcher is able to get the group to focus on questions of interest. Different approaches may be used to get the discussion going; for instance, the researcher may begin by asking participants to respond to a statement or a scenario in order to elicit input from all participants. To ensure the discussion stays on track, the researcher needs a question guide. In this guide, include questions that can help you encourage participation from all participants (e.g. 'Could we hear from someone who might have different views about this?') and structuring or transition questions to prompt participants to move to a different topic or question (e.g. 'Can we now move to the topic of . . .?). An advantage that focus-group discussions have over one-to-one interviews is that the researcher probably has less control and, therefore, less influence over the talk generated. The talk is likely to evolve in a more natural, spontaneous way than in the case of an interview. Because you have less control, however, you probably won't be able to use the checking or probing questions to verify your understanding of information or to request greater precision.

You need to record the focus-group discussion and transcribe your data. Researchers usually then carefully read through the transcribed text to identify the themes and sub-themes that were discussed (this procedure is discussed in Chapter 7, p. 102). Take note of interesting comments that could be used in your results; brief excerpts from the discussion can help readers understand the findings.

A focus-group discussion is harder to arrange than an interview. Not only should the room be undisturbed for the period of time needed, but also you need to arrange suitable seating and a table to ensure participants are facing one another. The microphone on the recorder needs to pick up all voices in the room. Consider where you will sit; you don't want to occupy a central position, but you also need to ensure you can intervene when necessary. You might consider using a whiteboard or flipchart to ensure the topics to be covered during the discussion are visible to all. As the facilitator, you need to welcome everyone, allow people to introduce themselves (name tags could be useful if people don't know one another) and close the discussion by thanking participants for their time.

Exercise 6.4

Focus-group discussion topics

Using focus groups as a data collection method is not suitable for all research topics. Identify topics from the following list that *would* be suitable:

1 Speaking practice in class: an investigation into high-school students' participation in speaking practice activities in co-educational and single-sex classrooms.
2 Teaching grammar in high-school classrooms: an examination into how teachers claim grammar should be taught and how they actually teach it.
3 Using standard British or US English as a learning model in the classroom: an examination of students' preferences for teacher, textbook and audio input.
4 Strategies used by administrative assistants to respond to English-language correspondence (email and letters) in the workplace.
5 Language-related difficulties experienced by graduate nursing students when communicating with English-speaking patients during their practicum period.
6 Reading your university textbook: an investigation into how first-year science students read textbooks in English.

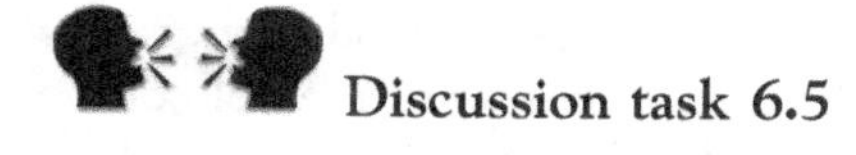

Discussion task 6.5

Focus-group discussion topics

Discuss the following questions in small groups:

1. Not all topics are suitable for a focus-group discussion because, for cultural reasons, it simply isn't appropriate to talk about some topics in public:
   a. Think of a couple of research topics for which you would not use a focus group to collect data.
   b. What would be an alternative data collection method for these topics that would be appropriate in your cultural context?
2. The best way to understand how a focus-group discussion can help you collect data is to experience one. Use Topic 3 from Exercise 6.4. Spend a few minutes in your group creating a question guide for the discussion facilitator. Then nominate the facilitator. This person should open the discussion appropriately, ensure the group moves through all the topics within the given time and close the discussion by thanking everyone for their time and their contributions. If you can record the discussion (for instance, by using the record function on your mobile phone), you will be able to play it back. As a group, reflect on how the facilitator used questions or comments to keep the discussion flowing and to ensure the participation of all group members.

Think-aloud protocols

Collecting data through think-aloud protocols allows insight into students' thought processes while completing an activity. Activities typically suited for this data collection method involve decision making, judgements or reasoning processes. Students are instructed to voice all thoughts that run through their mind ('think aloud') and these verbalizations are recorded and later analysed by the researcher. This data collection method has been used for a variety of different skill-based tasks involving writing, reading and translation. In addition, it can also be used to provide insight into how students understand the information layout of a text, or the wording of test items or instructions; for instance, it can be used to investigate how students use a website to do grammar and vocabulary practice activities, and how they understand and respond to test items (e.g. multiple-choice, true/false questions).

The following is an example of how think-alouds may be used to contribute to our understanding of how students revise their written work:

> The researcher wanted to investigate how students made use of the teacher's correction code symbols when preparing a second draft of the text. The teacher had used these symbols to indicate errors or weaknesses in the

> students' writing. The researcher recorded students individually as they verbalized their thoughts while redrafting their texts with the help of the correction code. In her analysis of the recordings, the researcher was able to identify to what extent students made use of the symbols when revising their texts, which symbols students found easier to understand and which symbols appeared more likely to result in the student successfully correcting an error.[2]

For most people, verbalizing one's thoughts while doing an activity does not come naturally, and students need detailed instructions on how to perform the given task while 'thinking aloud'; they may be shown a short video clip in which the technique is demonstrated, and they are usually also given a trial task in which they practise the technique before undertaking the exercise intended for data collection.

To ensure the student verbalizes his/her thoughts throughout the activity, you (or an assistant) should sit in the same room (at a discreet distance) while the student undertakes the task. This is usually done through gentle reminders when the student falls silent, which can be delivered verbally (e.g. 'What are you thinking now?') or visually by holding up signs with a symbol or a word prompting the student to continue verbalizing. You can also note down points in the exercise where students appear to hesitate, speak unclearly or correct themselves. After the task is finished, ask the students to describe what they were thinking at that moment. Some silence is needed, however, as students need time to convert thoughts into words, or to allow their thoughts to 'catch up' after verbalizing.

The student is recorded 'thinking aloud' while undertaking the task. For obvious reasons, it is not practical to attempt to record multiple students undertaking the same activity in the same room, so students are usually recorded one at a time. If you wish to collect data from multiple students simultaneously, the students need to be located in different rooms. The need for each student's 'think-aloud' performance to be monitored places a further limitation on the number of students who may undertake an activity simultaneously. This recorded data later needs to be transcribed and analysed. Like other forms of qualitative data, the analysis of think-aloud data may involve identifying different themes that emerge. An example of how this may be done can be found in the section on analysing interview data in Chapter 7 (p. 102).

Depending on the task, students should ideally be able to use their L1 during the think-aloud. This will allow them to verbalize their thoughts without having to concentrate on how they express themselves. In practice, code-switching is common as, typically, language students will use both the L1 and the L2 while undertaking a task. If you don't know the student's L1, translation assistance will be needed when transcribing the recordings. It would only be appropriate to require that the student uses the L2 while doing the task if the research question(s) specifically focused on the student's use of the L2. When calculating the time required for students to complete the activity, factor in additional time as students will need more time to complete the task than they usually would due to the think-aloud requirement.

Insights from the literature 6.2

Thinking aloud and data collection

The think-aloud approach to data collection is most typically used while participants undertake a task. This is known as *concurrent think-aloud* and it gives the researcher insights into the participants' thought processes while experiencing a particular task or activity. Participants can also be asked to think aloud after the activity, while watching a recording of themselves undertaking a task. This version is known as *retrospective think-aloud* or *stimulated recall*. The think-aloud technique is only suitable for certain research topics, as the act of thinking aloud may interfere with how participants undertake a task (Gu, 2014). If this technique is chosen and implemented with care, however, it can be an effective means of investigating how learners use the knowledge they have of the language or the information that is provided to them to complete certain tasks. Nevertheless, the participants' verbalizations will only be a partial representation of their thinking that the participants are able to make explicit; think-alouds won't provide insights into the participants' implicit knowledge or deeper, complex thought processes that elude verbalization (Bowles, 2010; Koro-Ljungberg et al., 2012).

The level of detail that participants are instructed to provide may vary depending on the research question(s). The most common type of think-aloud simply requires participants to verbalize their thinking while doing a task; the second type requires participants to also verbalize the reasoning behind the decisions they make when undertaking a task. To ensure this *metacognitive* approach is successful, the instructions need to be carefully worded so that participants are prompted to provide justifications for their answers (Bowles, 2010, p. 119). The person monitoring the procedure may also need to prompt the participants as required. The following are examples of research questions that would require a metacognitive think-aloud approach, as they enquire into how participants decide on the correct or appropriate response in a given context:

1. What factors do intermediate-level learners of English take into account when deciding on appropriate article use (zero/indefinite/definite) in a written text?
2. What factors do intermediate-level learners of English take into account when deciding on the appropriate use of either the simple past or the present perfect tense in a written text?
3. What pragmatic factors do intermediate-level learners of English take into account when deciding on the appropriate form of address when writing an email to their university lecturer?

4 What pragmatic factors do advanced-level learners of English take into account when formulating a request for an extension of an assignment deadline in an email to their university lecturer?

The think-aloud procedure does not come naturally to people, and Bowles (2010, p. 114) underscores the importance of detailed instructions for participants. Where possible, instructions should be delivered verbally and in writing in the participants' L1. The first step of these instructions should include a brief statement of the purpose of the activity and a simple explanation of why students need to verbalize their thoughts (e.g. 'I am interested in what you think about as you use the correction code symbols to revise your text. Please think aloud as you revise the text. Let me understand what is going through your mind.'). It is best not to explain the goal of the research to participants, however, as this could lead to students becoming overly conscious of the particular feature under study. Second, the instructions need to explain briefly what thinking aloud means (i.e. describe the desired behaviour), the language the participants should use and the amount of detail required. For example, if the researcher aims to compile data on how participants justified their answers, the instructions might be phrased as follows:

> Please say out loud the thoughts that go through your mind as you complete this activity. For each exercise, explain why you choose a particular answer. It may help to pretend you are alone in the room and you are speaking to yourself. You can use either your mother tongue or English, or you may combine the languages as you talk.

When coding the data, the researcher may begin with categories or themes that have been previously identified in the literature, before adding additional categories that emerge from the transcriptions. The analysis of the coded results should not simply focus on how many times a certain category (for instance, a particular learner strategy) appears, but should also take into account the order in which such categories appear, and the combination of different categories (or strategies) (Gu, 2014).

The researcher cannot always be confident about correctly interpreting a participant's line of thought from the verbalized data available; this may be because the idea was only partially verbalized or vaguely expressed. Where possible, Gu (2014) recommends checking one's coding of at least one section of the transcribed data with the participant to ensure their verbalization was correctly interpreted.

Rather than using think-alouds as the sole data collection method, Koro-Ljungberg et al. (2012, p. 742) propose using them in conjunction with interviews. In their study, they describe scheduling interviews with participants two days after the think-aloud exercise. Before the interview, the researchers reviewed the recording of the participant (in this case, a video) and noted instances where it was difficult to interpret what the participant was thinking, either because of gaps in the verbalization or because the participant completed an activity without adequately verbalizing how decisions were made. During the interview, they asked questions such as 'How did you know X was the right answer?' and 'Why did you refer back to a previous exercise here?'. To help prompt the participant's recall, excerpts of the recording were played back.

Discussion task 6.6

Discuss the following questions in pairs or small groups:

1. Do you ever verbalize your thoughts when doing a homework task (not necessarily related to English)? If so, how does this help you do this exercise?
2. Students can also benefit from participating in think-aloud protocols as they become more self-aware of their approach to tasks. How could this self-awareness help them become more effective language learners?
3. According to Koro-Ljungberg et al. (2012), the participant should preferably not be able to identify the person observing the think-aloud exercise as someone who is knowledgeable about the activity the participant is doing. If the participant did consider the observer an authority, how might this affect the participant's verbalization of his/her thoughts?

Notes

1 This is otherwise known as a university preparatory year or bridging year during which students improve their academic study skills and English-language proficiency.
2 This is a description of a Master's research project conducted by my former student Duygu Aktuğ under my supervision.

7 Your project chapter by chapter

Starting to write

Most people find writing an academic text difficult in their native language; writing a research project in a foreign language makes the writing task even more challenging. This section offers practical guidance on drafting each chapter of your project.

You are unlikely to start writing your research project at the Introduction and finish when you reach the Conclusion. It would probably be more effective to start writing the chapter you feel most confident about. This might be the Methods chapter or the Literature Review. Nevertheless, it is usually a good idea to draft the main gist of the Introduction early on, as this will give some direction to your work. Don't worry if you don't have enough to say when you begin to write a particular chapter; you can write notes to yourself such as 'Add definition', 'Check reference' or 'Discuss idea' to remind you that you need to add more information later. If you are unsure of what to say, leave a section empty and move on.

To help you begin the writing process, imagine you are telling your supervisor or a friend about your topic, using phrases such as the following: 'I think . . .'; 'I believe . . .'; 'I want to tell you why . . .'; 'I noticed . . .' Of course, when you revise your writing, you will delete these phrases as you reformulate your idea using more appropriate language. Nevertheless, beginning your work in a conversational style as though you were addressing someone can help the writing flow.

Don't be overly concerned about your use of language at the beginning; at this stage it does not matter greatly if your use of English is correct or not. Each chapter will need redrafting several times, so there is little point in trying to polish your language while working on the first draft. Once you see your own writing on the page, it becomes easier to add information to what is already there. The problem is the empty page! By the time you finally finish your project, you will have redrafted it many times and have had many opportunities to improve your writing and your use of language. Being critical about language use at this initial stage just creates an additional obstacle to getting ideas down and developing a flow in your writing.

Tip 7.1

Getting started

- Write the chapters you feel more confident about first. There is no requirement to write each chapter in consecutive order.
- If you are really having problems writing a chapter, try telling a good friend what you want to say (you can do this in your L1 or in English). Alternatively, record yourself on your phone as you talk through the chapter. Verbalizing what you intend to say, the main ideas you want to discuss, can help you actually write it.
- For each chapter, note down a list of topics or points you want to mention. Think about how they relate to each other and the order in which you want to discuss them.
- Don't focus on correct grammar and spelling at the beginning; you can revise these later.
- Start citing the authors you use from the beginning. If you don't, it is very easy to forget that an idea or a few sentences in your text were originally borrowed from someone else's work.
- As you read, make notes of definitions and important points you come across. These ideas can act as a springboard for your own ideas as you start to write.

The Introduction

The Introduction is one of the most important chapters of your work and you will probably draft and redraft this chapter several times. Although it appears early in the work, it doesn't need to be completed before drafting other chapters. It is advisable to create a basic draft of the Introduction early on, however, even if this is only several sentences, to sketch out what the study will attempt to demonstrate and the rationale. This will help you visualize more clearly the direction of your project. After drafting the Results and Discussion chapters, and as you start on the Conclusion, revisit the Introduction. This is a good time to redraft it. At this point, you will probably know a lot more about your topic in general and about your own study in particular and you will be better able to review the content and organization of this chapter and polish your writing.

Within the Introduction, you will need to do a number of things:

- Describe the situation, context, circumstances or background of your topic. This may include references to other studies.
- Signal the existence of a problematic issue, or something intriguing or puzzling that deserves study (this is effectively the justification for your research).
- Formulate your research question(s).

- State your hypothesis or thesis statement (if this is relevant to your study).
- Define any terms that are important to understanding the topic of your study or the approach you take (keep this brief, as you can provide additional definitions later in your work).
- Briefly describe how you will undertake your study (the methods).
- Inform the reader of how the project is organized (optional).

These first two sections of your Introduction have the aim of contextualizing your topic by indicating why it warrants attention. From this initially broad perspective, you then narrow attention to your specific research question(s), which articulates (or articulate) the purpose of your work; it may include a thesis statement – that is, a statement that expresses your particular position on the topic. Your research question(s) should ideally emerge from the foregoing context you provided.

Consider how you might show why extra work on the topic (i.e. your study) is needed or justified. If a considerable amount of published work already exists on your topic, the reader may wonder why you propose to do yet another study. Consider the following questions:

- What have other studies not shown or demonstrated to date?
- Can you conceptualize your topic as a sort of puzzle that you need to explore?
- What is it that you are going to contribute to the topic?
- What question(s) do you still have in your mind after reading the literature?

Note how other writers contextualize their own studies and indicate the need for further research. As you read journal articles for your Literature Review, try to identify the sentence(s) in the Introduction where the writer attempts to show this 'gap' in our current knowledge or understanding of the topic.

Finally, you could also include a short paragraph explaining the organization of your project. Sometimes you will see that writers add a 'road map' at the end of the Introduction – that is, a short paragraph that orients the reader by briefly stating the topic of each chapter. It explains how the whole project fits together. This is not obligatory; if you choose to include it, ensure it is no longer than a few sentences.

Exercise 7.1

Introductions

1 Read the Introduction of Chik's (2014) article on digital gaming and language learning in Appendix 1. To help you understand how the author has organized the information in this section, identify the following information (not all may be present):

- a background information on the topic;
- b research question(s);
- c references to previous studies;
- d definition of a key term;
- e the importance or relevance of the current study;
- f 'road map';
- g thesis statement.

2 Some writers begin the Introduction with a narrow focus (concentrating on something specific) and then broaden their focus to discuss the topic in a more general way. More commonly, writers begin with a broad focus and then narrow their focus as they formulate the research question(s). In Chik's Introduction, which approach has the author taken?

3 After reading this Introduction, you should be able to predict what the author will discuss in the article. Explain your answers.

4 Read the Introduction of Lee's (2011) or Chen's (2006) article (also in Appendix 1) and repeat Questions 1 and 2. These Introductions are longer and you may find multiple examples of the components of an Introduction. Identify similarities and differences in how information has been organized in the two Introductions you read.

5 Now start drafting your own Introduction. You may write sentences or just phrases at this stage. You may not be clear on just what your study will seek to do at this early point, but as you start drafting this chapter, you may find that your ideas become clearer during the drafting process.

Insights from the literature 7.1

The Introduction in moves

Our understanding of the rhetorical organization of Introductions in academic writing, in particular research articles, is largely based on the work of John Swales, who in the early 1980s published the results of an empirical study of how research article Introductions were structured. While his original research was based on an analysis of 48 research articles from the hard sciences, biomedical science and the social sciences, his findings have since been discussed in relation to a range of disciplines, including applied linguistics, and to both Master's and doctoral dissertations. Swales ([1981] 2011, pp. 28–9) originally identified a four-move structure, in which the four main moves are broken down into sub-steps. These moves are as follows:

Move 1: Establishing the field (showing the topic has a central place in the discipline, is important and is of interest, and stating current knowledge).
Move 2: Summarizing previous research.
Move 3: Preparing for present research (by indicating a gap, raising questions).
Move 4: Introducing present research.

In performing Move 1, Swales (2011) noted that authors frequently use the lexeme 'interest' while attempting to establish that their topic is of central interest (e.g. 'There has been recent interest in . . .'). In contrast, the notion of importance tends to be conveyed indirectly by referring to issues of significance, but without actually mentioning the lexeme explicitly. When describing previous research in Move 2, Swales identified differences in terms of whether authors or findings were foregrounded; he termed these a *strong author orientation* or a *strong subject orientation* respectively, and noted that the choice of approach depended on the particular stylistic effect desired. Typical verbs used in a strong author orientation include reporting verbs such as: 'suggest', 'propose', 'report', 'investigate', 'find', 'discuss', 'examine' etc. (Swales, 2011, pp. 47, 53). Move 3 essentially involves demonstrating how the author's work will contribute to the literature discussed; this involves some evaluation of previously mentioned studies to identify shortcomings or outstanding questions. The identification of a gap in literature provides justification for further work, and the writer then typically presents the purpose or intentions of the current study; this comprises Move 4 of the Introduction. Typical language used for this move might include the words 'purpose' or 'aim' (e.g. 'The purpose of the present study is to . . .'); alternatively, the writer may simply announce the intention to examine or evaluate something (Swales, 2011, pp. 70–5). Swales (1990) later revised this initial framework in his proposed CARS (Create a Research Space) model, reducing the four moves to three (Move 1: establishing a territory; Move 2: establishing a niche; Move 3: occupying the niche), each involving a series of steps comparable to those in the previous model.

Many genre-based studies have applied the CARS model to examine the formulation of Introductions in different academic disciplines. This has led to greater awareness of the flexibility in the order of steps comprising different moves and to suggestions of additional steps. For instance, Bunton (2002) applied Swales' CARS model to the introductions of PhD dissertations, and he proposed the addition of steps such as 'providing definitions', 'formulating research questions' and 'indicating the method used in the study'.

Cortes (2013) identified typical lexical bundles, or phrases, that are frequently used when formulating a move. For instance, in Move 1 (establishing a territory), typical phrases include: 'one of the most important'; 'play an important role in the'; 'it is well known that'; and 'studies have shown that'. For Move 2 (establishing a niche), Cortes found the following phrases: 'little is known about the'; 'in the context of'; and 'it should be noted that'. Move 3 (occupying the niche) is often manifested by phrases such as: 'the purpose of the present study is to'; 'the aim of this study is to'; and 'the purpose of this paper is to' (Cortes, 2013, p. 39). Lexical bundles such as these help writers organize their ideas and orient readers to important information within the text.

Swales' CARS model was developed using data emanating from the scholarly publishing tradition in English. A number of publications have identified differences between the structure of Introductions of research articles in English and those in other languages or cultural contexts. One such work was Soler-Monreal, Carbonell-Olivares and Gil-Salom's (2011) study of PhD Introductions in English and Spanish. According to their findings, while Spanish PhD Introductions included Move 1 (establishing a territory) and Move 3 (occupying the niche), Move 2 (establishing a niche) appeared to be optional. The authors concluded that academic conventions in this cultural context emphasize the need to contextualize the present work through a methodical review of related studies, but do not require that the author justify the present research by identifying limitations and unaddressed issues in previous research.

Comparable findings emerged from Loi's (2010) analysis of Introductions in Chinese and English research articles from educational psychology. Chinese Introductions were less likely to display Move 3 (renamed in Loi's study as 'presenting the present work'), and the discussion of previous literature in Move 1 was less detailed and contained fewer citations than in English-language articles. Not only would 'indicating a gap' (a step involved in Move 2) entail pinpointing shortcomings in previous work, a step that many Chinese writers might prefer to avoid, but also differences between the framing or contextualization of research in Chinese and Anglophone academic traditions are, the author surmised, partly due to the less competitive nature of establishing and occupying a research space in Chinese academic writing (Loi, 2010).

A third such study is Fakhri's (2004) analysis of research articles written in Arabic. Fakhri (2004) identified an absence of citations of prior studies; authors did not appear to contextualize their own research by attempting to establish a line of enquiry that had not yet been fully investigated. He pointed to the possible greater emphasis within this cultural context on presenting research in the form of *knowledge telling* (i.e. transmitting acquired knowledge) rather than *knowledge transforming* (i.e. extending the available body of knowledge).

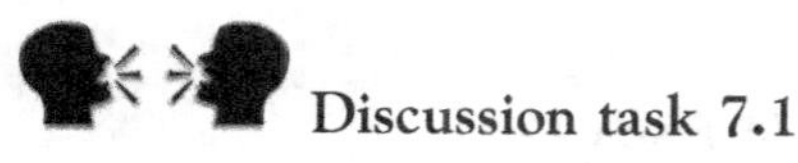

Discussion task 7.1

Introductions

Discuss the following questions in pairs or small groups:

1 The final paragraphs of Insights from the literature 7.1 discuss cultural differences in writing Introductions. Are you aware of any differences between writing conventions in your L1 and in English?

2 Insights from the literature 7.1 discusses typical phrases used in Introductions, as identified by Cortes (2013). Read the Introductions in Appendix 1. Underline phrases or expressions that you think could be useful to help you organize your writing or to formulate moves.

Tip 7.2

Useful phrases for the Introduction

The phrases below might help you formulate moves in your Introduction. They form part of the *Academic Phrasebank* (Morley, n.d.).

Establishing the importance of the topic

'X is an increasingly important area in the field of . . .'
'Recent developments in X have heightened the need for . . .'
'In recent years, there has been an increasing interest in . . .'

Providing a synopsis of the literature

'Previous studies have reported . . .'
'Recent evidence suggests that . . .'
'Several attempts have been made to . . .'
'Factors influencing X have been explored in several studies.'

Highlighting a controversy in the field of study

'To date there has been little agreement on what . . .'
'One major issue in early X research concerned . . .'
'Questions have been raised about . . .'

Highlighting inadequacies of previous studies

'Most studies in the field of X have only focused on . . .'
'Most studies on X were based on data compiled in Western contexts.'
'However, these results were based upon data from over 15 years ago and it is unclear if . . .'

Highlighting a knowledge gap in the field of study

'However, there has been little attention to . . .'
'There has been little analysis of . . .'
'Little is known about X and it is not clear what factors . . .'

Indicating the focus or objective

'This paper will focus on/examine/give an account of . . .'
'This essay critically examines/discusses/traces . . .'
'The aim of this study is to investigate the differences between X and Y.'
'This paper investigates the degree to which . . .'

The Literature Review

As the name suggests, the Literature Review chapter discusses and appraises previous studies related to your topic. This discussion provides both a context for your work and the opportunity to identify the particular contribution of your study. One of the purposes of this chapter is to demonstrate how your research question(s) is (are) justified in light of what has been done before. You need to show how your study 'fills a gap' in the body of literature that already exists on your topic. To do this, however, you need to be familiar with what has been previously written.

Preparing your Literature Review and undertaking your bibliographic search are interrelated activities. While drafting this chapter, it is likely that you will find references to additional articles or books of relevance. Journal articles in particular contain summaries of previously published work in the Introduction and Background chapters, and reading these can be very instructive.

In the Literature Review you will describe previous research relevant to your research question(s), summarize other authors' work and compare different perspectives on the topic. As you will refer frequently to other authors (whether by using summaries, paraphrases or quotations), you will need to use reporting verbs (the list in Appendix 4 may be helpful). At postgraduate level, the Literature Review of your thesis should be extensive and up-to-date, and you will need to critique previous work. At the level of an undergraduate research project, however, it is usually sufficient to describe previous studies and, if possible, indicate where additional work on this subject area might be warranted.

There are different ways of organizing the information in your Literature Review. As this chapter may contain a range of topics from different sources, drafting an initial outline of the chapter will help to identify how different studies might be related.

Probably the most common approach to organizing this chapter is in terms of *topics, theories or methodological approaches*. In this case, you need to be clear which topics (or theories) and sub-topics are most relevant to your own research topic. An approach that is too broad is likely to result in an 'unfinishable' research project or, alternatively, a study that says nothing in particular because it tries to say everything. There will always be topics that appear interesting but that you decide not to include.

To avoid becoming submerged in an ocean of ideas, terms and names, approach the reading of the relevant studies with a strategy in mind. For instance, identify the key concepts used to discuss your topic or the different positions taken by authors in their work. Some information might be repeated by different authors, but other information might only be found in a particular author's work. The next step involves bringing together, or synthesizing, positions and ideas you identified. It is not an easy task, even in your L1. Avoid being repetitive and exhaustive as you discuss different topics. Instead, identify commonalities, connections and differences between the various ideas or concepts, and ensure that your discussion is always related to your topic and relevant to your research question(s). It may take a number of drafts before you produce a satisfactory version.

One approach to organizing the discussion is from different *points of view*. In such cases, reporting verbs that express agreement, disagreement and suggestions will be useful (see Appendix 4). A further possibility is to order your discussion *chronologically*; this means giving priority to when the studies appeared, and sequencing the discussion from (usually) the earliest to the most recent publications. If you choose this approach, the transition words in Appendix 3 will probably be useful.

Some authors use a *mixture of approaches*; for example, they discuss different methodological or theoretical approaches, beginning with earlier approaches and continuing through to the present (chronologically ordered), and then they may discuss the different concepts or ideas that are relevant today (ordered according to points of view or relationships between different topics).

Some studies you discuss in your Literature Review will be worth examining in more detail. In this case, information about the background of the study could be important (such as where and how it was done and the results), as well as the study's research question. This is unlikely to be exactly the same as yours, and perhaps the motivation for the study was different. While you read, try to identify how this research might relate to your work. Remember, you are not always looking for authors you agree with; you are also looking for differences that you can discuss.

If you read a study involving data collection and analysis, make a note of the procedure followed and the characteristics of the sample group. This could be relevant when you compare previously published studies and discuss how these studies relate to yours. Finally, examine the findings. In a study involving data collection, these appear in the Results and Discussion sections; a literary study may not be organized by sections with sub-headings, which means that the main findings, arguments or conclusions are less clearly signposted, but are nevertheless likely to appear towards the end. Findings may also be restated in the Abstract and the Conclusion. Clarity on how the findings in studies relate to one another will be important for your synthesis of these works.

On a final note, the examiners of your research project will look carefully to see what you have read, and whether you have understood the key concepts and ideas related to your topic. One of the first things many examiners do when they receive a completed project is to turn to the list of references to check which authors the student claims to have read. Perhaps more than other chapters, the Literature Review is where you need to display the depth of your knowledge. It is important that you use appropriate academic sources, however (see Chapter 4). Your supervisor and the examiners are unlikely to take your work seriously if you have not based your Literature Review on credible and authoritative sources.

Exercise 7.2

The Literature Review

1 Read the excerpt below from Lee (2011, p. 90).
   a What approach does she take in the first paragraph of her Literature Review (i.e. in terms of topics, theories, methodological approaches, points of view or chronological order)?
   b Look at how she makes reference to previous studies. Underline the language she uses to introduce previous studies and the reporting verbs used to cite authors.

Example 7.1

Developing intercultural competence: blogs and ethnographic interviews

The need for language learners to develop intercultural communicative competence (ICC) has been strongly advocated as an essential component in L2 instruction. Byram's (1997) ICC model which presents a conceptual framework consisting of four interrelated components—*knowledge*, *skills*, *attitudes* and *awareness*—appears to be the most frequently adopted approach to develop intercultural competence (see pp. 50–63 for details). Within this framework, the goal is to promote cultural learning that goes beyond a superficial "facts only" approach. To become competent intercultural speakers, learners need to be open-minded to people of other cultures so that they understand cross-cultural perspectives with non-judgmental attitudes and respect (Bennett, 1993). In the process of developing ICC, learners are encouraged to reflect upon the cultural similarities and differences, and further develop the ability to tolerate differences that allow them to handle situations encountered with L1s. Common belief suggests that formal classroom instruction alone is not sufficient and close interaction with L1s is vital for students to gain ICC.

Among other approaches to intercultural learning, blog technology has been increasingly used to foster cross-cultural communication and awareness (e.g. Carney, 2007; Ducate & Lomicka, 2008; Elola & Oskoz, 2008; Lee, 2009b). Research findings have revealed that blogs afford students the opportunity to gain cultural knowledge from different perspectives (Elola & Oskoz, 2008; Pinkman, 2005). For example, using task-based activities, Lee (2009b) in her recent study of Spanish–American telecollaboration demonstrated how group blogs empowered students by raising cultural awareness through ethnographic interviews. Despite the favorable results, Carney (2007) argues that blogs open a new online discussion forum rather than a deeper cultural exchange due to the post–comment structure of blogs that results in brief exchanges and lack of continuity. Thus, teachers need to find ways, such as using guided questions, to stimulate students' high order thinking to build upon further discussions.

2 Read the excerpt below from Chen (2006, p. 37).
   a What approach does she take in the first paragraph of her Literature Review (i.e. in terms of topics, theories, methodological approaches, points of view or chronological order)?
   b Look at how she makes reference to previous studies. Underline the language she uses to introduce previous studies and the reporting verbs used to cite authors.

ABC Example 7.2

Studies on L2 learners' e-mail practice: a pragmatic perspective

Probably the earliest study on L2 learners' e-mail communication with professors was conducted by Hartford and Bardovi-Harlig (1996). They compared how international graduate students and U.S. graduate students made requests to professors via e-mail and reported four important findings: (a) international students used fewer mitigating forms in their request e-mails that produced a negative impact; (b) they used institutional explanations less frequently for their requests; (c) they mentioned their personal needs and time frames more often for their requests; and (d) they acknowledged imposition on the faculty members less often than U.S. students. [. . .] Subsequent studies on student-to-professor e-mail communication have similar findings. Biesenbach-Lucas and Weasenforth (2000) found that L2 students used fewer modal constructions and hedged expressions in their e-mails than did U.S. students; instead, their e-mails often contained inappropriate pleading for help from the professor. [. . .] Examining the same e-mail data, Biesenbach-Lucas (2005) further pointed out that L2 students demonstrated less initiative and weaker capability in using e-mail to interact with professors than did American students, particularly in providing progress reports, negotiating project topics, requesting professor responses, and offering potential response points for the professor.

3 Read the excerpt below from Chen (2006, p. 38). This is the final paragraph of her Literature Review. Note how Chen establishes that her study will differ in a meaningful way from previous studies and will thereby contribute to our knowledge. Underline the sentences where she does this.

Example 7.3

The above studies have demonstrated a variety of L2 learners' pragmatic problems occurring in their e-mail practice, particularly in student-to-professor e-mail communication. The pragmatic problems consist of not only the pragmalinguistic type such as modal use, hedged expression, and information sequencing, but also the sociopragmatic type such as status maintenance, politeness realization, and identity construction. These studies all point out the importance of developing pragmatic competence for L2 learners to carry out successful e-mail communication. However, there are several limitations in these studies. First, they are descriptive studies which neglect to adopt a critical approach. Although they examine L2 learners' e-mail practice from a sociocultural perspective, they seem to focus on the deviations or problems in L2 learners' language use but ignore how L2 learners' language use is an agentive choice made from multiple cultural and discourse resources available to them. Second, most of these studies are cross-sectional rather than longitudinal, which is likely to present L2 learners' language use in a preset, static manner rather than as a dynamic, evolving process. Third, most of these studies provide analyses of L2 learners' e-mail practice from the researcher's perspective, not including the participants' viewpoint. This etic view may not precisely reflect how the participants use e-mail and the second language in actual situations. More research in L2 learners' e-mail practice needs to be conducted with an emic and a critical approach, so that we can obtain deeper insight into the complex process of their development.

Describing methods

The Methods chapter describes the steps undertaken at the pre-collection phase and during the data collection and the analysis stages. Relevant factors usually described in this chapter include location, authorization for data collection, time period, numbers involved, medium of communication, piloting, the characteristics of the participants (or texts selected for analysis), how these were selected, the choice of data collection instrument and how this was used or the approach used to analyse texts. This detailed account enables sufficient insight into how the research was conducted so that readers may be in a position to replicate the study by following the same procedure.

As the information in this chapter is usually presented in chronological order, the use of linking words such as 'then', 'following', 'subsequently', 'before', 'after' etc. is common, as is the use of the passive voice. This allows the author to place the main focus on the action performed rather than the subject or agent undertaking the action. Some authors choose to make their presence explicit through the first-person pronoun ('I') to emphasize their agency through the data collection and analysis procedures. The first-person pronoun may also be useful in the event that several people were involved in the procedures and the author wishes to clarify the nature of his/her contribution. More information on first-person pronoun use can be found in Chapter 8 (p. 143).

The language used to explain the series of steps is often fairly predictable. The following exercises prompt you to reflect upon how events or actions are described in published research and in student writing.

Exercise 7.3

Describing data collection procedures

1. Read the Methods section of Chik's (2014) article in Example 7.4 below and answer the following questions:
   a. What function does each of the three paragraphs serve?
   b. Where did the study take place?
   c. What instruments were used to collect data?
   d. Who were the participants? How many were there?
   e. Identify the different steps taken by the author to choose the participants.
   f. Did the author conduct a trial or a pilot study?
   g. Why does the author use mostly passive voice in the second paragraph, but active voice in the third paragraph?
   h. Why did the author use participant-researchers?
2. Now read the following two examples of how Zeina and Zareen described the process of their data collection in the Methods chapters of their projects (Examples 7.5 and 7.6). What similarities do you notice between the use of language in Zeina's and Zareen's Methods chapters and the data collection procedure described by Chik?

Example 7.4

The Methods section in Chik (2014, pp. 88–9)

Data collection

This study set out to understand how gamers practice autonomous learning within communities by mapping the findings from a 12-month exploratory study on L2 gaming in East Asian contexts to Benson's (2011) framework for investigating out-of-class L2 learning. Yin (2009) defines a case study as 'an empirical inquiry that investigates a contemporary phenomenon in depth and within its real-life context' (p. 18) and observes that the case study method helps researchers to 'retain the holistic and meaningful characteristics of real-life events' (p. 4). Multiple case studies are justified when 'the single case is of interest because it belongs to a particular collection of cases', which share a 'common characteristic or condition' (Stake, 2006, p. 4). This study used a multiple case study approach to examine how Chinese-speaking gamers managed their digital gameplay for L2 learning, and to explore their everyday practices of digital gaming and L2 learning. Each case study consisted of an in-depth multi-method investigation of a young person's out-of-class digital gaming and L2 learning practices. This approach puts the focus on how gaming activities are situated in participants' lives, their perspectives on these activities, and the meanings that they attach to them.

In 2009, a participation call was sent to all Year 1 Chinese-speaking undergraduates in an English-medium Hong Kong university. Subsequently, 153 students responded by submitting background surveys on gaming practices and 500-word autobiographical language learning histories (LLHs) (Oxford, 1996) describing their L2 learning in out-of-class contexts. Among the respondents, about 50 undergraduates who explicitly mentioned using digital games for L2 learning were interviewed in depth. Following the interviews, 10 gamers from seven academic disciplines (M = 6, F = 4) were selected to participate in the one-year project (Table 1). These participants were selected primarily because they were able to articulate the ways they organized their gaming practices, both for entertainment and learning and because gaming was still part of their regular routines. The 10 participants came from China, Malaysia, and Hong Kong. All spoke either Cantonese or Mandarin as their first language, and learned English as an L2. Among the gamers, eight regularly played English-language games and two preferred Japanese-language games. The participants wrote extended LLHs on the roles of digital gaming in their L2 learning, joined a focus group discussion, blogged, recorded live gaming sessions, and participated in stimulated recall sessions.

In addition, the 10 participants took on the role of participant-researchers to interview five gamer friends to explore wider gaming practices in context. They then compiled a list of game-external Chinese-language websites and forums that they or their gamer friends used for game information and gameplay strategies (2004–2012). These websites and forums were hosted in Mainland China, Hong Kong and Taiwan, and their users frequently contributed in Chinese (which include Cantonese, Simplified and Traditional Chinese characters, Chinese code-mixed with Cantonese, English, or Taiwanese Hokkien). Though the servers are located in different regions, they appear to serve wider virtual communities of Chinese gamers. The archived collections of discussion threads on these websites served as 'funds of knowledge' (Moll, Amanti, Neff, & Gonzalez, 1992) in the context of digital gaming. From these online discussion forums, threads and texts relevant to L2 learning were selected for further analysis.

Example 7.5

Zeina's Methods chapter

Methods

The participants in this study were all students in their fourth year of a Bachelor degree in Arabic/English translation. The data were collected through a written test on their understanding of and ability to translate polysemous words administered in the Fall Semester of 2010. A test was chosen as it was considered to be the most convenient and efficient approach to identifying the level of ability of a group of around 40 students.

The test comprised two sections. The first consisted of a gap-fill exercise which tested students' awareness of the different meanings of polysemous words. The second section was a translation exercise involving phrases and sentences containing polysemous words (see Appendix for a copy of the test). While students were permitted to use a dictionary during the test, they were not allowed to talk to other students. A test was preferred to a take-home assignment as, in the case of an assignment, it would not have been possible to ascertain whether the student had sought assistance from others.

Permission was first obtained from the teacher of this course to take the final 30 minutes of a class to distribute the tests. Prior to distributing the tests, students were informed of the nature of the study and were given the option of leaving. Students were given 30 minutes to complete the test with the help of a dictionary. The second stage consisted of analyzing the students' work. A key with a range of answers considered to be acceptable for each item in the second section had previously been prepared and checked by a member of the Translation Department. Table 2 displays the percentage of incorrect and correct answers for each question. The following analysis shall focus on the incorrect answers.

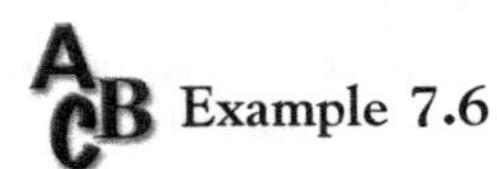

Example 7.6

Zareen's Methods chapter

Methods

This study was conducted at the University's Department of Foreign Languages. Participants in this study were students majoring in either a Bachelor's of English education or English/Arabic translation. A questionnaire containing 14 multiple choice items was designed with the assistance of the supervisor of this project. It was subsequently translated into Arabic by the author and this was then checked by a bilingual faculty member for accuracy. Permission was obtained from the administrators of the hostels where the data collection would take place to visit the hostels twice to talk to groups of students for the purpose of this research. The questionnaires were distributed to students in hostels for male and female students. The researcher had previously informed students in each hostel of the study in writing by using the hostel notice board, and orally by making an announcement to students in the dining hall during the evening meal. She also distributed leaflets describing the study to all students in the dining hall after her announcement. The researcher returned to the hostel for female students later that same week during the evening to distribute questionnaires to those willing to participate who were English majors. Students completed the questionnaires and then deposited them into a box that the researcher had brought for this purpose. The same procedure was followed by a male research assistant in the hostel for male students. To ensure the researcher obtained a total of 50 male and 50 female participants, a second visit in same week to the dining hall of each hostel was necessary.

Exercise 7.4

Your data collection procedure

If you did Exercise 6.3 from the previous chapter, reflect on the procedure you followed to collect data on the choice of language in lectures. Write 1–2 paragraphs describing this procedure. Use some of the phrases provided in Tip 7.3.

Tip 7.3

Useful phrases to describe your research procedure

As you read articles for your Literature Review, make a note of how other authors describe their research procedure in the Methods section of a research paper. Certain phrases, such as the ones below, recur. You might find some useful for your own work, although they may need to be adapted to fit the new context. The following phrases are part of the *Academic Phrasebank* (Morley, n.d.).

Describing the characteristics of your sample

'The initial sample consisted of 200 students, 182 of whom completed the questionnaire.'

'All of the participants were aged between 19 and 23 at the time of the study.'

'A random sample of students in their first year of study was recruited from the Biology department.'

'Forty-seven students studying Nursing were recruited for this study.'

'The project used a convenience sample of 32 first-year students of French and German.'

'Just over half the sample (53 per cent) was female; of these, 69 per cent were in their first or second year of study.'

'Semi-structured interviews were conducted with 17 male students aged between 22 and 26.'

Describing the process of collecting and analysing data

'Prior to commencing the study, permission was obtained from the University administration.'

'A pilot interview was conducted with the assistance of a teacher from the local school.'

'The students were divided into two groups based on their GPA score.'

'Questionnaires were distributed to 59 students in three different classes.'

'This test was repeated under the same conditions with students in their first year of study.'

'Twelve teachers were recruited using information provided by the administration of three schools.'

'The questionnaire was then translated into Arabic.'

'The translation was checked for accuracy by a lecturer before being distributed to the students.'

'Following this, interviews were conducted with four teachers.'

'Data were collected using a questionnaire and follow-up interviews.'

'The data were recorded on a digital audio recorder and later transcribed.'

'Finally, percentages were calculated using Microsoft Excel.'

'The answers to each of the questions were then analysed for semantic and syntactic acceptability.'

'After the interviews were transcribed, the information was coded.'

Insights from the literature 7.2

Moves and methods

You read about the use of moves in the Introductions of research articles. Do writers also organize their Methods section in terms of moves? What disciplinary differences are there in how this section is written?

Peacock (2011) examined the move structure of the Methods section of 288 published articles from eight disciplines; all studies included had an empirical data-driven approach with an Introduction–Methods–Results–Discussion format. Basing his approach on Swales' (1990) analysis of move structure in academic discourse, Peacock identified six distinct moves: M1 Overview; M2 Location; M3 Research aims/questions/hypotheses; M4 Subjects/materials/procedures; M5 Limitations; M6 Data analysis. Not all moves were obligatory and their order varied. In the field of language and linguistics, the typical Methods section had four moves: subjects; location; procedure; data analysis. Additional moves that may appear include: limitations; research aims; research overview. According to the results from Peacock's analysis, the Methods section in language and linguistics studies contained greater detail of each step of the procedure than in the hard sciences, and it comprised on average 25 per cent of the entire article.

Discussion task 7.2

Moving through the Methods section

1. After reading Insights from the literature 7.2, with a partner try to identify the different moves in Chik's Methods section in Example 7.4.
2. Do the same for Examples 7.5 and 7.6. Could the students' texts be strengthened by ordering the moves differently or by inserting an additional move?

Presenting quantitative data

Studies that involve a number of informants or that focus on different aspects of language use potentially produce a lot of numerical data. Using a program such as Excel in Microsoft Office will help you undertake basic calculations efficiently and accurately. This type of software can also convert your data into a graphic form so that your findings can be presented in a manner that the reader can easily absorb. Presenting just a few numbers in text form isn't difficult, but with a variety of numbers (or percentages) representing different phenomena, presenting them visually in a table or a graph is more effective than attempting to describe them.

Quantitative data can be presented in different ways. Before you decide on a particular graphic, experiment with a few options to see which one seems most effective for your purpose. If your study involves comparing two groups, such as males and females or students from two different departments or schools, seeing the contrasting data sets in close proximity can facilitate comprehension.

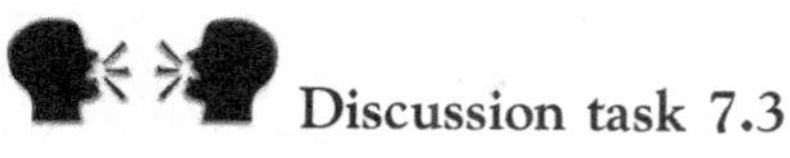

Discussion task 7.3

Choosing a suitable graphic for your data

Together with your partner, compare the graphics in the following four examples (A to D) from Zareen's study. Which one do you think displays the information most clearly?

Example A(i): getting high grades is important for my future career (males) (percentages)

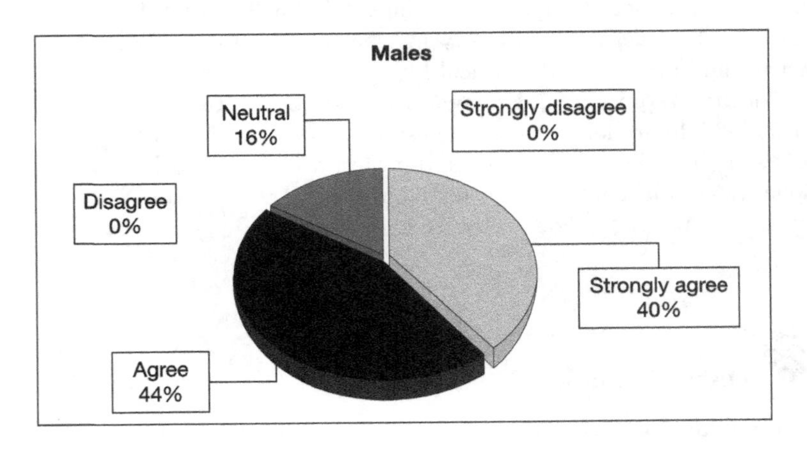

Example A(ii): getting high grades is important for my future career (females) (percentages)

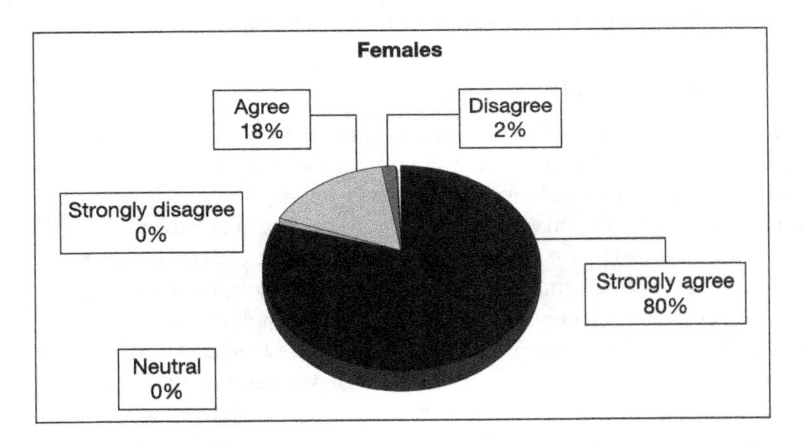

Example B: getting high grades is important for my future career (percentages)

	Strongly agree	*Agree*	*Neutral*	*Disagree*	*Strongly disagree*
Males	40	44	16	0	0
Females	80	18	0	2	0

Example C(i): getting high grades is important for my future career (males)

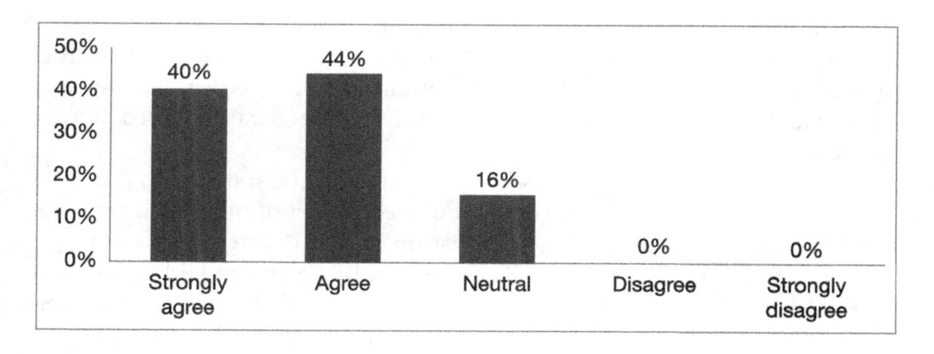

Example C(ii): getting high grades is important for my future career (females)

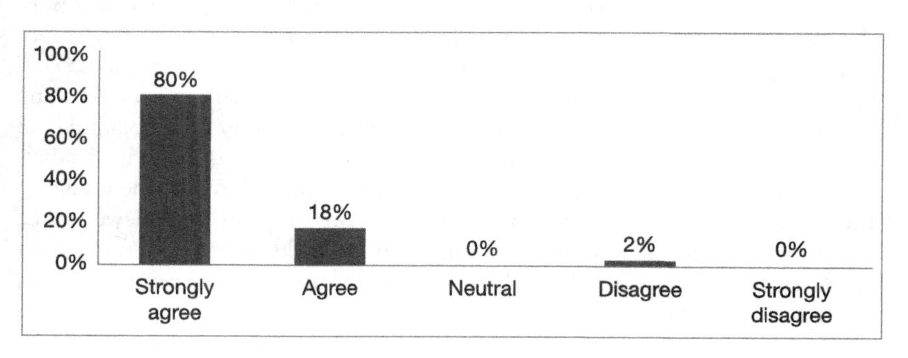

Example D: getting high grades is important for my future career (males and females)

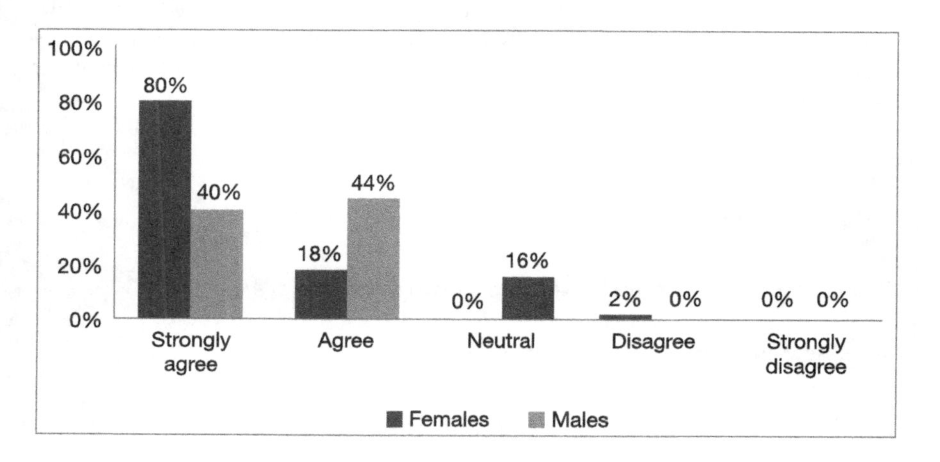

Analysing and presenting qualitative data

Data gathered from questionnaires or test results, interviews, open questions or focus-group discussions generate descriptive, personalized responses, known as qualitative data. As this information is not numerical, it needs to be displayed and analysed in a different way from quantitative data compiled from a questionnaire or test.

Once you have the transcript of your interviews (or you have collated all the answers to your open questions), you need to identify the main topics or themes mentioned. This can be done by writing a label or category for each topic in the margin of the transcript. Keep the label or category fairly general at this stage. After reviewing several transcripts, you will probably find that the interviewees tend to mention similar topics or issues, although the details or examples may differ.

The second step involves transferring the labels or categories to a separate page and using each as the heading of a column. Example 7.7 shows excerpts from the answers to two questions given by three different students. To protect their identities, Zareen has replaced their names with numbers ('ST02', 'ST04' and 'ST05'). After transcribing their answers, Zareen began the process of coding the content. As you can see, she has written labels in the margin. Example 7.8 illustrates the second stage of the process; Zareen has transferred these labels to a table and they have become categories into which Zareen is now able to transfer the examples from her interview transcriptions. She interviewed three female and three male students about their attitudes towards achievement at university, so her final table will contain more examples and categories than the few illustrated here.

After creating her table, Zareen then needed to describe these results in her project. The categories helped her organize what she wanted to include in this section. For each category, Zareen described in general terms the information mentioned by the participants, noting particular tendencies and unexpected findings. Occasionally, she included a quote from the participants; for example, she used a phrase from one interviewee that expressed an idea particularly well and put the identity of the speaker in code form (e.g. 'ST04') in brackets after the quote.

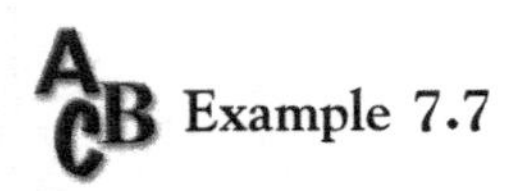

Example 7.7

Transcription of students' responses to two questions

Interview question: Do you always attend class?

Follow-up question: When do you miss class?

when

reason

when

reason

reason

activity to catch up

I usually go to class at the beginning of the semester but then I start to miss the class on Friday. I want to go home on Friday afternoon so I sometimes don't go to class in the morning. I have had enough of the classes and teachers by then and I don't feel like sitting in the classroom anymore. Also, it takes me a long time to get home. Sometimes I don't get back to the university in time for class on Monday so sometimes I miss class then as well. If we have a quiz or an exam in one class, then I sometimes miss my other classes because I want to study. Though I usually don't really study, but it just gives me more free time so I don't feel so pressured. Otherwise it is too much stress, too much pressure. If I don't like the teacher then I guess I sometimes miss his class. Then I just ask my friends what they did in class but I don't go. (ST02)

reason

reason

activity to catch up

I always go to class except when I am sick. Even if I don't like the teacher, I still go because I know the teacher takes attendance and if I miss class then I am not sure what to study. Once I missed class because I overslept but I only did that once. Then I went to the teacher's office to ask him what he did in class but I couldn't find him. If I am sick then I start to get worried if I miss more than one day, because then I don't know if I can catch up. (ST04)

It depends on the class. If the teacher takes attendance then maybe I attend more classes. But if he doesn't then sometimes I don't go. It depends on whether I like the class. Sometimes I am too tired to go to classes all day, so I go to one and then I go back to the hostel. I don't think you have to attend all the classes to pass the course. Even I know some students who always attend and then they failed the course. I guess I attend more classes if my friend is in the same course because then it isn't so boring for me. But sometimes my friend tells me let's not go, and then we both don't go to class. Also, sometimes I don't understand what the teacher's talking about in the class so I don't want to go. (ST05)

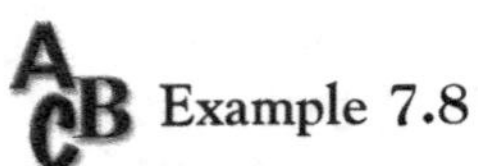

Example 7.8

Table showing thematic categories

Days of week	*Reasons for non-attendance*	*Reason for attendance*	*Peer influence*
I start to miss the class on Friday. (ST02) Sometimes I don't get back to the university in time for class on Monday so sometimes I miss class then as well. (ST02)	It just gives me more free time so I don't feel so pressured. Otherwise it is too much stress, too much pressure. (ST02) If we have a quiz or an exam in one class, then I sometimes miss my other classes. (ST02) If I don't like the teacher then I guess I sometimes miss his class. (ST02) Once I missed class because I overslept but I only did that once. (ST04)	I still go because I know the teacher takes attendance and if I miss class then I am not sure what to study. (ST04) I start to get worried if I miss more than one day, because then I don't know if I can catch up. (ST04)	

Attitude towards attendance	*Activity in place of attendance*	*Actions to catch up*	
	I sometimes miss my other classes because I want to study. Though I usually don't really study, but it just gives me more free time. (ST02)	Then I just ask my friends what they did in class but I don't go. (ST02) Then I went to the teacher's office to ask him what he did in class but I couldn't find him. (ST04)	

Exercise 7.5

Coding qualitative data

Write the labels for the information given by ST05 (final paragraph in Example 7.7). Then add the information to the appropriate column in Example 7.8. There is one extra column in case you need a new category.

Reporting results

The visual presentation of numerical data should be accompanied by a description of your findings in one or more paragraphs. Ensure you also refer to each graph or table in your text (e.g. 'see Table 2' or 'as can be seen in Graph 3'). Tip 7.4 lists phrases commonly used when reporting results. Do not mention every result shown in the graph or table, but rather synthesize the findings and describe results that stand out in some way. Look at the graph in general terms. What trends can you identify? What should the reader focus on? It can be challenging to achieve the right balance between a general report of your findings and a detailed account of selected points. What information from Zareen's results in Discussion task 7.3 would you describe in general terms? What would you specifically draw the reader's attention to?

Exercise 7.6

Describing your results

1 Below are two descriptions of the results from Zareen's graphic in Discussion task 7.3. Which one is more effective? Explain your answer.

Example A

Figure 3 shows that 80 per cent of girls 'strongly agree' with the statement 'Getting high grades is important for my future career' compared with 40 per cent of males, but more males 'agree' than females. Also, 16 per cent of males gave a 'neutral' answer to this statement, but no females gave this answer. Finally, 2 per cent of females disagreed with this statement, but no males did.

Example B

As can be seen in Figure 3, twice the number of females 'strongly agree' that high grades are important for their future career than males. When viewed in general terms, however, the contrast is less stark; 98 per cent of females 'agree' or 'strongly agree' with the statement compared with 84 per cent of males. While a small number of females disagree with this statement (2 per cent), a markedly higher number of males (16 per cent) answered with 'neutral'. It is unclear how this answer might be interpreted; it might indicate that these males partly agree and partly disagree, or it might also indicate that they had not formulated any particular view on the matter.

2 Use the questionnaire in Example 6.2 (p. 63) to collect data from ten people in your class and/or friends. Decide how you will present these results. Finally, write a paragraph to describe your results.

Tip 7.4

Useful phrases to describe your results

These phrases are part of the *Academic Phrasebank* (Morley, n.d.).

Highlighting significant data in a table/figure

'It is apparent that very few . . . (see Table 2) . . .'

'As can be seen in Figure 9, only a minority of . . .'

'As Table 2 shows, . . .'

Highlighting significant, interesting or surprising results

'The most striking result to emerge from the data is that . . .'

'An interesting trend that can be observed from these results is that . . .'

Reporting results from questionnaires and interviews

'Of the 130 originally contacted, 90 students completed and returned the questionnaire.'

'Of the total of 123 students who completed the survey, 66 were female and 57 male.'

'The majority of respondents felt that . . .'

'A minority of participants (17 per cent) indicated that . . .'

'Over half of those surveyed reported that . . .'

'Almost two-thirds of the participants (64 per cent) said that . . .'

'Of the 148 patients who completed the questionnaire, just over half indicated that . . .'

'In response to Question 1, most of those surveyed indicated that . . .'

'Some participants expressed the belief that . . .'

Discussing results

Following the initial presentation and reporting of data comes the discussion of findings. This may appear as a separate chapter or it may be included in either the Results or the Conclusion chapters; it depends on the tradition followed at your institution. Similarly, the practice in research articles also varies. In some studies, the presentation of results and the discussion may appear in the same chapter, in others a brief discussion of findings may be incorporated into the Conclusion, whereas in other cases, the Discussion may constitute a separate chapter of its own. Each journal establishes the practice it wishes authors to follow.

The difference between the Results and Discussion chapters essentially lies in the purpose of each. The objective of the Results chapter is to present the findings and answer the question 'What did I discover?'. The Discussion chapter guides the reader towards an interpretation of the findings; here, you attempt to respond to the questions 'Why did I get these results?', 'What do these findings mean?' and 'How can I explain these findings in light of the literature?'. Logically, readers need first to see a description of the results to understand the interpretations and conclusions presented in the Discussion.

Writing the Discussion chapter can be challenging as one needs to review the literature in the light of one's findings and pinpoint salient issues that illuminate or contextualize aspects of the study. It is not easy to interpret findings clearly and convincingly, and simultaneously demonstrate how these relate to the literature. One function of this chapter is to highlight unanticipated or unusual results. Surprisingly, identifying the novel element may not be straightforward. After investing so much time and energy in your study, you might find all the results equally interesting. Talking through the results with an interested listener may help you identify unexpected and thought-provoking elements of the findings. Findings that confirm (or refute) your initial expectations (these were probably stated in the Introduction) or that support findings from prior studies also require detailed discussion. Don't attempt to discuss your results exhaustively, however; the key is to be selective.

In some studies, it may be just as important to discuss the method or approach used in the study as the actual findings. If your study involved a novel approach to collecting or analysing data, or the approach was less commonly employed in your cultural context, a critical discussion of the suitability of this method in light of your experience should be included. Alternatively, the method you used may not have been novel, but, in hindsight, it may not have been the most appropriate for your context or the study's objectives. This realization also requires balanced discussion with the aim of informing future researchers of this valuable insight.

One section of your Discussion chapter should address the question 'why did this study result in these findings?'. Apart from considerations of the methods used, to some extent the findings may be explained by the profile of the study participants, or the purpose and functions that the texts serve. Also, reflect on whether an understanding of the sociocultural context of the participants (or the context in which texts were produced) may shed light on aspects of your findings. The explanations you provide probably don't exhaust the range of possible interpretations, but they are the ones you consider to be most likely, or most justified in light of your knowledge of the context, your experience undertaking this study and your understanding of the literature. To signal your degree of conviction in the different explanations you discuss, use adverbs ('possibly', 'probably'), modal verbs ('might, could') or expressions that show a degree of uncertainty ('it appears', 'it seems'); the linguistic term for these words is *hedges*. Chapter 8 contains a section on how to 'hedge' claims (p. 157). Common phrases used in Discussion chapters may be found in Tip 7.5.

Your discussion should be informed by your knowledge of the relevant literature. This will require returning to your Literature Review chapter (and the wider bibliography you assembled) to identify how the literature can clarify the issues, questions and tendencies that emerged in your findings. You might consider undertaking another brief literature search for material on very specific topics. For instance, if the results from your study indicate that some underlying social issue may be an important factor in explaining a particular tendency, information relating to social norms or values of your environment could be helpful. Avoid basing such interpretations on your personal opinion or experience.

Exercise 7.7

The Discussion section

Below is an excerpt from Chik's (2014, pp. 95–7) Discussion section. Identify instances where Chik:

a mentions salient findings;
b synthesizes findings;
c relates the findings to the literature to confirm, question or extend claims or findings from previous studies;
d uses cautious language when interpreting findings;
e refers to the sociocultural context;
f identifies issues or phenomena that are hard to explain; and
g pinpoints findings or issues that require further exploration.

Discussion

The present study set out to examine the ways gamers practice autonomy within community by managing their gameplay both as leisure and as learning practices. [. . .] In line with findings by Piirainen-Marsh and Tainio (2009), L2 gamers learned an L2 from gaming through textual and social interaction in community; however, it was not quite clear what could be learned beyond L2 vocabulary. This may help explain how Swedish gamers would perform better than non-gamers in a vocabulary test (Sylvén & Sundqvist, 2012). The other two dimensions—pedagogy and locus of control—highlight certain limitations of L2 learning through gaming. The lack of structured materials or instructions (pedagogy) appears to restrain progress in L2 learning. Findings on locus of control suggest the distribution of control among individual, community and artefacts. To some degree, the exercise of control could be limited by the age of the gamer or the available language interface of a game. If the language interface of a COTS game is only available in an L2, all consequent learning could be incidental rather than intentional. On the other hand, if a gamer chose to play an L2 game and applied learning strategies, L2 learning would be intentional. The choice of game genres caters to individual preferences and gears L2 learning in certain directions, and this personal preference is an underexplored area in gaming study. [. . .]

Secondly, this study identified a new dimension, trajectory, to expand Benson's (2011) framework in light of the practice of autonomy within gamer communities. Put in context, the original framework was theorized as a template to explore how individual learners achieve learning or to explore how learning could be understood in contexts beyond the language classrooms. In addition to managing gaming practices, Gee and Hayes (2011) found that gamers also transferred literacy and life skills learned from gaming to their formal learning, and this process took place over adolescence and young adulthood. Findings from the present study also indicate that L2 gaming is a long-term leisure activity, and gamers were shown to have actively managed their gaming practices by using both personal experience and community resources. Borrowing Goffman's (1968) concept of 'career' as 'any social strand of any person's course through life' (p. 119), the addition of trajectory extends Benson's (2011) framework to include a temporal component in understanding L2 learning through gaming as a persistent and managed career.

Thirdly, by situating L2 gaming in the East Asian social and economic contexts, support and affordances within the online communities might have contributed greatly to L2 learning. Studies have shown game-external paratexts to be complex and rich texts which could be conducive to L2 learning (Apperley & Walsh, 2012; Sykes & Reinhardt, 2013; Thorne et al., 2012). This study confirms that the consumption and production of paratexts was common within the online Chinese gaming communities. In addition, gamers actively seek and give L2 learning advice on online discussion forums and blogs, thus creating 'funds of knowledge' (Moll et al., 1992) for other gamers. [. . .]

Tip 7.5

Useful phrases for the Discussion chapter

Most of these phrases are part of the *Academic Phrasebank* (Morley, n.d.).

Stating results

'The results of this study show/indicate that . . .'

'The most interesting finding was that . . .'

'Another important finding was that . . .'

'The results of this study did not show any significant increase in . . .'

Discussing unexpected outcomes

'Surprisingly, X was found to . . .'

'However, no differences were found in . . .'

'Contrary to expectations, the results from . . .'

'This finding was unexpected and suggests that . . .'

Referring to previous research

'The findings of the current study are consistent with those of Jones (2001) who found . . .'

'These results are consistent with those of other studies and suggest that . . .'

'However, the findings of the current study do not support the previous research. For example . . .'

'This study has been unable to demonstrate that . . .'

Explaining results

'There are several possible explanations for this result.'

'A possible explanation for this might be that . . .'

'It seems possible that these results are due to . . .'

Interpreting with caution

'These data must be interpreted with caution because . . .'

'However, with a small sample size, caution must be applied, as the findings might not be transferable to . . .'

Noting implications

'This finding has important implications for developing . . .'

'One of the issues that emerges from these findings is . . .'

Offering suggestions for future work

'Further research should be done to investigate the . . .'

'Future studies on the current topic are therefore recommended.'

'A further study with more focus on X is therefore suggested.'

The Conclusion

For many, writing the Conclusion can be a bit frustrating. You may reach the end of the project thinking that you have exhausted what you wanted to say, and you don't know how to avoid being repetitive in the Conclusion. This is perhaps more likely to be the case if you have a separate Discussion chapter, as maintaining a distinction between these two chapters can be difficult.

The Conclusion will be shorter than the Introduction. Writers may restate their research question(s) early in the Conclusion. Rather than copying the sentence verbatim from the Introduction, it can be reformulated. Important findings should be highlighted and these can be linked to a broader social, educational or theoretical context. This indicates how your research has contributed to the body of literature on this topic area. When mentioning how your findings might be interpreted, keep a 'big-picture' focus and avoid discussing particular issues in detail; this was the purpose of the Discussion chapter.

If relevant, identify any limitations to the study or findings; limitations are expected due to the particular characteristics of the sample used during data collection or the choice of texts analysed, or the methods used to collect and analyse data. Perhaps something occurred during either the data collection or the analysis stage that may have impacted your findings. Such limitations indicate that the findings may not necessarily be generalizable to a wider population (or a broader range of texts) or that the theoretical interpretation may not be extended to other texts or other dialects. It is also an indication that further research or a replication study may be needed. Being transparent about the study's limitations is not a sign of weakness; on the contrary, it signals that the researcher is aware of factors that may have influenced the study's outcome. You are likely to see other authors identify limitations to their study in the articles you read during your review of the literature.

Stating the implications of the study contributes to making the practical significance of your findings explicit. This component of your Conclusion answers the question 'So what?'; that is, if these findings are true, what does this mean for language learners, teachers, translators and interpreters, or our understanding of a particular literary period or genre? Keep any implications you identify brief. Implications are logically followed by recommendations (this component may not be applicable to all topics); keep these brief and realistic. Recommendations may be placed in a separate subsection; again, this depends on the tradition followed at your institution.

Exercise 7.8

Conclusions

Read the Conclusion of Chik's (2014) article in Appendix 2.

1 Examine how the author has organized the information in this section. Find the following information:
   a the research question(s);
   b the main findings;
   c implications;
   d limitations.
2 Do the same exercise with the Conclusion of either Lee's or Chen's article (also in Appendix 2).
3 In the Conclusions you have just read, underline any standard phrases that you might also use in your Conclusion.

Insights from the literature 7.3

From the Discussion to the Conclusion in moves

Ruiying and Allison (2003) investigated the structure of the Results, Discussion and Conclusion sections in applied linguistic research articles. The authors identified both a variety of names for these sections and differences in how these sections are organized. In some cases, the Results (or Findings) and Discussion sections may be separate, while in other cases a separate Discussion section is absent and the discussion of findings may occur within the Results section. Although not common practice, writers may also indicate they have joined the two sections into one by using the title 'Results and Discussion'. Basing their approach to analysing move structures on Swales' (1990) work, Ruiying and Allison (2003, p. 374) identify three main moves in the Results section: M1 Preparatory information; M2 Reporting results; and M3 Commenting on results. The first move essentially functions as a connector between the preceding section and the presentation of results, reminding readers of the methods and instruments used. This move is not obligatory. In M2, the text may be accompanied by the presentation of findings in visual form, whether through figures, tables or graphs. In M3, writers indicate how the reader should interpret the findings in light of the current knowledge base; this usually involves relating findings to the literature. Writers may also attempt to offer explanations for their findings or signal limitations in their generalizability (Ruiying & Allison, 2003, p. 374). M2 and M3 occur in a cyclical manner; that is, the presentation of results may be interspersed with the writer's commentary.

Where a separate Discussion section is included, this usually comprises a selection of the following moves: M1 Background information; M2 Reporting results; M3 Summarizing results; M4 Commenting on results; M5 Summarizing the study; M6 Evaluating the study (limitations); and M7 Deductions (or recommendations and implications) from the research. The main emphasis is on commenting on results (M4). Not all results are necessarily commented upon in the Discussion section, however; rather, the writer may choose to focus on results that confirmed expectations or were unexpected or problematic in some way. Where M1, M2 and M3 are included, these are brief and their purpose is primarily to contextualize the commentary. If M6 and M7 are included in the Discussion section, reference to these issues will likely also appear in the Conclusion section, and an indication of limitations (M6) may appear in the Results section. Thus, according to Ruiying and Allison (2003), the treatment of M6 and M7 in the Discussion section depends on how the writer approached these topics in the adjacent Results and Conclusion sections.

The Conclusion section comprises moves previously seen in the Discussion section. Typically comprising three moves (M1 Summarizing the study, M2 Evaluating the study and M3 Deductions from the research), Ruiying and Allison (2003, p. 379) note that the focus of the Conclusion section is on the overall study rather than specific findings or the evaluation of particular research procedures.

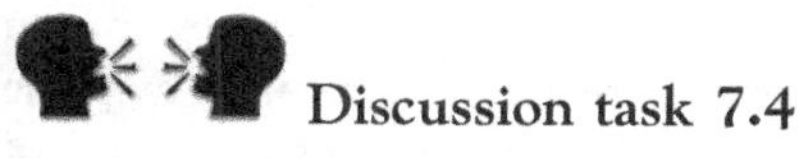

Discussion task 7.4

Discuss the following questions in pairs or small groups:

1. What are the requirements at your institution for the organization of the Results, Discussion and Conclusion sections? Are you expected to write three different chapters (i.e. Results, Discussion and Conclusion) or two (i.e. Results and Conclusion)?
2. Many writers find it challenging to to ensure that these three chapters are distinct, as there is potentially quite a bit of overlap of content. Underline points in Insights from the literature 7.3 that can serve as a reminder of what to write in each chapter.

8 Features of academic writing

Sounding 'academic' in writing

The style of academic texts varies considerably depending on the type of publication and the discipline. For your research project, your goal should be a fairly formal academic style. As communication in our daily lives doesn't usually involve this style of writing, achieving an appropriate academic style will require practice and multiple drafting attempts. Anxiety about style can hinder your writing flow, however. To avoid this, start drafting your text in a conversational tone and allow a more formal style to emerge gradually in subsequent drafts. To build your awareness of what constitutes an appropriate academic writing style, focus on the use of language in academic texts. For instance, in place of commonly used, multifunctional words such as 'get', 'do' and 'put', you will likely often find more precise, less common words such as 'obtain', 'attain', 'undertake', 'perform', 'place' or 'assign', depending on the context. At the level of textual cohesion, you may also identify phrases that show how ideas are related or appear to help the reader (and the writer) move through the text. Sharpening your awareness of academic style necessitates reading on two levels: for content and for language use.

This chapter examines different aspects of academic writing such as the integration of sources, appropriate vocabulary and language functions. One of the most important features of academic writing involves relating your work to previous research and explicitly signalling this through author citations. You may choose to integrate ideas from another author's work into your own by using summaries, quotations and paraphrases. How well you manage to situate your study within the wider discourse on your topic will be one of the criteria used to judge the quality of your work.

While drafting your research project, you will have to 'do' certain things with language or perform certain actions linguistically. For instance, you will need to define certain terms or inform your reader how the sections of your work are related. You might think of phrases used to perform such actions as language functions. The function of a definition is to make explicit to the reader how certain concepts will be used in your work. Other language functions commonly found include, for example, describing procedures, comparing and contrasting phenomena, explaining causes and effects, and arguing a point of view. This chapter will briefly look at how language is used to perform some of these functions. While only a few examples are provided here, the objective is to prompt you to start noticing how authors employ language for purposes such as these. Consider creating a small database of different phrases that you consider particularly effective.

As language functions typically involve 'fixed' phrases or formulaic expressions, it is usually acceptable to copy functional phrases used in a text you are reading and, where appropriate, use them in your own writing. In many cases, formulaic expressions need to be learnt and used as chunks as they may not admit changes (or only to a very limited degree). For instance, the phrase 'in light of the aforementioned . . .' is often used to conclude a discussion and to introduce a claim or argument. The phrase 'in light of' does not admit changes, but the final noun phrase can be substituted for another, although the range of nouns that typically appear in this position is limited. Adopting such formulaic phrases, or 'building blocks', and making them part of your emerging writer's voice can be a valuable strategy to improve your academic style. Formulaic language is, by definition, not original language, but rather an accepted, standardized way of expressing something. A particular function (such as 'concluding a discussion') can be formulated in many different ways and, as you become a more experienced writer, you will begin to use a greater variety of formulations. It is important that you don't understand this as an invitation to copy and use extensive chunks of text, however. Functional language is usually limited to phrases, and doesn't generally extend to sentences. Copying a sentence or even a part of a sentence that expresses an idea that originated with a particular author would likely lead to accusations of plagiarism.

Summaries, quotations and paraphrases

A fundamental part of academic writing entails relating your own work to the work of others, or 'situating' your work within the established disciplinary discourse. This means that you need to use the literature you read in various ways; for instance, you will need to summarize ideas or findings from previously published studies, explain how an author defines a concept and show how your work differs from (or is similar to) related studies. To do this, you will use summaries, paraphrases or quotations. The following exercises will explore important differences between them.

Exercise 8.1

Summaries, quotations and paraphrases

1 Read the sentences below; for each one, indicate whether this is true for a summary, a quote or a paraphrase. Write 'S', 'Q' or 'P' after each sentence (in some instances, multiple answers are possible):
   a uses exactly the same words;
   b may omit some words from the original sentence and use [. . .];

- c restates the idea using similar words (approximately the same length or a bit shorter);
- d restates the idea using similar words (much shorter in length);
- e uses quotation marks;
- f does not use quotation marks;
- g includes a citation of the author;
- h does not include a citation of the author;
- i includes the year of publication;
- j does not include the year of publication;
- k gives the page number of the original source;
- l does not give the page number of the original source;
- m uses a reporting verb such as 'said', 'explained' or 'stated'.

2 Why should you use quotations, summaries and paraphrases? Read the following list of reasons and underline all those that are legitimate.

- a They show I have read other authors.
- b They show I can recognize and understand the main ideas connected to my topic.
- c My ideas seem stronger if I can show that other writers have a similar opinion.
- d They provide context for my own work.
- e I need to show that some authors disagree with an idea or opinion I want to discuss.
- f I want to show that other authors disagree with each other.
- g The views of other authors are more important than my views.
- h Other authors give important examples that I can use to support my idea.
- i They fill up a lot of space in my work.

3 Do you have problems deciding when to use a quotation, a paraphrase or a summary? In the following cases, which would you use (in some instances, multiple answers are possible)?

- a The idea expressed by this author is very important, but the exact words he/she uses to express this idea are not particularly special.
- b The exact words of a published author will make my ideas and my argument sound more credible.
- c The exact words of this author will make my English sound better.
- d The exact words the author uses are important to understand the idea correctly.
- e The author uses several important terms that I think originate with this author.
- f The details are not so important; it is the general idea I want to use in my work.
- g I need to express in one paragraph what the author discusses in one chapter.

Paraphrasing

Paraphrasing an author's idea involves retaining the general idea as expressed in the original text, while expressing it in different words. Maintaining the same formal academic style while reformulating an idea can be challenging in a second language. In unsuccessful paraphrases the original meaning may be lost or difficult to understand, or the paraphrase may simply be ungrammatical.

Alternatively, if too few changes are made, the sentence will be too faithful to the original to be considered a successful paraphrase. Never insert into your work verbatim a sentence or part of a sentence that represents an idea originally formulated by another writer, unless it is accompanied by quotation marks and an author citation. Incorporating some of the 'useful phrases' from the *Academic Phrasebank* (Morley, n.d.) is not considered plagiarism, however. These phrases are routinized formulations that commonly recur in academic texts. Even if you do borrow from the *Academic Phrasebank*, minor changes to the phrase will be needed to ensure it fits into the context of your text. The idea or excerpt you choose to paraphrase should be short – one to two sentences at the most. Rather than trying to paraphrase a whole paragraph, try summarizing the text instead. Finally, do not paraphrase terminology. The correct use of the appropriate terms is important; otherwise the meaning of a passage may be altered or even lost.

A common mistake is to attempt to paraphrase a sentence word by word. This makes the task very difficult for the writer and the result can be equally difficult for the reader to understand. The following technique will help you avoid this:

- Read closely the passage that you want to paraphrase.
- Put the passage to one side so you are not looking at it.
- Note down the key words you remember from the passage that express the main idea. (Whether you use English or your L1 makes little difference at this stage.)
- Look at the passage again; are these a good choice of key words?
- Put the passage aside again. Translate any words you wrote in your L1 into English. Find synonyms for as many words as you can. (It is advisable to check the meaning and use of these synonyms in a good dictionary to make sure they are appropriate in this context.) Do not find synonyms for terminology, however.
- Start to write the main idea in the passage using your list of key words. (You may not need all of them.) You may need several of attempts at this.
- When you feel comfortable with what you have written, read the original passage again. Have you expressed the same idea? Is your passage sufficiently different from the original? Are any words the same? If a few words are the same, this shouldn't be a problem; but if you have whole phrases or even clauses that are the same, this is probably a sign that you need to make more changes.

Tip 8.1

Paraphrasing

Typical changes we make to a sentence when paraphrasing include the following:

- *Use synonyms*: 'studies'/'research'/'investigation'; 'society'/'community'/ 'social environment'/'culture'/'civilization'; 'caused by'/'brought about by'/'triggered by'/'instigated by'.
- *Change the word class*: 'India'/'Indian'; 'the assessment of students at Foundation level'/'assessing Foundation students'.
- *Use a synonym and change the word class*: 'learners who attain top grades'/'high-achieving students'.
- *Use a more general word*: 'the tuition fees charged by universities'/'the cost of tertiary study'.
- *Change the voice from active to passive (or vice versa)*: 'The departmental committee awarded the project a high grade'/'The project was awarded a high grade.'
- *Combine two sentences by using participle phrases*: 'The students completed the questionnaire. They then did a short test.'/'After completing the questionnaire, the students did a short test.'
- *Use different prepositions and transition words* (see Appendix 3 for a list).
- *Use nominalization*: 'Many students were unable to pass the exam'/'The high rate of exam failure'.
- *Rearrange the sentence constituents (phrases or clauses)*: 'Students were interviewed and then they completed a short test.'/'Students completed a short test after being interviewed.'
- *Ignore the words you think are not essential.*

It is not enough to use just one of the above strategies in your paraphrase. A good paraphrase employs several of these strategies; you will, for example, find synonyms, change the word class of particular words, rearrange the sentence constituents and use a different conjunction. You will not use all words from the original in your paraphrase; some can be ignored. You choose to paraphrase because the idea is the most important thing – not the exact words. There is no rule regarding the length of paraphrases; while they are usually shorter than the original as some parts will be unimportant for your purposes, the use of more elaborate formulations may result in a paraphrase longer than the original.

Tip 8.2

Synonyms

The synonyms you find in the dictionary usually have slightly different meanings. Consider the different connotations conveyed by 'cheap' and the various synonyms of this adjective in the sentence below:

> The university offers *cheap/inexpensive/economic/affordable/low-cost/competitively priced/cut-price/bargain-priced* degree programmes.

You may have to change the structure of a sentence when you use a synonym. This may not only mean using a preposition, but also it may mean changing the sentence from active to passive voice (or vice versa):

1 'Some Malaysian universities *attract/appeal to* many foreign students.'
2 'Many foreign students *are drawn to* some Malaysian universities.'

If you don't know whether the meaning of the synonym is appropriate, or whether using this synonym will require a change in sentence structure, look for example sentences of this word. Good dictionaries provide examples of words in context.

Exercise 8.2

Paraphrasing techniques

1 Read the original sentence below, taken from Chik (2014, p. 88). This sentence has been paraphrased in four different ways (a–d). Which paraphrased version do you prefer? Do all four paraphrases accurately reflect the content of the original? Read carefully the version you prefer; which paraphrasing techniques (see Tip 8.1) can you identify?

Original

'The growing body of research on L2 gaming suggests that digital gaming is not necessarily an individual activity: it is also a community- or team-based activity that involves gaming partners, either in physical proximity or in virtual gameworlds.'

a 'Far from being a solitary activity, studies on L2 gaming reveal the social or community orientation of digital gaming through the involvement of peers, whether in person or virtually.'

b 'Prior research has uncovered the social orientation and team spirit of L2 gaming, due to the participation of co-gamers.'

c 'Increasingly, research is pointing to the collaborative dimension of digital gaming, which involves cooperation between gamers in person or virtually.'

d 'One of the most important characteristics of digital gaming appears to be the strong collaborative nature of gamers; rather than constituting a solitary activity, it appears to be intensely social.'

2 Now repeat the exercise with the second example from Chik (2014, p. 92) below.

Original

'These examples suggest that though many L2 gamers prioritized gaming pleasure over L2 learning, some gamers appropriated L2 gaming for learning by turning incidental learning into intentional learning.'

a 'Although evidence suggests that L2 gamers were more motivated by enjoyment than L2 acquisition, some gamers combined gaming with learning opportunities.'

b 'Some gamers managed to blend purposeful language learning with gaming, but for most, gaming was purely entertainment-oriented.'

c 'Gaming is a context in which language acquisition can occur, whether purposely or incidentally, although most gamers are primarily attracted by the entertainment value of gaming.'

d 'While much L2 learning during gaming occurs incidentally, gaming provides some gamers with the opportunity to target language learning; admittedly, however, gaming is for most merely a diversion.'

Exercise 8.3

Paraphrasing practice

Read carefully the two excerpts from Chik (2014, p. 87) below. In each one, part of a sentence appears in italic. Use the steps described on p. 117 to paraphrase the idea in italic. The surrounding text is provided to contextualize the idea; you don't have to include this in your paraphrase unless you wish to.

Paragraph 1

'In addition to online gaming interaction, *current research on digital gaming identified in-game text consumption and game-related text production as providing affordances for L2 learning*. Good games engage players not only in playing the game, but also in reading and writing about them on interest-driven websites.'

Paragraph 2

'These game-related texts are not just practical texts for instructions and strategy training, *they are also imaginative and creative outputs developed by gamers and circulated in online gaming communities*. These texts are often highly sophisticated, with rich lexical items and syntactic structures, and of multiple genres.'

Citing the author

When paraphrasing, you need to cite the author of the source you used. This can be done in two ways. The reference may be an integral part of the sentence (an *integral citation*), introduced by the author's name and the year of publication. This approach has the effect of foregrounding the author, particularly when the citation appears early in the sentence. Alternatively, the author's name and the year of the publication may appear in parentheses at the end of the paraphrase. This citation is not a component of the sentence and is known as a *non-integral citation*. Integral citations are usually followed by a reporting verb. As illustrated by the list of reporting verbs grouped semantically in Appendix 4, these may convey quite different shades of meaning.

If you wish to paraphrase (or summarize) more than one sentence, or more than one idea, it is usually good practice to indicate that the subsequent sentence or idea also originates with the author you cited previously. To avoid repeating the author's name, use a *reference reminder*. This is a cohesive device that signals to the reader that you are attributing additional information to the same source. Such 'reminders' include: 'as the author points out', 'in their study', 'this study suggests' etc. This cohesive device is used if the reference referred to appeared within the preceding sentence; that is, it should refer to a previous integral citation, not a non-integral citation. The following two examples from Chik (2014, pp. 86, 87) demonstrate how a reference reminder ('the authors') may be used across adjacent sentences (Example 1) or with an intervening sentence (Example 2) (my italic):

1 '*Sykes and Reinhardt (2013)* further examine possible contributions of digital gaming in light of five key areas in L2 learning (goals, interaction, feedback, context, and motivation). By mapping L2 learning theories onto gameplay designs and principles, *the authors* provide a potential blueprint for the implementation of game-mediated L2 learning activities in classroom contexts.'
2 'Turning to console-based gameplay, *Piirainen-Marsh and Tainio (2009)* show L2 gaming could be utilized as learning resources in naturalistic settings and the game avatars could become the L2 "teachers". Although the two Finnish teens mainly conversed with each other in Finnish while playing *Final Fantasy* X, they repeated or used the English phrases spoken by game avatars. *The authors* used Conversation Analysis to analyze gameplay sessions and found patterns of other-repetition.'

Exercise 8.4

Citing the author

1 The Literature Review is the obvious place to find examples of author citations. Look at the excerpts from Lee's and Chen's Literature Reviews in Exercise 7.2 (pp. 91–3). Find an example of an integral and a non-integral citation in each excerpt.
2 Return to the paraphrases given in Exercise 8.2. Insert an author citation into each of the four paraphrases. Use integral and non-integral citations.
3 Add an author citation to your paraphrased sentences in Exercise 8.3. Use integral and non-integral citations.

USING AND CITING INFORMATION FROM SECONDARY SOURCES

The author of the book or article you are reading will signal the incorporation of ideas and information from other authors through author citations. If you wish to use in your own text information that has been attributed to another author, but you haven't actually read the original text by this author, you need to cite this author as a secondary source. The convention for citing secondary sources signals that you haven't personally consulted the original text and states the source where you learned about this author's work. While it is always preferable to consult the original work, this is frequently not feasible.

The following is an example of citing a secondary source using a paraphrase and a quotation:

> While gamers usually converse during the activity in their L1, Piirainen-Marsh and Tainio (in Chik, 2014, p. 87) demonstrate how L2 language practice occurs through the echoing by gamers of phrases spoken by avatars during a game.

The writer signals that the paraphrased information about the study by *Piirainen-Marsh and Tainio* was extracted from *Chik*. The writer provides the year of publication of Chik's work (*2014*) and the page where Piirainen-Marsh and Tainio are cited in Chik (*p. 87*). In the list of references, only include the work you read (in this case *Chik*); don't include the secondary source (in this case *Piirainen-Marsh and Tainio*).

Quotations

Incorporating a quotation (often abbreviated to 'quote') entails using the exact words from a source text, whether a phrase, a sentence or several sentences, and enclosing this borrowed chunk of text in quotation marks. To show the source of this information, you must cite the author's name, the year of publication and the page number. This is important, as the reader might want to check the original source to understand the broader context from which you extracted this short passage. Students usually find using quotations to be much easier than using paraphrases, as the quoted material is inserted verbatim. Nonetheless, quotations can be misused and this can detract from the quality of your writing. In this section we will look at the things you should consider when using quotations in your work.

Identifying the key information: Be selective about what you choose to quote. The use of a quotation signals that the original formulation of the idea is important; it indicates that this particular formulation captures the idea so well that it would be difficult to achieve the same effect with a paraphrase. A common mistake of inexperienced writers is to select a long passage and use it as a quote, without considering why the entire passage is so significant.

Embedding the quote: Students often make the mistake of 'parachuting' quotes into their work. When you insert quotes, they need to be 'embedded' in your own writing. This means that you need to connect the quote to your own writing through the adjoining text.

Frequency: Quotes tend to be far less common than paraphrases. In some journal articles you read, there may be none. This is not uncommon. In your own work, consider carefully whether a quote is warranted or whether a paraphrase would be preferable. Use them sparingly. Also, take care not to include multiple quotes from a single source (unless there is a very good reason to do so). Otherwise it will appear that you lean too heavily on the original words of a particular author, or even that you transfer wholesale portions of an original text to your own.

Omitting words: Avoid using the whole sentence in your quote if only part of the sentence is pertinent to your work. Take the phrase you need, or select different parts of the same sentence and omit other parts. You need to show you have omitted words by inserting an ellipsis ([. . .]) in their place.

Citing the source: You must cite the source (including the page number) for all quotes. The citation should appear either directly before or directly after the citation. Do not neglect to do this just because you mentioned the author's name earlier on.

Reporting verbs: A quote is normally introduced by the author's name and a reporting verb (see Appendix 4 for a list). It may take you some time to work out how the meaning of some closely related reporting verbs differs. Pay attention to how reporting verbs are used in journal articles.

The information in Appendix 5 clarifies how to use quotes according to the APA referencing system.

Exercise 8.5

Using quotations and citing sources

Look at the following passages from the Literature Review chapter of one student's work on using games with children in the English classroom. Her use of quotations and author citations needs revision. Find the problems and correct them.

> According to Tongue, Moon & Brumfit (1991): 'Games are activities that children naturally and universally engage in.' Bedson, Lewis and Maley (1999) and Kiryk (2010) agree that games are fun activities with rules and a goal that promote interaction, thinking, learning, problem solving strategies, and oral fluency. Some games require oral or written interaction, and this enables players (students) to practice language. What is more, Bedson, et al. state that, 'the key to a successful language games is that rules should be clear and the ultimate goal should be defined well.' (1999, p. 6). According to Bedson, et al. say games promote children's analytical abilities. For Hadfield (1999), there are two kinds of games. 'The first kind is a competitive game, which means the player or teams (students) race to be the first to reach the goal. The second kind is the cooperative games, in which players or teams (students) work together towards a common goal.
>
> The challenge element is an important component of games. Players should experience a degree of struggle throughout all or parts of the game. These challenges increase the player's determination to succeed and the motivation to complete the game. 'When the players and the games have gotten more challenging, student's learning experience will be heightened'. (Kiryk 2010)

Exercise 8.6

Using quotations and paraphrases in a paragraph

1 For this exercise, you will write a paragraph. The topic sentence and a final sentence for your paragraph are provided; treat these as though they were your own writing. In the body of your paragraph, you will make three related points. The information for these three points comes from Chen (2006) and is labelled 'Supporting Information'. You will integrate excerpts from this supporting information either as a paraphrase or as a quotation. You can also add information. Use both integral and non-integral author citations in your paragraph and cite the information from Crystal (2001) (in Supporting Information 2) as a secondary source.

Topic sentence (your writing)

When formulating a request to lecturers in an email, judging the appropriate level of directness is a difficulty many students experience and it was one of the most persistent challenges experienced by Chen's (2006) informant Ling throughout her student years.

Supporting Information 1 (Chen, 2006, p. 42)

'Ling tended to use an inductive, or story-telling, approach to structure her messages in all her e-mails. She usually started a message with a self-identification (e.g., "This is Ling. I'm in your xxx class.") followed by a pre-request without giving a specific purpose (e.g., "I need help from you" or "I have some questions I need to ask you"). Then she provided lengthy personal details or contextual information explaining why she needed to make the request, and finally she placed her request act or purpose statement (e.g., "I want to ask you to write a recommendation for me") at the end of the message.'

Supporting Information 2 (Chen, 2006, p. 42)

'Such an inductive approach, however, is likely to be viewed as an ineffective discourse structure by those working in an institutional context where e-mails are often read quickly. As Crystal (2001) notes, "an email writer should assume that information located at the end of the message might never be seen, if the reader decided not to scroll down any further".'

Supporting Information 3 (Chen, 2006, p. 42)

'Ling's continued use of the inductive approach to structure her e-mails is probably not just an idiosyncratic practice but a common cultural practice for Chinese native speakers in making requests.'

Final sentence (your writing)

Thus, the challenges experienced by students, particularly those using English as an additional language, are of both a linguistic and cross-cultural nature.

2 Now do the same exercise for this second example.

Topic sentence (your writing)

Students' emails may sometimes appear to be too direct, or even rude, due to the students' lack of awareness of the pragmatic implications of a chosen formulation.

Supporting Information 1 (Chen, 2006, p. 43)

'Two types of request strategies at the lexico-syntactic level were identified in Ling's request e-mails: Want Statements (e.g., I want/need/hope you . . .) and Query Preparatory (e.g., Can/Could/Would you . . .).'

Supporting Information 2 (Chen, 2006, p. 43)

'Ling used Want Statements more often than Query Preparatory in her e-mails sent to professors during her master's studies; moreover, she often put an intensifier "really" before the verb "need" or "hope" and followed by the word "help" in both pre-requests and request acts to increase the illocutionary force.'

Supporting Information 3 (Chen, 2006, p. 44)

'Using Want Statements to convey a help-needed tone might help her to gain some attention from professors, yet this strategic choice is likely to cause two pragmatic problems from the target culture's perspective. First, her frequent use of Want Statements along with the word "help" is likely to project a negative image as a needy, helpless student, which is quite the opposite from the attitudes such as independence and confidence that a graduate student is expected to demonstrate in U.S. academic culture.'

Final sentence (your writing)

Students can thus clearly benefit from explicit instruction in email conventions within the target culture during their early student years, rather than be left to discover conventions by trial and error.

Insights from the literature 8.1

Why cite?

Citations in academic writing have a range of pragmatic functions and author citations are one of the clearest mechanisms by which academic writing as a form of social interaction becomes most evident. It is a mechanism by which the writer can interact with his/her supervisor, the likely reader of a paper written at university, or, if the paper is intended for publication, with other academics.

Acknowledging sources through citations is an integral part of academic work and a number of studies have enriched our understanding of how academics cite and what motivates their selection of author citations. By interviewing academics from the 'hard' and 'soft' sciences, Harwood (2009) explored citation practices within the domains of computer science and sociology. Harwood identified 11 different reasons for using citations, extending far beyond simply supporting claims through referring to prior work. Five examples of these functions (and a few of the related sub-functions) from his study are as follows. *Signposting citations* help to keep the argument on track and to save space by omitting detail that the reader can consult in the cited publication. *Supporting citations* help writers justify choices they make in their research such as topic, methods or claims made. *Credit citations* allow writers to acknowledge their debt to other writers for ideas; they also help writers protect themselves by signalling that another person is the originator of an idea. *Position citations* enable writers to identify different viewpoints and show how these may have evolved over time; for instance, the writer may cite earlier studies and then later studies with a view to showing the development of an idea. Through *engaging citations*, writers dialogue critically with their sources; this may mean that the author shows different degrees or shades of agreement or disagreement with the sources cited. Citations can have multiple functions, however; for instance, when using a citation to justify a choice of research method (supporting citation), the writer may also be crediting another author with the idea of using a particular approach (credit citation).

How students interact with their sources and incorporate citations for different purposes within their own writing may provide a signal to the quality of their writing and the standard of their research. In her analysis of high- and low-rated Master's theses, Petrić (2007) noted low-rated theses displayed a much narrower range of citation functions. Tending towards greater descriptiveness in their references to the literature, these students used citations primarily to attribute information to particular sources to facilitate the knowledge retelling process.

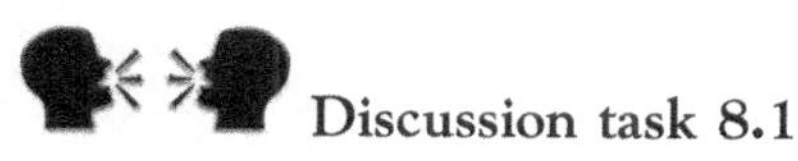

Discussion task 8.1

Why cite?

Try doing this exercise with your partner. Underline the author citations in the Introductions written by Chik (2014) and Lee (2011) in Appendix 1. Can you find examples of the five citation functions identified by Harwood (2009)? Discuss different possible answers for each citation:

1 signposting;
2 supporting;
3 credit;
4 position;
5 engaging.

Tip 8.3

Misuse of citations

In-text citations are a very important feature of academic writing. They are often misused, however, whether intentionally or simply due to lack of awareness. The following examples illustrate how in-text citations may be misused or simply used inappropriately. These practices should be avoided.

The writer:

- invents a reference;
- invents information and attributes this to an author;
- attributes information to an author that cannot be found in this author's work;
- attempts to build a strong claim by referring to a minor study with very limited generalizability;
- cites a source he/she has not actually read at all (and without indicating this is a secondary source);
- inserts references for information that is self-evident or widely recognised as factual or accepted practice.

Avoiding plagiarism

All academic writing incorporates the work of other authors in some way. This is usually done by summarizing, paraphrasing or quoting from another's work or by simply citing an author when referring to ideas, data or specific terms borrowed from this person's work. If borrowed material is not adequately referenced, allegations of plagiarism could well arise.

Exercise 8.7

Test your understanding of plagiarism

Read the seven examples below before you continue reading this section. Which ones constitute examples of plagiarism?

1 Zurab copied several examples of how to formulate emails for different purposes from a book entitled *How to write effective emails at work*. He inserted these examples into his own work without citing the author of the book.
2 Zurab found some statistics showing that the use of email as a means of communication between faculty members and students had increased over the last five years. He used these figures in the Introduction of his project. He didn't cite the source of these statistics.

3 Zareen copied a couple of graphs displaying achievement levels of university students in different Middle Eastern countries over the past three years. She inserted these graphs into her project, but she didn't indicate where these graphs originally came from.
4 Zareen found a paragraph on levels of achievement in single-sex and coeducational schools. This was perfect for her work! She copied the paragraph and changed the order of some sentences. Then she put half of the final sentence in quotation marks and she cited the author's name, the year of publication and the page number after the quotation marks.
5 Zakia read an article about the portrayal of gender roles in Arab literature in the 1900s. She particularly liked how the author defined a term and she used this definition in her work. She copied the sentence with the definition word for word and she cited the author's name.
6 Zakia found an essay on gender roles in literature on the Internet. She decided that her supervisor could never have read that particular website, so she copied one paragraph from this essay and inserted it into her own work. She did not cite the source.
7 Zeina read a chapter on the denotation and connotation of words. The author mentioned that the connotation of a particular concept in one language may differ from the connotation of this concept in another language. Zeina particularly liked how the author expressed this idea, so she inserted the sentence into her own text, changing a few words and adding a few more words at the beginning. Now it seemed like it was her sentence, so she didn't cite the original author.

Tip 8.4

What is plagiarism?

Your university may have a definition of plagiarism on its website. This definition can be found on the website of the University of Hong Kong:[1]

> Plagiarism is copying the work of another person without proper acknowledgement. There are two parts in the definition: copying and the absence of proper acknowledgement. It gives the impression that the work is the original work of the author when in fact it was copied.

Remember to cite the source in the following situations:

1 You took an idea from a text you read or a specific term that originated with one author that is not generally viewed as common knowledge.
2 You took data from a text you read; these could be numbers, percentages or even graphs or other diagrams.
3 You took a sentence (or more) from a text you read.

Common problems with borrowing information from a text that would be considered to be plagiarism include the following:

1 You didn't cite the source of a passage (or phrases, sentences or paragraphs) that you took from another author.
2 You borrowed a passage from an author but you didn't use quotation marks around all the borrowed text, so it looks like some of that text could be yours.
3 You borrowed a passage and you changed a few words or you changed the order of some of the information.

Discussion task 8.2

Justifying one's actions

Common justifications for behaviour that leads to plagiarism include the following. Do you recognize any? In pairs, discuss whether you have heard these justifications used by students at your university. Can you think of any additional justifications that are used in your context?

1 I can't remember where I read (or heard or watched) it before.
2 I'll make a few changes to the sentence but keep most of it; it will help me write faster.
3 I was in a panic because I ran out of time so I found a student essay on the Internet and submitted it.
4 The writer is saying it so well; I can't possibly say it any better.
5 I've read this sentence so many times and I've even added a few words of my own; it feels like it's mine.
6 I am sure my instructor has never seen this book before, so there's no way she'll be able to catch me.
7 There are 50 students on my course so I'm sure my instructor will never really read my essay carefully.

Exercise 8.8

Incorporating sources and recognizing plagiarism

Try this task individually first, and then discuss your answers in small groups.

This is a paragraph from Chen's (2006, p. 36) article on students writing emails. Below are six attempts at paraphrasing this paragraph. Read through each one and critique the paraphrasing technique. Remember, terminology should not be paraphrased.

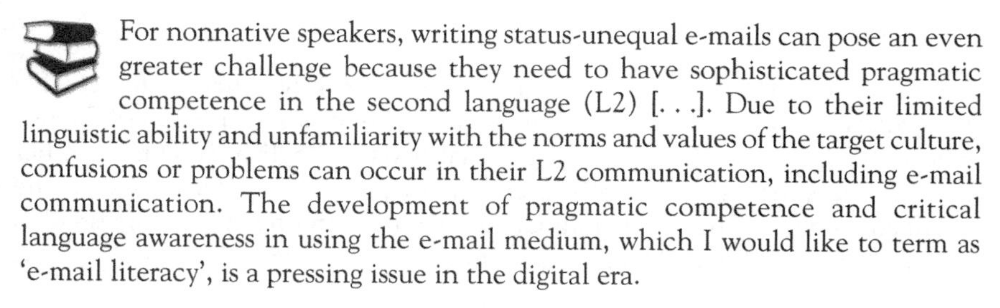

For nonnative speakers, writing status-unequal e-mails can pose an even greater challenge because they need to have sophisticated pragmatic competence in the second language (L2) [. . .]. Due to their limited linguistic ability and unfamiliarity with the norms and values of the target culture, confusions or problems can occur in their L2 communication, including e-mail communication. The development of pragmatic competence and critical language awareness in using the e-mail medium, which I would like to term as 'e-mail literacy', is a pressing issue in the digital era.

Example 1

Writing status-unequal emails can be challenging for non-native speaking students due to the need for sophisticated second-language pragmatic skills. Misunderstandings can occur in L2 communication owing to limitations in linguistic ability and familiarity with the norms and values of the target culture. The development of pragmatic competence and critical language awareness in email communication needs to receive greater attention in the current digital era.

Example 2

For students who are non-native speakers of English in particular, writing emails to a higher status individual can be difficult because it involves sophisticated pragmatic competence in the second language. Communication problems arise through limited linguistic ability and unfamiliarity with the target culture. Email literacy, or the development of pragmatic competence and critical language awareness, is an important skill in the digital era.

Example 3

According to Chi-Fen Emily Chen, composing emails to a higher status individual can be particularly challenging for non-native English speakers. Linguistic ability is limited and many target culture norms will be unfamiliar. Email literacy skills include the development of pragmatic competence and critical language awareness, and these are increasingly important in the digital era.

Example 4

In her article entitled The Development of E-mail Literacy: From Writing to Peers to Writing to Authority Figures, published in the journal *Language Learning and Technology* in 2006, the author Chi-Fen Emily Chen introduces the term 'e-mail literacy', which she claims involves pragmatic competence and critical language awareness in using the email medium. Instruction in email literacy in the digital era is important because many students lack sophisticated pragmatic competence in their L2.

Example 5

Misunderstandings occur in email communication and these may be more likely to occur, according to Chen (2006), in the case of non-native speakers of English who may lack experience of writing formal texts in English. Results from her study indicate that critical linguistic skills may be weak and the awareness of the email communication may be limited. Literacy skills are thus a 'pressing issue' in the current age (Chen, 2006, p. 36).

Example 6

Email communication between status incongruent individuals often requires sophisticated linguistic ability and advanced pragmatic skills, which can be even more challenging for second-language users. Chen (2006) demonstrates how limitations in a student's English-language communication skills and a lack of insight into target culture norms may lead to misunderstandings of a pragmatic nature. The teaching of 'e-mail literacy' skills, which Chen (2006, p. 36) defines as a combination of medium-specific pragmatic and linguistic expertise, is vital in view of our reliance on digital communication.

Insights from the literature 8.2

Approaches to plagiarism

Plagiarism is a broad term used to describe different forms of inadmissible behaviour related to the notion of academic integrity. It encompasses paying someone to write a paper for you and submitting the paper in your name, and recycling parts of an assignment or the entire assignment from a different course, to less clear-cut cases in which writers may have consciously or unconsciously borrowed ideas or chunks of text from a source without providing the appropriate citation. Plagiarism is commonly viewed as a transgression that requires some sort of punitive measure, which may involve lowering the final grade through to failing a course. Increasingly, universities use text-matching software to facilitate the detection of plagiarism. Such software identifies and highlights sections of a given text that also appear in other texts within its vast database.

Viewing plagiarism from the perspective of language acquisition, research has highlighted the fact that copying key words or chunks of language can actually be part of the process of learning how to express oneself appropriately in a second language (Pecorari, 2003). Howard (1995) coined the term *patchwriting* to refer to the copying of sections of text that are inserted into the student's own writing. She claims that this differs from prototypical plagiarism in that the writer does not intend to plagiarize but rather borrows from the source as a way of helping him/her understand the material (Howard, 1995, p. 801). In addition to assisting, comprehension patchwriting also helps novice writers to develop their language use and composing skills through copying an admired model (Pecorari, 2003). Thus borrowing from source texts helps students understand the material and develop their ability to express themselves in the desired academic style and so may also be seen as a way in which students experiment with language in an unfamiliar register (Pecorari & Petrić, 2014).

In recent decades, many universities have developed specific policies to help staff identify and deal with problems related to plagiarism in students' work. The main focus of these policies has been oriented towards punitive measures. In distinguishing between the severity of plagiarism cases committed by students in their coursework, universities usually attempt to identify whether the student intentionally presented work as his/her own, or whether the result was simply due to poor referencing and paraphrasing skills (Yeo & Chien, 2007). If intentional deceit can be shown, some form of punishment may be foreseen; if lack of skills or carelessness was to blame, then remedial work is recommended. Additional factors such as the amount of work plagiarized (i.e. a paragraph or a whole paper) and whether the student had been previously found to plagiarize are also taken into account. According to the results from a recent survey of plagiarism policies at Australian universities by Kaktiņš (2014), it appears that, at least in their policy documents, Australian universities are beginning to acknowledge that, for students to learn how to interact with academic texts in the sophisticated ways required of them, they need pedagogical support, and that a solely punitive approach to dealing with plagiarism is not pedagogically sound. Such a change in mind-set may, indeed, be due to the recognition that novice writers frequently find that copying text models plays an important role in the process of expanding their linguistic repertoire and developing more sophisticated academic writing skills (Pecorari & Petrić, 2014, p. 278).

Discussion task 8.3

Avoiding plagiarism: your experience

Discuss the following questions in small groups:

1. Does your university have an official policy on plagiarism? Do you know where to find this policy on the university website?
2. Have you ever been aware of instances of plagiarism in assignments submitted by students in your department? Describe what the student(s) did.
3. Do you think that in some cultures the concept of plagiarism might be understood differently from the definition given earlier in this chapter? Explain your answer.

Using the language of the discipline

Each subject area has its own discipline-specific vocabulary, comprising typical words and terms that recur in texts about a particular topic. Pay attention to recurring words and phrases in texts that seem specific to your topic or typical of academic writing in general. It would be advisable to start using some of these words or phrases in your own writing. This can contribute positively towards your developing academic writing ability and also assist you in expressing ideas more precisely and (hopefully) convincingly.

How can you recognize important words and terms from your topic or field of study? One approach is to start underlining key words and phrases in the texts you read for your Literature Review and creating your own database. Exposure to the same key words in different contexts can sharpen your awareness of the meaning and use of such words. Some words may appear frequently in many academic texts; these are probably words typical of academic writing in general. Other words you might find only when you read about a specific topic area; these are more likely to be specialized terms.

Academic language: style and register

When we discuss style, we focus on the level of formality; the term *register* refers to language that is typical of a particular discipline or occupation (although, admittedly, there is some variation in the definition of these two linguistic terms). Academic writing tends to be quite formal in style, although the level of formality varies depending on the type of publication and discipline.

Differences between disciplines are most visible in the particular vocabulary items that recur in texts from a given field of study. Differences can also extend to the syntactic level. As students of English language, education or translation, you are familiar with many of the specialized terms found in your coursebooks. If you consult the textbooks or journal articles from computer science or chemistry, not only will you find many unknown terms, but you may also notice differences in how ideas are expressed and how texts are structured. An example of this is the use of the first-person pronoun 'I'. It would be uncommon for the authors to use 'I' in a research article in the fields of computer science, chemistry or engineering, but you will find it used in studies in applied linguistics and education. A second example of disciplinary differences concerns the use of the passive voice. In the fields of engineering or chemistry, repeated, uninterrupted use of the passive voice in texts would not be considered unusual, while it would not be recommended in applied linguistics or education. Much of the language used in academic texts is not discipline-specific, however, but simply reflects a 'general' academic style. For instance, words may express a more precise meaning than their 'everyday' synonym or may simply have a formal-sounding ring. Formal academic language usually enables the writer to express ideas more concisely. As fewer words are used to express the same idea, the text becomes denser.

The first step in learning how to use the vocabulary typical for your field of study is to notice recurring 'academic-sounding' words and terms in books and journal articles. Some students create a collection of words or phrases frequently used when discussing a particular topic. The second step is to notice how these words are used within phrases and sentences: what other words do they occur with? Do they occur more frequently in specific sections of a text (e.g. when giving a definition or explaining the data collection procedure)? The following exercise will help you identify specialist words (terminology) and more general academic words.

Exercise 8.9

Noticing terminology and academic vocabulary

Look at the first paragraph below taken from the Literature Review of the article by Lee (2011). (Sentences have been numbered for convenience.) The examples of terminology are underlined and the examples of formal academic words are in italic. They appear below in the two lists.

(1) Within the social constructivist framework, researchers *advocate* that CALL provide catalytic conditions for active involvement in *constructing knowledge*, critical reflection on content, and collaborative interaction with peers (Benson, 2001; Blin, 2004; Leahy, 2008; Meskill & Ranglova, 2000; Murphy, 2006; Schwienhorst, 2008). (2) As such, Dang (2010) claims that these elements are prerequisites for the development of autonomous learning. (3) Among other CALL applications, electronic tandem language learning (e-Tandem) permits L1s of two different languages to work together via the Internet in order to study each other's language and culture. (4) Over the years, many e-Tandem projects have been created in European countries including Germany and Spain. (5) E-Tandem is *underpinned* by principles of *reciprocity* and *autonomy*, which allow both parties to benefit equally from the exchange and hold each party responsible for their own learning by deciding what, when, and how to *execute* learning tasks (see Brammerts, 2001 for review). (6) Within the CMC context, researchers view online learning as an extension of classroom-based learning, which gives students more control of their own learning and *promotes* greater interaction and cognitive engagement (e.g., Hewitt, 2000; Jeong, 2004; Lee, 2005; Sykes, Oskoz, & Thorne, 2008). (7) Unlike real-time CMC, asynchronous communication gives students more time to reflect on their ideas, which *fosters* critical thinking (e.g., Abrams, 2005; Arnold & Ducate, 2006; Jonassen, 2003; Lamy & Goodfellow, 1999). (8) Lee (2009a), for example, reported that a discussion board *enabled* student teachers to *gain* an in-depth understanding of teaching principles and practices through *critical reflections* on others' postings. (9) While *critical reflection* on the content is *crucial* for promoting learner autonomy, Lamy and Hassan (2003) stress that such an

expectation needs to be explicitly explained to students. (10) In addition to cognitive and social dimensions of language learning, affective factors, such as attitudes toward learning tasks, affect how learners *engage in* online learning. (11) Thus, tasks need to be *attainable* and take into account students' interests and motivation in order to inspire learner autonomy (Dang, 2006; Lee, 2002; Levy & Stockwell, 2006).

Terminology: 'social constructivist framework', 'CALL' [computer-assisted language learning], 'catalytic conditions', 'autonomous learning', 'electronic tandem language learning (e-Tandem)', 'CMC' [computer-mediated communication], 'online learning', 'classroom-based learning', 'cognitive engagement', 'asynchronous communication', 'critical thinking', 'teaching principles and practices', 'learner autonomy', 'cognitive and social dimensions', 'affective factors', 'learning tasks'.

Formal academic words: 'advocate', 'constructing knowledge', 'underpinned', 'reciprocity', 'autonomy', 'execute' (tasks), 'promotes', 'fosters', 'enabled', 'gain' (an understanding), 'critical reflections', 'crucial', 'engage in', 'attainable'.

Other than 'CALL' and 'electronic tandem language learning', the terms in this list are not unique to applied linguistics or education. They would also be understood in disciplines such as psychology and sociology, although perhaps used slightly differently. This is because these disciplines are all representative of the 'soft sciences' and they share, to some extent, a basket of common terminology. Academic texts from the 'hard sciences', such as physics or chemistry, however, would be unlikely to contain these terms, and you would probably find texts from these disciplines difficult to understand without specialized knowledge. An interesting exception to this is 'catalytic conditions'. This term appears to be frequently used in the hard sciences (chemistry and physics) to describe a context that induces a reaction. It is not common in applied linguistics or education; however, the fact that it is used occasionally can be viewed as an example of inter-disciplinary cross-fertilization.

Task

Do the same exercise using the Introduction of Chik's (2014) article in Appendix 1.

Exercise 8.10

Stylistic choices

This exercise will help you think about stylistic choices in academic writing. The sentences below are based on the first four sentences of Lee's (2011, p. 91) Methods section. These sentences have been rewritten in 'everyday' language. Reformulate them so they better reflect formal, written academic style. Lee's original sentences are in the answer key; you are likely to have alternative, equally appropriate sentences, however.

1 'This project looked at students from the US who went on two study abroad programmes at the University of Granada in Spain.'
2 'To give students more chance to find out about Spanish culture and mix with the locals outside of class, the researchers designed together the project for intercultural learning.'
3 'The project had three big blog tasks. They were described in the syllabus and were worth 60 per cent of the coursework.' [You can combine these two sentences.]
4 'We used blog technology to get students to think critically about cross-cultural topics and FTF [face-to-face] interviews for real-time intercultural conversations with locals.'

Linking words

Using academic language appropriately is more than knowing how to use formal words and terminology; it also involves knowing how to formulate your ideas convincingly and how to develop a paragraph that flows logically. Using linking words, such as 'firstly', 'as a result' or 'moreover', can help you achieve this. Linking words are a broad class of words that include adverbs, conjunctions and prepositional phrases. They help the writer 'do' things within the text, such as structure the paragraph, signal the order of information and indicate the purpose of an action. From the reader's perspective, these words signal how certain parts of the text relate to each other and, in this sense, they guide the reader through the text. The list of linking words in Appendix 3 has been arranged according to the functions or meanings they express.

Although some linking words may have similar meanings, selecting a suitable transition word, knowing where to place it in the sentence (i.e. at the beginning of a sentence, somewhere in the middle or at the end) and choosing the appropriate punctuation can be challenging. Some linking words can be potentially problematic because they are polysemous (e.g. 'besides' can express the meaning of 'in addition to' but can also express a concession). Apart from noting how they are used in texts you read, an excellent way to explore how linking words are used in academic writing is through conducting guided corpus searches using, for instance, the *Corpus of Contemporary American English* (Davies, 2008).

Insights from the literature 8.3

Linking words and semantic relationships

Connectors or linking words such as 'however', 'thus', 'therefore' and 'because' are adverbials used to link sentences or parts of sentences (clauses or phrases) and are an important means of creating cohesion within a text. Aside from their linking function, these words also signal the relationship between sentence constituents. Biber et al. (1999, p. 875) identified different types of relationship that such adverbials can signal, such as enumeration (listing related items) and addition, summation (drawing conclusions), result (signalling the outcome), contrast (showing differences) and concession (signalling reservations or limited commitment). Drawing on Biber et al. (1999), a brief description of each semantic category follows. All examples below are concordance lines extracted from the *Corpus of Contemporary American English* (Davies, 2008).

1 *Enumeration and addition*: Typical adverbials in this category include 'first(ly)', 'second(ly)', 'finally', 'lastly', 'next', 'also', 'further(more)', 'likewise', 'moreover', 'in addition', 'aside from' and 'besides'. These adverbials allow the writer to connect related items in a certain order; these do not have to be close to each other within a text, but may be interspersed by several sentences or even in different paragraphs. Some adverbials in this category are prepositional phrases. Not limited to a purely additive function, some adverbials signal that the additional item is also similar ('similarly', 'analogously', 'relatedly', 'by the same token').

Examples

- '*Moreover*, academically successful students were recorded to do more homework, study harder, be less likely to skip class and have higher educational demands.'
- '*By the same token*, it is preferable not to use *tu* but *vos* (i.e. the second-person singular) in Nicaraguan poetry since that is how people speak in daily life.'
- '*Relatedly*, we also expected that families would be focused on communication skills such as expressing one's needs, wants and discomforts.'
- '*Besides* its harmful effect on the health of young people, noise indirectly affects their work.'

2 *Summation*: These are adverbials that signal that the writer wishes to sum up or draw a conclusion from the aforementioned text. They are often used after the writer has presented a variety of different points of view or details and have the function of signalling to the reader how this information should be interpreted. Some adverbials in this category are prepositional phrases. Typical examples are 'in conclusion', 'thus', 'overall', 'to conclude', 'to summarize' and 'in sum'.

Examples

- '*In sum*, three-year-olds demonstrated varying degrees of accuracy for specific aspects of syntax and morphology in separate studies.'

- '*To summarize*, in each word-learning session the child completed four comprehension and four production trials.'
- '*Overall*, this study showed that English-speaking students learning Spanish outperformed English-only learning peers on cognates that were presented in English.'

3 *Result*: Adverbials expressing result signal that the following information should be interpreted as the outcome or consequence of the preceding information. Typical examples include 'consequently', 'accordingly', 'as a result', 'hence', 'in consequence', 'thus' and 'therefore'. The examples below illustrate the typically variable position of the adverbials 'accordingly', 'therefore', 'thus' and 'hence' within a sentence.

Examples

- '*Accordingly*, the children's performances were relatively stable across the paper and computer test versions.'
- 'For instance, omissions of the infinitive marker "to" were demonstrated by only seven children and *hence* were classified as an uncommon error.'
- '*Hence*, there is a need to design narrative tasks that are both interesting to adolescents and sensitive to age-related changes in language use that occur during this developmental period.'
- '*Therefore*, stories from children raised in different cultures may differ and may require assessment that is culturally sensitive.'
- 'They also did not read the required chapters assigned for class and the discussion, *therefore*, remained minimal.'
- 'These results *thus* suggest a promising strategy for achieving behavioural improvement in children with social adjustment problems.'
- '*Thus*, when assessing children to determine if they do or do not stutter, this second type of sample should be considered in addition to the standard conversational sample.'

4 *Contrast*: This category of adverbials signals differences, contrasts or alternatives. Typical examples include 'instead', 'on the contrary', 'contrary to', 'in contrast', 'by comparison', 'on the other hand' and 'conversely'.

Examples

- '*Contrary to* the conventional belief that self-ratings are unreliable, the present study showed that self-rated proficiency measures were sensitive predictors of bilingual listeners' speech-recognition abilities.'
- '*Conversely*, teachers who have more confidence in their ability to affect change may be more willing to retain the difficult-to-teach student in general education.'

5 *Concession*: When writers make concessions, they express reservations about certain information in the text. Examples include 'nevertheless', 'nonetheless', 'however', 'in spite of this', 'despite this' and 'besides'.

Examples

- '*Nevertheless*, this individual was apparently brought up by English-speaking parents or caretakers at home.'
- '*Nonetheless*, their sample included preschoolers only and the mental and linguistic verbs occurred very rarely.'
- '*Despite this*, some care should be taken when interpreting the results.'
- '*Besides*, data were also analysed based on frequencies as well as percentage.'

According to Biber et al. (1999, p. 886), linking adverbials are more commonly used in academic writing and conversation than in literature and newspaper texts, and a greater variety is used in academic writing than in other text types. Relatively frequent linking adverbials in academic writing include 'thus', 'then', 'therefore', 'hence', 'however', 'nevertheless' and 'on the other hand'. While the most common position for linking adverbials, according to Biber et al. (1999, p. 890), is the initial position, examples such as 'thus' and 'therefore' also tend to occur in medial position, immediately following the subject or an auxiliary verb.

Charles (2011) built on findings in Biber et al. (1999) by examining the phraseology and functions of a selected group of adverbial linking words of result, 'thus', 'therefore', 'then', 'hence', 'so' and 'consequently', in a corpus of academic writing. While these linking words appeared more commonly *inter-sententially* – that is, to link ideas expressed across sentence boundaries – others were also used *intra-sententially* to show the relationship between information in different clauses or phrases within a sentence. For instance, 'thus' is frequently used in an intra-sentential position after the main clause followed by a gerund verb, which frequently expresses a result or outcome of an event or process described in the preceding clause.

Example

- 'All index entries are stored as Latin and Cyrillic texts, *thus* enabling the use of both scripts in online searches.'

The author noted that adverbials such as 'thus', 'therefore' and 'hence' may be particularly salient in a text when occurring in sentence initial position followed by a comma. If overused, from the reader's perspective, such adverbials may be perceived as interrupting the flow of the text and contributing a jerky effect (Charles, 2011, p. 55). When used intra-sententially, as in the examples below, the adverbial is less salient.

Examples

- 'It is *therefore* important to recognize the limitations of generalizing the findings to all colleges in the state.'
- 'Most of the great biographies are written about people who are dead, and *thus* the biographies are unauthorized.'

Charles (2011, p. 59) favoured drawing novice writers' awareness to how specific adverbials are used in writing. As students are often presented with lists of adverbial linking words, grouped semantically, students may believe they can be used interchangeably. By highlighting how they are used in discourse, both in terms of their position and their function in a sentence, novice writers may become more aware of inappropriate usage of these adverbial linking words.

For many novice writers, these adverbials are an organizational device that assists them in structuring their work by creating overt linkages between ideas and information. While more experienced writers may also rely heavily on these devices in early writing drafts, repetitive or superfluous instances of such discourse devices are likely to be edited out of subsequent drafts. It is quite usual to become less reliant on surface-level linking words to signal relationships as one's ideas crystallize and become more precise.

Results from Bolton, Nelson and Hung's (2002) study of native English-speaker (British) and non-native English-speaker (Hong Kong) writing indicate that overuse of such linkages is a noticeable feature of students' writing, regardless of whether they are native or non-native English speakers. As their repertoire of connectors is limited, students tend to overuse what they have at their disposal, when compared to the frequency of use of such items in a corpus of published academic writing. While Hong Kong students appear to rely heavily on connectors such as 'so', 'and', 'also', 'thus' and 'but', the British students' texts typically overused 'so', 'therefore', 'thus' and 'furthermore' (Bolton, Nelson & Hung, 2002, p. 180). Overusage of particular linking words can also be due to L1 influence. For instance, in Mohamed-Sayidina's (2010) view, the pronounced preference for additive transitions ('and', 'also', 'in addition', 'furthermore' etc.) among advanced-level users of English with Arabic as their L1 may be explained by the dominance of such linking words in written Arabic.

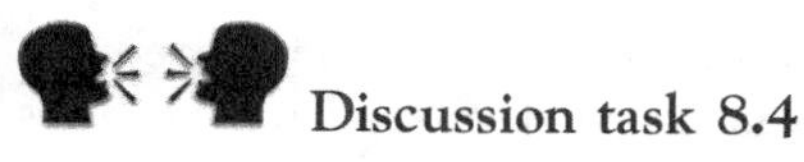

Discussion task 8.4

Functions of linking words

Discuss the following questions in pairs or small groups:

1 Underline the linking words in the Introduction and Conclusion sections in the articles by Chik (2014) and Chen (2006) in Appendices 1 and 2. Discuss

the function of each one (refer to functions presented in Insights from the literature 8.3).

2. Both authors use the linking words of the type 'first', 'second', 'third' and 'finally' in the Conclusion but not in the Introduction. What function do these words serve in each text? Why are they used in this section but not in the Introduction?
3. Are you aware of overusing certain linking words in your writing? Identify alternatives for the overused examples you named.

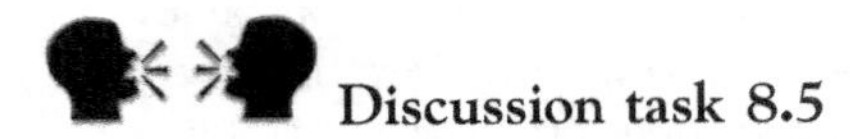

Discussion task 8.5

Textual cohesion and linking words

In the following examples (a–d), Chen (2006) has used multiple linking words (underlined) in a paragraph to signal the relationship between the different ideas expressed.

1. Discuss the function of each linking word in relation to the other linking words in the paragraph.
2. For each paragraph, consider alternative linking words that could be used (multiple answers may be possible here). Changes to word order or punctuation may be needed. You may also omit a linking word.

(a) 'However, there seem to be no fixed, standard e-mail writing rules for users to observe, especially since e-mail is a hybrid discourse inheriting features of both written and spoken language. On the one hand, e-mail users may feel liberated from the restriction of traditional letter writing rules; on the other hand, they may struggle to produce an appropriate e-mail to meet the recipient's standards.' (p. 35)

(b) 'First, Ling's language use in e-mail was identified as distinctive because her e-mails normally contained a wide variety of discourse strategies. Second, she used e-mail to communicate in English more frequently and more diversely compared to the other Taiwanese graduate students. Moreover, she had a year of e-mail exchange experience with international pen-pals when she was a college student in Taiwan. Ling's e-mail practice, thus, constituted an information-rich case for the present study.' (p. 38)

(c) 'However, Ling also pointed out that she adopted this style in her e-mails only when writing to the professors who had used this style in their emails to her. If the professors had not used this style, she did not. Her use of e-mail style, therefore, was not simply a personal choice but mainly depended on the way those authority figures wrote e-mails to her.' (p. 41)

(d) 'Thus, she established her own rules in writing these status-unequal e-mails by either guessing what might be appropriate or observing how native speakers interacted in other types of communication practice. Such implicit learning without guidance made the acquisition of the hidden rules not only slow but also limited. In addition, this acquisition process was rather complicated as Ling's language use was intertwined with the change of her identity construction and value choices.' (p. 50)

The pronoun 'I'

Students are often unsure whether it is appropriate to use the first-person pronoun 'I'. In academic writing, 'I' is less common than in the descriptive or expository-type essays typical of school or early university years. Whether it should be used or not depends not only on the discipline and the text type, but also on the location in the text and your purpose as the writer. While preparing the Literature Review, you may notice the use of 'I' in applied linguistics and literature. Note how the author uses it and where. Instances in a research article where 'I' typically appears include when the author wishes to show how his/her approach to the topic is different from previously published research (typically when introducing the research question(s) or when interpreting findings) or where the writer describes the procedure (in the Methods section). The passive voice is very common in descriptions of research procedure, but the occasional use of 'I' helps the writer avoid repeating the same structure too often. The use of 'I' in the Methods section also helps clarify who undertook the data collection. This is important to know, as the type of responses given in questionnaires and interviews may be influenced by who is asking the questions or distributing the forms. Some students use the term 'the researcher' in place of 'I' to make it clear that they undertook these procedures. This can be seen in Examples 7.5 and 7.6 by Zeina and Zareen (p. 96).

Students often make the mistake of presenting their ideas or arguments with 'I think'. The use of 'I' and a cognitive verb such as 'think', 'believe' or 'consider' is usually not appropriate. When presenting an idea or an argument, it is usually advisable to avoid personalizing it through explicit self-references; alternative, more objective-sounding formulations are preferable. As you read journal articles and academic books, pay attention to how the writer describes the procedures used in the Methods section and how an argument is presented. In your own work, it is probably better to minimize the use of 'I'. Some institutions may even penalize students for using 'I' in their research project.

Exercise 8.11

The use of 'I'

Read the Methods section from Zareen's project. The section has been rewritten to include seven examples of 'I'. Redraft the section using the passive voice and other structures so that 'I' is used only once.

When you finish, compare your text with the original version in Example 7.6 (p. 96).

Zareen's Methods section

Methods

I conducted this study at the University's Department of Foreign Languages. Participants in this study were students majoring in either a Bachelor's of English education or English translation. I designed a questionnaire containing 14 multiple choice items with the assistance of the supervisor of this project. I subsequently translated it into Arabic and it was then checked by a bilingual faculty member for accuracy. I obtained permission from the administrators of the hostels where I would collect the data to visit the hostels twice to talk to groups of students for the purpose of this research. I distributed the questionnaires to 50 students (English majors) in the girls' and boys' hostels. The researcher had previously informed students in the hostel of the study in writing by using the hostel notice board, and orally by making an announcement to students in the dining hall during the evening meal. The researcher returned later that same week during the evening to distribute questionnaires to students who volunteered to participate. The same procedure was followed by a male research assistant in the boys' hostel. The second step consisted of analyzing the results from the 100 questionnaires; I describe this analysis in the next section.

Insights from the literature 8.4

The problematic first-person pronoun

Students are often not provided with instruction on the use of first-person pronouns in their academic writing. This may be because their lecturers are themselves not clear on how appropriate personal pronoun use may be, a predicament that is not helped by the omission of guidelines relating to the use of personal pronouns in academic writing textbooks (Harwood, 2005a). In light of this, students may be told personal pronoun use is inappropriate in formal academic writing and be encouraged to avoid it. Before the use of computers to compile electronic corpora of written texts, it was understandably difficult to attain an overview of how language was used in particular disciplines (Harwood, 2005a). Since the use of specialized corpora to investigate writing practices, however, studies have revealed both the frequency with which personal pronouns are used in academic writing and the discipline-specific differences in their usage.

Despite of the amount of information currently available on the use of personal pronouns in written academic discourse, we still cannot speak of there being clear parameters surrounding the use of 'I' and 'we' in academic writing, but we do have greater clarity regarding the frequency of pronoun use in particular disciplines, and a better understanding of the functions that pronoun use serves.

Hyland (2002a) related pronoun use to the writer's negotiation of his/her identity within the written text, noting that disciplinary differences exist. An examination of 240 research articles from eight different disciplines revealed that writers in the humanities and social sciences tend to have a stronger projection of their individual identity, expressed through the use of first-person pronouns, compared to writers from disciplines in the hard sciences. Indeed, 75 per cent of all such pronoun use occurred in the soft sciences. Hyland (2002a) explained this frequency of usage in terms of the greater subjectivity in the research process and the lesser degree of precision in the creation of knowledge; projecting a strong, authoritative author stance through the use of personal pronouns can strengthen the presentation of a claim or its interpretation. Additionally, authors may use pronouns to signal explicitly that the interpretation of the results is their own. By comparison, in the hard sciences authors avoid foregrounding their personal contribution to the research process or personalizing the interpretation of results.

Despite evidence that authors of published research do tend to commit themselves to claims or arguments made during the work through pronoun use, students and novice writers may lack confidence in their authority and avoid using pronouns for these purposes. Hyland (2002b, p. 1104) noted that novice writers displayed a preference for alternative formulations that effectively remove themselves from claims, such as the passive, or attributing an agentive role to tables, data or sections of the work (e.g. 'The table displays . . .', 'This chapter introduces . . .').

Interviews with students revealed that these novice writers did not feel it appropriate to insert themselves into the text, either because they felt the resulting subjectivity was inappropriate or they did not consider themselves in a position to assume an authoritative role (Hyland, 2002b). Additionally, cultural factors may also contribute to this reticence in personalizing claims or claiming ownership of arguments. Hyland (2002a) pointed out that this type of individualistic stance may jar with more collectivist cultures that may value highly a collaborative stance and consensus building.

Personal pronouns can serve a range of functions in academic writing; that is, a variety of reasons may underlie the writer's motivation for using 'I' or 'we' at different points in the text. Harwood (2005b) identified a series of reasons for pronoun use in his corpus-based study of published research articles from both hard and soft disciplines. According to his analysis, self-promotion is a common reason for pronoun use and this typically occurs at the beginning and the end of a research article. At the beginning of a research article, authors may use 'I' or 'we' to make their stance and contribution explicit. This helps orient the reader to the novelty or the 'newness' of the work. The author may use pronouns at the end of the article to individualize claims or arguments again, thereby refocusing the reader's attention on the writer's achievements or contributions.

One form of self-promotion can be seen when the writer attempts to 'mark the difference' between his/her work and the approach taken by a different author (Harwood, 2005b, p. 1222). When highlighting the difference, the writer often begins by describing the approach taken by another study and then continues by using a pronoun and a conjunction such as '*however*' or '*nevertheless*' (e.g. 'I claim, however, that . . .', 'Nevertheless, we view . . .'). A second instance where personal pronouns are common is when recounting the study's procedures (Harwood, 2005b). Here, a writer may insert himself/herself into the text in order to underscore innovative approaches he/she has taken, to alert the reader to how the researcher dealt with complications that may have arisen, and, finally, to lend weight to the image of the author as a meticulous, attentive researcher (Harwood, 2005b). A further common function of pronouns, according to Hyland (2002b), is to acknowledge one's debt to those who lent some form of assistance to the research. Such acknowledgements commonly appear at the end of the paper or in a footnote.

Exercise 8.12

First-person pronouns

According to Hyland (2002a, 2002b) and Harwood (2005b), the use of the first-person pronoun in academic writing may serve a number of purposes. Some of these are listed here:

1 help organize the text (to provide signposting for the reader);
2 explain experimental procedure;
3 personalize claims;
4 show the writer's familiarity with the field through self-citation;
5 underscore the importance of the writer's work through self-promotion
6 introduce the research question(s);
7 make public acknowledgements;
8 clarify the use of terminology.

Task

Look at the following examples of pronouns used in published work. For each example, identify the purposes for the pronoun use. For instance, Example 1 corresponds to 'help organize the text' from the list above. All examples are concordance lines extracted from the *Corpus of Contemporary American English* (Davies, 2008); pronouns are shown in italic.

1. 'In closing, *we* would like to propose a few novel and intriguing application areas that in our opinion deserve further investigation by the research community.'
2. '*We* believe that this paper in no way exhausts the possible investigations that can be performed with this data.'
3. 'While working on this article, *I* was supported by a Harkness Fellowship from the Commonwealth Fund.'
4. 'All of the interviews were recorded and transcribed. *I* supplemented the information gained from them with more than 250 randomly generated public interviews with ordinary citizens.'
5. '*I* thank the three anonymous reviewers from the *American Journal of Public Health*.'
6. '*I* then offer some suggestions for how to address this problem.'
7. '*I* extensively argue elsewhere – so *I* will pay little attention to the issue here – that *we* can corroborate Indian and Irish narrator recall through comparison with other autobiographical accounts and with evidence contemporaneous to the events recalled.'
8. 'Even though this category is a product of modern Western scholarship, *I* would argue that it is reasonable to discuss Chinese cultural phenomena in nonindigenous terms if the criteria and motivations are made explicit.'
9. 'To answer this question, *I* will trace the source of Chinese nationalism, examine the formation of such sentiments, and analyze the causes for anti-Western nationalism in China from 1989 to 1999.'
10. 'Before proceeding, *I* shall trace the theory back to its source, consider its early propagation, and examine the various theorists of intertextuality.'
11. 'In this paper *I* elucidate Montaigne's conception of the self to show how it underlies his argument for toleration.'
12. '*I* use the term "local" as a general reference to residents of metropolitan Las Vegas.'
13. 'Before considering the test results, *I* describe the impact of incentives on five groups.'
14. '*I* propose to view the history of the New Philology as consisting of three phases.'
15. 'In the current study, *we* propose that collegial connections foster a sense of belongingness needed to promote long-term commitment to teaching.'
16. 'The Renaissance was a turning point. *I* use the term in its widest sense to describe the period from 1300 to 1600.'
17. 'In this article *I* use the term "conscientization" to refer more broadly to the process by which all sectors of society, particularly privileged ones, become newly aware of the presence of injustice.'
18. '*We* predict that these errors, which are already infrequent, would be even less common in the writing of braillists who do not so frequently use computer braille.'

19 'Therefore, *we* question the effectiveness and efficiency of using large print as a primary reading medium with this population.'
20 'In this article, *I* consider three general issues raised by Haier and Jung (2008). First, *I* discuss the use of drugs for intellectual enhancement. Second, *I* reflect on prediction of performance based on biological measures. Third, *I* query whether biology can tell us what intelligence and creativity are. *I* conclude that biological assessments raise as many questions as they answer.'

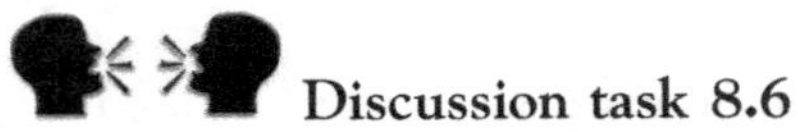

Discussion task 8.6

The first-person pronoun and writing conventions

Discuss the following questions with your partner or in a small group:

1 Academic writing traditions are culture-specific. How texts are composed in the English-language scholarly tradition may be quite different from what is considered appropriate for academic texts in other languages. Consider what you have learned about the use of the first-person pronoun in academic writing in English; how does it compare to the use of the first-person pronoun in academic texts in your L1? What similarities do you find? What differences?
2 Chen (2006) uses two personal pronouns ('I' and 'we') in her Conclusion (see Appendix 2). What functions do these pronouns serve in each example?

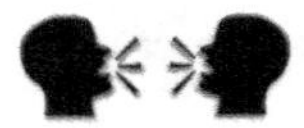

Discussion task 8.7

The use of 'I'

Consider the phrases below. Imagine you wrote these phrases in your work. You are now revising the chapter. Which phrases will you keep? Which will you change? For each phrase, choose one of the following four options. Discuss your answers with your partner.

Options

1 This is an appropriate formulation for a formal academic text and I will keep this phrase.
2 I've seen other writers use this, but I am not sure if this is considered 'good style'.
3 I write like this sometimes, but I don't think it is appropriate.
4 This is wrong. I have to change it.

Phrases

a 'I collected data over a four-week period.'
b 'Data were collected over a four-week period.'

a 'It is argued in this study that . . .'
b 'This study argues that . . .'
c 'I argue in this study that . . .'

a 'It is shown in Table 2 that . . .'
b 'Table 2 shows . . .'
c 'I demonstrate in Table 2 that . . .'

a 'I think we can interpret these findings in different ways.'
b 'These findings can be interpreted in different ways.'

a 'In my opinion, we should consider an alternative interpretation.'
b 'This study proposes an alternative interpretation.'
c 'An alternative interpretation is possible, however.'

a 'I claim that . . .'
b 'This study claims that . . .'
c 'It is claimed in this study that . . .'

a 'I initially planned to collect data from . . .'
b 'The initial plan entailed collecting data from . . .'
c 'Data were initially planned to be collected from . . .'

a 'I undertook the second stage of my data collection in May.'
b 'The second stage of the data collection was undertaken in May.'

a 'I visited the participants in their offices to interview them.'
b 'I interviewed participants in their offices.'
c 'Participants were interviewed in their offices.'
d 'The interviews were conducted in the participants' offices.'

Paragraph structure

Paragraphs are the building blocks of your project and provide a visual clue as to the organization of each chapter. In each paragraph, the reader should usually be able to identify a central or main topic; there may be a single main topic, or one topic may lead into a second topic within the same paragraph. Consider the length of your paragraphs; they should neither be too long nor too short (unless there is a good reason for this). By scanning each page of your work, you will quickly see where potential problems lie. Long paragraphs are often an indication of rambling or the clustering of too many different topics. In either case, slashing sections or weeding out topics to form stand-alone paragraphs would be advisable. A very short paragraph may occasionally be acceptable, particularly if the writer is providing information to the reader about the organization of the text. Normally, however, if your paragraph has only one or two sentences, this signals an underdeveloped or fragmented idea. While you needn't be concerned about this during your first attempts at drafting a chapter or a section, you do need to be attentive to paragraph structure when redrafting and revising your work.

Paragraphs normally contain a topic sentence; this is known as the controlling idea of the paragraph. When skim reading, one frequently reads just the first sentence of each paragraph, in anticipation that this conveys the main idea expressed in this paragraph. The reader would normally expect the remaining information in the paragraph to relate in some way to this topic sentence. Although the topic sentence most frequently appears towards the beginning of the paragraph and is very often the opening sentence, this doesn't have to be the case as it is possible for the topic sentence to appear at the end of the paragraph, preceded by a discussion of related points. Nevertheless, this is less usual and, in most cases, it is harder to draft a paragraph with the topic sentence in final position.

While drafting and redrafting, you are likely to find different ways to develop your paragraphs. After the topic sentence, a common move writers make is to *restate* or *reformulate* their main idea (or topic sentence); while doing so, the writer may provide *examples* or a brief *explanation* or *definition* of a term or word used. In restating the main idea, the writer may *expand* it to express a more general concept or the writer may *narrow* or *refine* the idea, perhaps by stating what it is not, or by limiting it in terms of location or time. The writer will often need to buttress the idea or claim expressed in the topic sentence with *supporting information*; this may be in the form of one or two sentences illustrating the idea or claim, or it may consist of brief examples (phrases) included in the writer's expansion or narrowing of the idea. This supporting information may be a *summary* of an idea or argument originating with another author and may possibly include a *quotation* (in both cases, the writer will cite the author). The writer may then *analyse* the veracity or the applicability of examples or ideas introduced as supporting information, and *discuss* their limitations or applicability to a different context; in doing so, writers are likely to display their degree of *agreement* or *disagreement* with the additional information and examples provided. In some cases, the writer may include a *concluding sentence* to the paragraph, thus wrapping up the brief discussion of this point.

Paragraphs often have a *general to specific* structure; that is, the opening one or two sentences are likely to be more general than the information that follows. This is logical; one would expect the writer to first introduce the topic or claim in broad terms before discussing finer aspects of it. While providing examples or definitions, reformulating, expanding or narrowing an idea, or providing supporting information, the writer is likely to cite the work of other authors. It would be advisable to check your paragraphs to ensure you support your claims with appropriate author citations.

Be aware, however, that not all paragraphs contain all the moves mentioned here, and they may not even have a clearly identifiable topic sentence. Many students do have problems developing a paragraph, however, especially in a second language, and structuring the paragraph around a topic sentence can be very helpful. When revising your work, it might be useful to try identifying 'stronger' and 'weaker' paragraphs in your writing. Your supervisor will probably also point out paragraphs that need more supporting information or paragraphs that lack focus, either because you discuss too many different things or because the information needs to be reorganized.

Exercise 8.13

Paragraph structure

Analyse the development of the paragraph below from Chen's (2006, p. 36) Literature Review. Identify the function of each of the four sentences. (The sentences have been numbered for convenience's sake.) The following terms will be helpful (one sentence may have more than one function):

a topic sentence;
b explanation;
c narrowing;
d examples;
e discussion;
f reference to the literature;
g concluding sentence;
h restatement/reformulation;
i expansion;
j supporting information;
k analysis;
l summary;
m (dis)agreement.

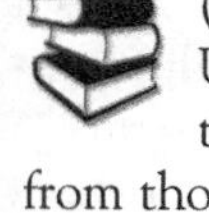

(1) In their study of Chinese-speaking students' e-mail interaction with U.S. professors, both Chang and Hsu (1998) and Chen (2001) found that the request strategies that Chinese students used in e-mails differed from those of U.S. students. (2) U.S. students tended to structure their request e-mails in a direct sequence placing the request act at the beginning of the message, but their linguistic forms of the request act were more indirect involving more lexico-syntactic mitigating forms. (3) In contrast, Chinese students tended to structure their request e-mails in an indirect sequence using many pre-request supportive moves and placing the request act at the end, while their linguistic forms of the request act were more direct with fewer lexico-syntactic modifications. (4) These findings are consistent with studies on Chinese speakers' oral and written requests (Kirkpatrick, 1991, 1993; Nash, 1983; Zhang, 1995a, 1995b), which indicates that Chinese-speaking students probably transfer the request strategies that they normally use in Chinese to the English request e-mails written to professors.

You can try the same exercise using the paragraph in Exercise 8.9.

Definitions

You will probably need to define certain terms that you mention early in your Introduction or Literature Review chapters. Many definitions tend to be written in a fairly formulaic way so, assuming you understand the concept, formulating a definition at an appropriate point could give you a point of entry into your Introduction. Typically, you might cite an author or even quote a sentence or phrase from a definition formulated by an author you have read. This is what Chik does in Examples A and B below (Example 8.1). In Example B, this strategy is particularly effective because it allows Chik to highlight two different terms ('paratexts' and 'attendant discourse') that are used in the literature to refer to texts that accompany games ('game-related texts'). In Example C, Lee wishes to distinguish two related terms and she uses author citations to support her differentiation. Author citations are not essential in definitions, however; Lee has not included them in Example D, probably because the concept is broadly understood in the field and is not traceable back to a particular scholar or school of thought. In Example E, Chen has taken the initiative of coining her own term ('e-mail literacy'), preceded by a definition ('pragmatic competence and critical language awareness'). Note the use of the first-person pronoun ('which I would like to term') to underscore that this is Chen's original contribution.

A definition may be short and explain only one aspect of the term (such as Example D), or it may describe multiple features, encompassing one or more sentences. Example F is a two-step definition comprising both the meaning and the purpose of the concept 'case study'. In Example G, the extended definition of 'trajectory' allows the writer to enumerate elements included in the term. This helps to minimize misunderstandings, as Chik uses the term differently from its conventional meaning. Example H is a three-step extended definition; Chen provides a brief explanation of each term, gives examples and then finishes by signalling possible social implications of using the group of statements covered by each term.

Extended definitions are neither necessary nor appropriate for all phenomena or concepts you want to define. Frequently, a simple definition such as Example D will suffice; alternatively, you may want to show conflicting perspectives by contrasting definitions used by different authors (not all authors agree on the same definition!).

You may find it difficult to define a concept in your own words. While you read, make a note of definitions provided by other authors; you could use these (or part of them) in your own work (provided you cite the author). Also, consult a specialized dictionary, such as the *Longman Dictionary of Language Teaching and Learning*, or a dictionary of translation or linguistic terms. You will likely find such dictionaries on the reference shelves of the library. Remember to cite the author(s) if you use one of these definitions in your work.

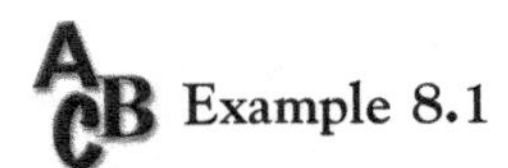

Example 8.1

Definitions

Example A

The authors defined a learning community as 'consist[ing] of individuals who come together to accomplish a specific end or goal' (p. 70). [Chik, 2014, p. 87]

Example B

Game-related texts, such as walkthroughs, video tutorials, fan fiction and fan art, have been described as 'paratexts' (Apperley & Walsh, 2012; Consalvo, 2007), or 'attendant discourse' (Sykes & Reinhardt, 2013). [Chik, 2014, p. 87]

Example C

Personal blogs are collections of online journals that foster self-expression and self-reflection (e.g., Lee, 2010; Yang, 2009), whereas collective blogs involving an entire class or small groups promote interactive and collaborative learning (Lee, 2009b). [Lee, 2011, p. 87]

Example D

For the purpose of the study, self-directed learning refers to learners taking responsibility for planning, monitoring and evaluating their own learning. [Lee, 2011, p. 103]

Example E

The development of pragmatic competence and critical language awareness in using the e-mail medium, which I would like to term as 'e-mail literacy', is a pressing issue in the digital era. [Chen, 2006, p. 36]

Example F

Yin (2009) defines a case study as 'an empirical inquiry that investigates a contemporary phenomenon in depth and within its real-life context' (p. 18) and observes that the case study method helps researchers to 'retain the holistic and meaningful characteristics of real-life events' (p. 4). [Chik, 2014, p. 88]

Example G

Trajectory concerns the management of out-of-school gaming practices over time, which is not only restricted to the amount of time or energy or money one spends on digital gaming. Trajectory is also about managing one's practice from one game to another. While the concept of trajectory is not part of Benson's framework, it is added here to account for noticeable patterns in the data, especially when considering practices of autonomy within community. [Chik, 2014, p. 94]

Example H

Two types of request strategies at the lexico-syntactic level were identified in Ling's request e-mails: Want Statements and Query Preparatory (terms in Blum-Kulka, House, & Kasper, 1989). Want Statements indicate the speaker's desire that the hearer carry out the act (e.g., I want/need/hope you . . .); Query Preparatory contains reference to preparatory conditions for the feasibility of the request, such as ability, willingness, and possibility (e.g., Can/Could/Would you . . .). The latter is generally considered more indirect, and thus more polite, than the former. [Chen, 2006, p. 43]

Exercise 8.14

The language of definitions

The writer can formulate a definition in different ways. Some of these options are listed here. For instance, the writer may begin a definition by providing a more general description of the phenomenon. Read the eight definitions in Example 8.1 (A–H) and, for each one, decide which option(s) the writer has used. The examples may contain more than one of the approaches described below; alternatively, some of the approaches listed may not appear in the definitions.

1 gives a general description of the phenomenon;
2 gives a more general term for the phenomenon;
3 describes what the phenomenon does or what we use it for;
4 gives examples of what the phenomenon is;
5 gives examples of what the phenomenon is not (usually the antonym);
6 explains why the phenomenon occurs;
7 identifies or categorizes sub-types of the phenomenon;
8 gives a reason for the name;
9 differentiates this phenomenon from another related phenomenon.

Exercise 8.15

Writing definitions

1 Read one of the three Introductions in Appendix 1. Find a term that you think could be defined for the reader. Formulate a definition for this term. The phrases you identified in the previous exercises and the phrases in Tip 8.5 will help you.
2 Choose two terms from your field of studies (i.e. applied linguistics, language teaching, translation or literature). Write an extended definition for each term, using the examples above and the phrases below to help you. In place of the term, leave a blank space, so the reader does not know what you are defining. See if your neighbour can guess the term that you have defined.

Tip 8.5

Useful phrases for definitions

The following phrases are part of the *Academic Phrasebank* (Morley, n.d.).

'The term X is generally understood to mean . . .'

'The term X has been applied to situations where students . . .'

'In broad terms, X can be defined as . . .'
'In the literature, the term X tends to refer to . . .'
'X can be defined as . . .'
'X can be loosely described as a . . .'

Giving examples

Examples are frequently used in academic writing to clarify a concept and are also often used in definitions and to support an idea or argument. Examples can provide a concrete illustration of an abstract idea, or they may point to the variety of forms a concrete phenomenon can have. As such, they support your line of reasoning or argumentation, providing the example helps the reader correctly interpret the intended meaning. By the same token, not providing an example puts the onus on the reader to imagine an appropriate example or application of the phenomenon. How often you provide examples in your work depends on a number of factors such as the topic or the type of research being conducted. Research that relies on the analysis of data from texts, such as Lee's or Chik's work, is likely to contain more examples than a more theoretical study. The inclusion of examples also depends on the section of text you are writing, as you are probably less likely to insert examples in the Methods chapter than in the Introduction and Literature Review. As you prepare your Literature Review, take note of how authors introduce examples in their work; sometimes explicit language is used, but other times no explicit signalling is given.

Exercise 8.16

Identifying examples

Read the following excerpts from articles written by Lee (2011) and Chik (2014) and underline the language used to give an example. There may be more than one instance in each excerpt.

1 'In addition to cognitive and social dimensions of language learning, affective factors, such as attitudes toward learning tasks, affect how learners engage in online learning.' (Lee, 2011, p. 89)
2 'The advent of Web 2.0 technologies (wikis, blogs, podcastings) brings new dimensions to online learning. Blogs, for example, are used in various ways depending on their pedagogical purposes.' (Lee, 2011, p. 87)
3 'Thus, teachers need to find ways, such as using guided questions, to stimulate students' high order thinking to build upon further discussions.' (Lee, 2011, p. 90)

4 'To facilitate the interviewing process, the instructor provided students with guidelines and they spent one class practicing interview techniques, such as asking structural and contrast questions.' (Lee, 2011, p. 93)
5 'For weekly assignments, students read topic-specific readings, participated in cultural activities (e.g., film, play, excursions) and/or conducted interviews with L1s. For example, one of the topics addressed immigrants in Spain.' (Lee, 2011, p. 93)
6 'The following comments drawn from the reflective reports illustrate their optimistic experiences.' (Lee, 2011, p. 97)
7 'The above student built on the message that her partner composed to construct new meanings by using information from other sources, such as *Wikipedia* and personal communication.' (Lee, 2011, p. 101)
8 'The following is an example of how the student responded to her L1 partner.' (Lee, 2011, p. 101)
9 'Over the years, many e-Tandem projects have been created in European countries including Germany and Spain.' (Lee, 2011, p. 89)
10 'However, digital gaming is not sanctioned in schools in East Asia, where it is frequently viewed as addictive and non-educational (see, for example, Gentile, Choo, Liau, Sim, Li, Fung, & Khoo, 2011).' (Chik, 2014, p. 86)
11 'Thorne's study illustrates natural and autonomous learning moments of native speakers of two different languages teaching each other in the multilingual *WoW* gameworld.' (Chik, 2014, p. 86)
12 'The findings suggest that gamers generally do not prefer educational games, but many were aware of the pedagogical potentials of in-game texts such as game dialogues and visual cues.' (Chik, 2014, p. 92)
13 'When a discussant asked about using role-playing games (RPGs) for English learning (2008-04-27, 11:01, Chinese forum), nineteen RPG games were listed half an hour later with evaluations of their language learning potentials (e.g. "*Mafia: The City of Lost Heaven*: you can read a lot of gangster language, slang, it is quite authentic").' (Chik, 2014, p. 92)
14 'A lot of gamers were proud of their specialist vocabulary knowledge, for example, "street slang learned from GTA" or "pilot's vocabulary learned from *Flight Simulator*".' (Chik, 2014, p. 94)

Exercise 8.17

The language of examples

1 Using the examples in Exercise 8.16, create your own list of functional phrases (similar to the one provided in Tip 8.5) used to signal examples in academic writing. Compare your list with your neighbour's.
2 Now go to the *Academic Phrasebank* website (www.phrasebank.manchester.ac.uk). Find the section on giving examples. Are there any phrases that are quite different from the ones on your list? Write down a few that could be useful for your own work.

Hedging your claims

Think of the common meaning of 'hedge'. You are probably thinking of a noun, and you may have in mind the shape and colour of the living fence between you and your neighbour. In academic writing, we use 'hedge' as a verb in a metaphorical sense. If you hedge your claims, you demonstrate to the reader the degree to which you stand behind your claim; that is, hedges (used here as a noun) allow you to caution the reader regarding the degree to which the statement or claim is accurate some or all of the time, or the extent to which it may be generalized to apply to other contexts. You can visualize how this metaphorical use relates to the concrete meaning of 'hedge'; hedges signal limits, both in your garden and in academic writing. If you restrict yourself to talking about certainties, things you can present as facts, you will run out of things to say quite quickly. Using hedges allows you to talk about a wider range of issues as you can vary the degree to which you present them as significant, likely or applicable to other contexts. By hedging a claim or an evaluation, you avoid alienating your reader by presenting a claim as conclusive, and thus allow greater space for agreement.

Just like a verdant hedge, hedges in academic writing come in a variety of forms. The most typical approach to hedging a claim involves using verbs and adverbs that leave room for a divergent explanation or alternative viewpoints. Look at the following example (adapted from Lee, 2011, p. 102). Which modal verb do you think the author used in her work? (See the note at the end of this chapter for the answer.)

> Further studies *might/must/should* consider the investigation of learners' perceptions of autonomous online learning using other social networking tools.[2]

If you use verbs such as 'demonstrate', 'show', 'prove', 'cause' or 'result in', you present your idea or your results as though they were facts. Such claims are usually difficult to defend, as a clear cause and effect relationship is actually very difficult to establish. You could easily be accused of being over-confident or of ignoring counterevidence. Alternatively, if you present your claim with a verb such as 'seem', 'appear', 'signal', 'tend', 'indicate', 'contribute to' or 'suggest', you acknowledge that alternative factors might also play a role, or that the data in your study have limitations. Frequently, such verbs are combined with a modal verb to further soften the claim (e.g. 'might', 'may', 'could'). In addition to verbs, adverbs are a convenient way to tone down the force of your claim (e.g. 'possibly', 'probably', 'conceivably', 'likely'). You can also use phrases to limit the claim to your particular data set context (e.g. 'according to the results from this study', 'within this cultural context').

Although it is quite normal to use more than one hedging device in a sentence or when expressing an idea across several sentences, it is possible to 'over-hedge'. The secret is to achieve the right balance between being assertive in your claim (i.e. expressing sufficient confidence in what you are saying) and being prudently cautious (i.e. not overstating or exaggerating your claim).

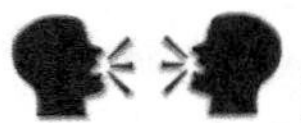

Discussion task 8.8

The effect of hedges

In pairs or small groups, answer the following questions:

1. Read the Conclusion of Chik's article in Appendix 2. Underline all the hedging expressions the author uses. In each case, discuss why the author decides to hedge her statement.
2. Compare the use of hedges in English (for example, in the Conclusion you have just read) with the use of hedges in academic writing in your L1. Do you use the same sort of hedging devices? Would you use more or fewer hedges when writing an academic text in your L1?

Exercise 8.18

Cautious language

1. Go to the *Academic Phrasebank* website (www.phrasebank.manchester.ac.uk). Find the section on using 'cautious' language. Judging from the different groups of phrases you see, in which sections of an article are writers most likely to use cautious language?
2. Write down a few phrases from this page that could be useful for your own work.

Insights from the literature 8.5

Exercising caution

One feature that characterizes academic writing is the tendency to moderate claims by signalling the writer's degree of commitment to the validity of claims made in relation to the writer's own work or another writer's work. Hedging entails the use of a variety of linguistic devices that may be employed to modify claims, and they thus respond to the reader's expectation that the writer will explicitly signal the degree of confidence the writer has in the information given (Hyland, 2000). By conveying the right degree of 'modesty and assertiveness' (Hyland, 2000, p. 179), writers can hope to convince the reader of their standpoint. Hedges enable a writer to express strong belief in the importance or veracity in a claim; known as *boosters*, these include adverbs such as 'obviously', 'undoubtedly', 'clearly' and 'naturally', but they also include adjectives such as 'important', 'significant' and 'convincing' and verbs such as 'will', 'cause', 'demonstrate', 'show' and 'confirm'. Hedges are more commonly described as a means to soften or mitigate the writer's stance or to introduce an element of doubt.

Such hedges are known as *down-toners*. Typical examples of these include adverbs such as 'possibly', 'perhaps', 'probably' and 'conceivably', adjectives such as 'likely', 'apparent' and 'potential' or verbs such as 'may', 'would', 'could' and 'might' (modal verbs) or 'seem', 'appear' and 'indicate'. In addition, particular phrases have a hedging function such as 'to a certain extent' or 'to a degree', in contexts such as the following:

> Students' positive response to the use of a bilingual glossary *may*, *to a certain extent*, be attributed to their being accustomed to this approach from their school days.

As illustrated in the example above, hedges may appear in clusters; that is, writers don't usually employ just one hedge when expressing an idea, but may include a number of different hedging words, especially when the idea expressed extends across the length of a paragraph.

By hedging, writers protect themselves from criticism and disagreement by allowing for the possibility of alternative interpretations. By stating something in factual terms, it becomes easy to dispute it. By claiming that one's interpretation is simply one possibility, albeit a strong one, the writer concedes to readers a degree of liberty in how they interpret information and the writer becomes thus less vulnerable to counterarguments (Hyland, 1998).

According to research by Hyland (1998), hedging is not used equally across the different academic disciplines. Broadly speaking, in the humanities and social sciences hedging appears much more frequently (up to twice as frequently in some cases) than in the hard sciences and engineering, with biology positioned in the middle. Hyland (1998) claims this is due to the greater tendency the hard sciences to present information in a factual or objective light and avoid elements that signal personal involvement in the text. Down-toners, or mitigating devices, were more common than boosters across all disciplines included in his study.

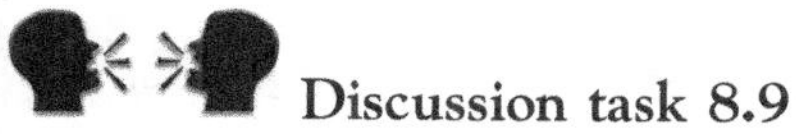

Discussion task 8.9

Playing with hedges

Before doing this task, you need to read Insights from the literature 8.5. Review the difference between down-toners and boosters:

- Down-toners limit the extent of your commitment to a claim and may introduce an element of doubt.
- Boosters express your confidence in the truth of a claim.

1 Below are excerpts from the Results and Discussion section from Lee's (2011, pp. 98, 100) article on the use of blogging with language learners. Underline all the words or expressions Lee uses to hedge statements or claims.
2 Working with a partner (Person A/Person B), make the following changes, then read your new text to your partner:

   Person A: increase the use of hedges to express lack of confidence (down-toners).
   Person B: delete all hedges expressing lack of confidence (down-toners) and replace them, where possible, with boosters.

Excerpt from Lee (2011, pp. 98, 100)

The results coincide with the findings found in studies conducted by Carney (2009) and by Lee (2010), who found that the comments did not show in-depth discussions of the content but rather surface level issues. The findings suggest that while students were capable of socializing with each other through discussing cross-cultural topics, they had limited ability to engage in high-order thinking. It is possible that the lack of continuity due to the post–comment structure of blogging may have affected the quality of critical reflection, as argued by Carney (2007). Garrison et al. (2001) suggest that teacher presence and scaffolding play a facilitative role in giving subject matter expertise and guidance to students during social interactions. To this view, teachers could use guided questions to cultivate reflective thinking to foster further discussions. [. . .]

Despite the fact that students gained cultural knowledge and awareness from online exchange, the findings confirm the previous concerns raised by the students about the lack of substantial comments to generate critical thinking. It is possible that students were not accustomed to reflecting. They may also have felt reluctant to express their candid thoughts in an open source blog platform because they did not wish to make others feel uncomfortable or to provoke an unfriendly learning situation.

Notes

1 University of Hong Kong. *What is plagiarism?* Retrieved 2 July 2010 from www.rss.hku.hk/plagiarism/page2s.htm.
2 Further studies *might* consider. . . .

9 Research logistics

Time management and revisions

Undertaking your research project necessarily means investing a lot of time and energy in this work over an extended period. Students who work steadily on their project usually need at least several months to produce their first draft; many need much more time because their work is interrupted by other activities. To finish your project within one semester, you will need to think carefully about how to organize your time to minimize interruptions, and combine your study obligations with family and/or work responsibilities. Creating a plan for your project and identifying the steps involved in doing your research can help with time management.

Study habits

Think about how you organize your day and your week. People often differ as to when they prefer to do certain activities. Which of the following apply to you?

- I prefer working in the evenings (I'm a night owl).
- I prefer getting up early and working (I'm an early bird).
- I like to do different things simultaneously (I like multitasking).
- I like to work on one thing and then do the next thing (I prefer to focus on one thing at a time).
- I find time to study whenever I can during the day.
- I save a special time of day (or one day of the week) for study.
- I only study when I feel like it.
- I am easily distracted by noise from the TV, people talking, my mobile or the Internet.
- When I sit down to study, I find it easy to concentrate.
- I can study anywhere.
- I need to study at my special study desk with all my books around me.
- Talking to someone about what I am studying helps me understand important ideas.
- I never talk to anyone about things I'm working on.
- I plan my time when I do my assignments and I do them step by step.

- I leave my assignments and homework until the last minute.
- Sometimes I don't even do my assignments or homework; I copy from my friend.

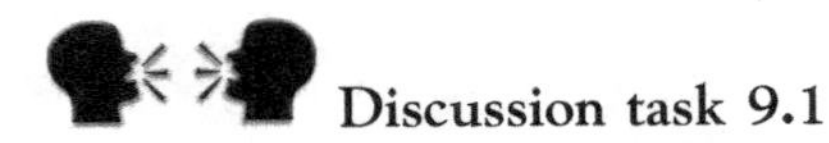

Discussion task 9.1

Discuss the following questions in pairs:

1. After reading the list above and identifying your study habits, consider which ones are likely to be 'useful' habits for doing your project.
2. Everybody has some 'bad' habits. Which are yours?
3. Changing bad habits is hard. Think of one thing you want to change about how you study while you work on your project.

Demands on your time

Before beginning your project, think of all the responsibilities you have that require your time and energy. These may be responsibilities you have at the university (attendance, course work, assignments, exams) or within your family. Consider how you will juggle your different responsibilities and dedicate the time necessary to complete your research. Will you have one or two days a week (at least) when you can solely work on your project? Will you have some mornings or afternoons each week when you can work on one aspect of your project? If your answer to these questions is not a clear 'Yes', reconsider whether this is really the best time to do your project. It can be quite a frustrating experience for both you and your supervisor if you are unable to dedicate the time you need to your work. Consider whether it might be advisable to delay working on your project until the holiday period or until the following semester.

Exercise 9.1

Planning your time

Zeina decided on her topic (translating polysemous words) and discussed the plan for her project in detail with her supervisor. Together they decided what she needed to do and when. They parted with the understanding that Zeina would send in her first chapter within the next month so her supervisor could see her work. Eight months later, Zeina visited her supervisor. Her supervisor couldn't remember who Zeina was. Zeina had to explain her project again and show her project proposal form. Zeina then told her supervisor that she had had a baby three months ago and had not been able to come. Instead of looking happy and congratulating Zeina, her supervisor looked slightly irritated.

1 Why was the supervisor irritated? How could this situation have been avoided?
2 Are you about to get married, have a baby, start a new job or move to a different city? If so, think about how this might affect your plans to work on your project.

Finding people to support you

Other members of your family and your close friends ought to know that you will be working on your project over the coming months, and be aware of the effort and energy it will require. You will need a quiet place at home where you can work undisturbed; you will need to leave your books and papers around your work desk; and you will need to be a bit 'unsocial' for a period of time. If your family and friends understand your needs, they will be better able to support you.

For some tasks related to your project, you could ask friends or family members to help you. Perhaps you have a friend who is doing a similar topic; this means that you can share the literature you find. If you need to distribute questionnaires in a classroom or the hostel, it is possible that a friend or family member could help you do this. If you delegate the task of distributing questionnaires to someone else, ensure you write down exactly what you want this person to tell the students about the study and the instructions you want this person to give them. The students' answers may be influenced by the information they receive from the person facilitating the procedure, so it is important that they all receive exactly the same information. Family members and friends who are quite fluent in English might also be able to help proofread your work.

Revising your work

Writing is a continual process of redrafting. While producing multiple drafts of each section, expect to change the order of sentences or paragraphs and to add and delete information. You may even delete an entire section if you find yourself losing the main focus to your work. Once you are generally satisfied with the overall organization and content of your work, the revision process begins.

Revise each section or chapter in light of the specific purpose of the chapter (see Chapter 7 for a reminder). As you revise, you will need to read both for organization and sentence-level language use. Deal with the organizational issues before you address specific language issues, as you are likely to make numerous changes to your sentences as you reorganize information.

With regard to organization, consider the following points in each chapter of your work:

- What are the objectives of this chapter?
- How does each paragraph contribute to this broader purpose?
- Are your ideas ordered in the most effective manner to achieve the objectives of this chapter? Is there a logical flow to your ideas? Can you identify places where you appear to jump from one idea to another?

- Readers need to understand where you are leading them and they appreciate being reminded occasionally of your research question(s). Do you provide your reader with sufficient signposting?

After revising the content, you need to read again to revise for language use, punctuation and the appropriate use of the chosen citation style. It is quite normal not to recognize problems in sentence-level language use in our own writing. As the writer, we know intuitively what we meant to express even if the words don't actually convey this meaning. Changing how you normally read your work will help you identify weaknesses in your writing. Try these techniques:

- Read each line of a paragraph separately by covering the rest of the text with a ruler or piece of paper. Reading line by line helps you focus on sentence structure, word choice and punctuation.
- Alternatively, use the return function on your computer to make line breaks after each sentence in one paragraph of your work. Read this paragraph sentence by sentence.
- Read each paragraph aloud. Listening to yourself helps you find problem areas. Alternatively, use the record function on your mobile phone and listen to the recording. Does your writing seem to flow logically?
- Try to identify your specific problem areas. For instance, if you know you often make mistakes with, for example, article use, go through and circle every noun. In each case, identify whether an article is required.

Exercise 9.2

Redrafting and revising

As part of her research project on gender and student achievement, Zareen had a section on gender and cheating at her university. She conducted a survey of students' practices and their views on cheating and wrote up the results. This is a very preliminary draft of the results on cheating.

Summary of findings

According to the data that researcher collected from the students at the University through questionnaires and interviews with teachers, no one main reason may be adduced to answer the question why students cheat. This section will discuss the main findings from the study.

Both female and male students do cheating but females tend to be more innovated and arrive at new methods for cheating. Males are more likely to believe cheating is wrong although the majority also admitted to doing it. Accordingly students' views, the most succeed strategy to reduce cheating is having several invigilators in the exam room. Teachers' attitudes also affect students' behaviour because sometimes teachers just ignore students when they cheat. Both female and male students of English major are more likely to cheat from others of different disciplines. Female students in second and last year are more likely to cheat from others while male students in fourth year are more likely to cheat than other males. Some students have never cheated before. Interesting is that only a minority claim they have never seen any cheating during tests and exams.

Task

Redraft the paragraph. Reorganize the information to ensure it flows logically, add information that you believe is missing (this will entail using your imagination) and correct any problems with grammar or word choice. Finally, identify the type of table or graph that would display the results most appropriately.

Getting help with language

It is not the responsibility of your supervisor to ensure your work is written in acceptable English. Your project is a demonstration of what *you* are capable of at the end of your Bachelor's degree. Nevertheless, your instructors appreciate how challenging it is to write a project in a second language and will assist, although the extent of the assistance you receive depends on the supervisor. Some may give quite detailed feedback on language use, while others may tell you to revise the language yourself. In any case, it is highly recommended that you have people who can help you revise your work, whether they are family members or friends. You may even have a student colleague working on his/her project at the same time as you, and you can help one another by reading and editing each other's work. Consider how a *support network* might work for you.

If your university has a *Writing Centre*, make use of the support they offer. Again, it is not their responsibility to edit your work. They may agree to edit one section to show you the type of errors you tend to make; you will then have to read through the rest of your work to find other examples of these same mistakes. They can also help you organize your writing and understand how to use quotes and paraphrases correctly and how to cite the sources you use. They may also organize workshops on different aspects of the writing process; keep a look out for these and attend some of them. Both the input and the opportunity to talk about your work can be very useful.

Presenting your work: the oral examination

Once you finish writing up and revising your project, you are ready to present it formally in front of a committee who will evaluate your work and your presentation. Not all universities require an oral presentation (viva voce) or defence of the student's work at undergraduate or even postgraduate level. If this is a requirement at your university, consider it as an opportunity to broaden your experience. Presenting your work will allow you to practise skills such as public speaking, the use of Microsoft PowerPoint, responding to challenging questions and convincing your audience of your views. These are all transferrable skills you will likely use later in your professional life. This section will give you advice on how to prepare your presentation and what to expect. As the exact procedure varies depending on the institution, you will need to enquire into the procedure at your university. The following is a description of how an oral presentation may proceed.

Your supervisor, or a committee, will arrange the day and select the examiners. These people need some time to read your work, so don't expect to be invited to give your presentation immediately. In some institutions, this is a public event and other people such as family members, friends and other students may also attend. In other institutions, this is a 'closed-door' event, which takes place exclusively between you and the examiners.

As is the case with other formal events, your presentation will consist of a series of steps. The following is one example of how the event may be structured:

1 Your supervisor will start by formally introducing the examiners, you and your research topic.
2 You then have around 15 minutes to present your work.
3 Your supervisor will then ask the two committee members for their comments and questions. They will probably have between two and four questions or comments each. You will have time to answer after each question.
4 When the committee members have finished questioning you, your supervisor will ask you (and anyone else present) to leave the room. This is when they decide on a grade for your project (including your presentation).
5 You will be invited to re-enter the room to receive your grade. You may also be informed of certain minor corrections you need to do in response to points raised by the examiners. In this case, you will need to resubmit a final copy of your research project.

Advice for your presentation:

1 Speak to your audience directly and avoid burying your head in your notes.
2 Don't go through your whole project exhaustively; rather, give a short introduction to the topic (its importance and your motivation for choosing it), and then outline the methods you followed before moving to the main findings or results. You might mention any difficulties you had along the way. Rather than methodically going through your results, concentrate on the findings that relate more directly to your research question(s) and that appear more representative. Mention any implications your findings have (that is, what do your findings mean to language teachers or learners or translators?) and one or two recommendations. The committee members have all read your work and they won't take kindly to a blow-by-blow account of your results or recommendations.
3 Highlight what you learned about your topic and about doing research; the committee members will likely be interested in how your skills as a young

researcher developed. Also, all projects have limitations; perhaps there is something you would do differently if you were to repeat the project. Acknowledging this demonstrates your awareness of the research process.

4 The most challenging moment during your presentation is when the committee members ask you questions, as it is difficult to predict what they will ask. Answer each question as clearly as you can. You can refer to what you have written in your project but you can also mention things you did or learned but perhaps did not include when you wrote the final version of your study. You may also be asked to relate the findings in your work to a specific context. The examiners want to see if you can find an application for your work in real life or extend your findings to a different context.
5 You can use PowerPoint (or a similar application such as Prezi) if you wish, but this is usually not obligatory. If you use it, make sure you use it well. When it is used poorly, it detracts from the presentation. If you don't know how to make good use of PowerPoint for a presentation, either ask someone to help you or read up on how to use it well (the Internet is a great resource for advice on this). If you don't have time to improve your skills, consider not using it.
6 The committee members have taken the time to read your work, attend your presentation and talk to you about your topic and your academic interests. This may be the last time you have the undivided attention of your instructors; despite your nerves, try to enjoy the event – it has all been organized for you!

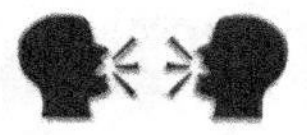

Discussion task 9.2

Discuss the following questions with your partner or in a small group:

1 What have you heard from your instructors and peers about the oral examination at your institution?
2 The procedure at your institution may differ from the one described above. If so, in what way(s) is it different?
3 If you know people who have successfully completed their oral exam, what positive things did they have to say about the experience? Were there any negative comments?
4 How will you prepare for your oral exam?

Insights from the literature 9.1

Preparing for the defence

For most students, the oral examination (or viva voce) is an unfamiliar and intimidating event. Frequently, little information is available to students about the oral examination experience; some institutions do not allow anyone in the room other than the examiners and the student being examined, so it is impossible to learn about the procedure first-hand. In such situations, most students rely on second-hand information from their instructors and peers. Such information can be very subjective, however, and students' experiences and perceptions may differ considerably. Rarely do institutions provide students with a description of the procedure or formally prepare students for the event. Procedures for oral examinations have usually been developed within an institution over time, and thus frequently follow 'customary practice' rather than objectively established assessment guidelines (Park, 2003, p. 48).

Before undergoing an oral exam, most students don't view the event in a positive light. According to research by Wellington (2010), common emotional reactions include fear of a negative outcome (e.g. failing the oral exam), anxiety about their performance (e.g. not being eloquent enough, not responding appropriately to questions) and anxiety about the examiners' personalities and questions (e.g. some examiners are 'harder' than others, examiners' academic interests may be different from yours). Not all emotions are negative, however; students also look forward to this event for reasons such as the following: it is an opportunity to receive feedback from a group of specialists who have gathered just to talk to you; the event gives a 'stamp of approval' to the completion of your degree; it gives you an opportunity to raise questions, learn more about your topic of interest and perhaps get ideas for further study; it also allows you a chance to share your interest and enthusiasm on the topic with others, and show how much you have achieved (Wellington, 2010). After successfully undergoing an oral exam, many students actually view the event quite positively (Carter, 2012).

Although one common fear regarding the oral examination concerns not knowing what questions will be asked, research shows that the general question types are quite predictable (Wellington, 2010). These question types include introductory questions in which the student is asked to summarize the key points and to explain his/her motivation for choosing the topic; questions regarding the choice of theoretical framework and the choice of works in the Literature Review; questions regarding the methods, the sample and the data analysis; and questions regarding the application of the findings (Wellington, 2010).

In addition to anticipating the questions that will be asked, students may find that preparing a brief overview of their research project helps build their confidence. By practising their opening move, students feel better able to cope with questions and responses from the examiners. An additional recommendation involves rereading important literature quoted in the study in order to review the main ideas that influenced the work (Carter, 2012).

From the perspective of academic staff, the oral exam also constitutes a mechanism by which an institution can attempt to verify whether the student truly authored the study (Carter, 2012; Park, 2003). Not only does our dependency on the Internet lend itself well to a 'copy–paste' mentality, but the electronic age also facilitates the 'ghost-writer' phenomenon, whereby a student pays someone to write a research paper or thesis that the student then presents as his/her own. By enquiring into aspects of the Literature Review or methodology, for instance, examiners can attain greater confidence regarding authorship and academic integrity.

Discussion task 9.3

After reading Insights from the literature 9.1, discuss the following questions with your partner or in a small group:

1 In your view, should oral exams be open to the public (i.e. should family members and other students be able to attend)? Or should they take place behind closed doors? What are the advantages and disadvantages of each?
2 Consider your friend's or your neighbour's research topic. If you were an examiner for this research project, what questions would you ask?
3 Thinking of your own oral exam, what positive things would you like to get out of the experience?

Appendix 1

Introductions from published articles

Chik, A. (2014). Digital gaming and language learning: Autonomy and community. *Language Learning & Technology*, *18*(2), 85–100.

Introduction

Many of the most popular commercial off-the-shelf (COTS) games played in China, Hong Kong and Taiwan are developed and published by Japanese and American game developers. COTS games are 'designed purely for fun and entertainment rather than for learning' (Whitton, 2010, p. 199). These games are first released in Japanese- or English-language versions, and bilingual Chinese versions are often released at a much later date, if at all. In these regions, English is taught as a compulsory subject in schools, while Japanese is popular as a language for informal learning, but not widely taught in schools. Chinese-speaking East Asia, then, presents an interesting context to study digital gaming and second language (L2) learning because gamers frequently use an L2 to play digital games outside the classroom. While gamers are playing L2 games, many are also using L2 gameplay for L2 learning. Some are playing and learning autonomously, while some are seeking support from communities (Chik, 2012). This paper seeks to understand the ways gamers practice autonomy within community by managing their gameplay both as leisure and as learning practices in different dimensions (location, formality, locus of control, formality, and trajectory).

Lee, L. (2011). Blogging: Promoting learner autonomy and intercultural competence through study abroad. *Language Learning & Technology*, *15*(3), 87–109.

Introduction

The traditional teacher-driven classroom has become pedagogically limited in making language learning a student-centered instruction that stresses learners' capacity to learn autonomously. According to Little (2003), autonomy entails decision-making, critical reflection and social interaction. Autonomous learners are responsible for their own learning and are actively involved in the learning process by setting personal goals, planning and executing tasks, and reviewing their progress (Dam, 1995; Little, 1996). Teachers play a supportive and facilitative role in the autonomous learning by encouraging students to take an active part in decision-making and problem-solving, and offering them guidance. From a social constructivist view, the development of autonomy is a result of interplay between social and reflective processes (Little, 2003). Benson (2003) notes that during social interaction, students work collaboratively with others through which they develop high order thinking skills by observing, analyzing and evaluating information.

While there are many ways to foster autonomous learning, computer-assisted language learning (CALL) is increasingly recognized as a powerful means for developing learner autonomy (Benson, 2004, Lee, 2005; Murphy, 2006; O'Rourke & Schwienhorst, 2003). The advent of Web 2.0 technologies (wikis, blogs, podcastings) brings new dimensions to online learning. Blogs, for example, are used in various ways depending on their pedagogical purposes. Personal blogs are collections of online journals that foster self-expression and self-reflection (e.g., Lee, 2010; Yang, 2009), whereas collective blogs involving an entire class or small groups promote interactive and collaborative learning (Lee, 2009b). Blogging fosters learner autonomy, as students take charge of making their own decisions as to what, how much and when to publish their work (Lee, 2010). Accordingly, students develop the awareness of their ability to plan, understand and regulate their own learning (Baggetun & Wasson, 2006; Ward, 2004).

Given that blogs are asynchronous CMC, students construct knowledge at their own pace, which enables them to reflect on the content (Armstrong & Retterer, 2008; Campbell, 2003; Murray & Hourigan, 2006; Richardson, 2005). In addition, Lee (2010) points out that blogs increase students' participation and motivation because they are intended not only for a sole instructor but rather for a broad audience. While blogging presents pedagogical potentials with regard to autonomous learning, the accessibility to networking influences participation levels (Belz, 2002; Lee, 2004). Lacking Internet access at home or in school creates learner stress and frustration. Consequently, the level of engagement diminishes and the quality of work suffers (Peterson, 1997).

With the aforementioned benefits, blogs have been increasingly implemented in L2 instruction across contexts. Research findings have shed light on our understanding of the effectiveness of blogs for developing reading and writing skills (e.g., Bloch, 2007; Churchill, 2009; Ducate & Lomicka, 2008; Lee, 2010; Murray & Hourigan, 2006). To promote intercultural learning, blogs have been incorporated into conventional classes and study abroad programs (e.g., Elola & Oskoz, 2008; Lee, 2009b; Sun, 2009). Existing CALL research, however, has not yet given much attention to issues of autonomy, as suggested by L2 researchers (Benson, 2006; Blin, 2004; Chapelle, 2001; White, 2003). To gain new insights regarding the emergence of autonomy beyond the classroom, the current study explored how blogs in conjunction with ethnographic interviews foster learner autonomy. Using a social constructivist approach, this study involved 16 American undergraduate students who participated in a blog project to develop their intercultural competence over the course of one semester of a study abroad program. As a course requirement, the blog project aimed to use (a) personal blogs to give students individual spaces to write and reflect upon their experiences with the host culture and people on a regular basis, and (b) a class blog to open a social place where both students and L1s shared and exchanged cross-cultural perspectives using teacher-assigned topics. Real-time ethnographic interviews with local L1s as part of the class blog afforded abroad students additional opportunities for FTF intercultural exchanges. The combination of two modes of communication (CMC and FTF) was used to optimize students' learning potential according to their learning styles and personal needs. Importantly, blogs and ethnographic interviews enabled students to develop cultural insights independently and collaboratively outside of class. The study examined the impact of reflective blogs on self-directed learning from students' perspectives. Furthermore, factors that affected autonomous learning within the virtual learning environment were explored.

Chen, C.E. (2006). The development of e-mail literacy: From writing to peers to writing to authority figures. *Language Learning & Technology*, *10*(2), 35–55.

Introduction

The development of information and communication technology along with the widespread use of the Internet has rapidly promoted e-mail as a common interpersonal communication medium. With its high transmission speed and less intrusive nature, e-mail has been widely used for both personal communication and institutional communication, particularly in academic and business institutions (Baron, 2000; Crystal, 2001). The wide use of the e-mail medium, however, does not necessarily mean that it is used without difficulty. While people can write e-mails to peers in any manner they like, research has shown that people in the workplace tend to feel uneasy writing e-mails to those perceived as higher in status when initiating communication, suggesting new ideas, making requests, and expressing disagreement or criticism (Baron, 1998, 2000; Kling, 1996; Murray, 1988, 1995). They usually need to spend more time planning and composing such status-unequal e-mails in which various face-threatening acts are involved.

An important reason for the challenge of using this medium, particularly for status-unequal communication, is that e-mail, unlike face-to-face talk, lacks paralinguistic cues such as vocal inflection, gestures, facial expressions, and a shared mental and physical context (Murray, 1995). These paralinguistic cues usually constitute metamessages that convey social meaning (e.g., relationships between and attitudes toward each other) and serve as social lubricants. Without these paralinguistic cues, the metamessages sent via e-mail are revealed solely by how the written words are chosen, expressed, and organized. Wording and message structuring, thus, become more crucial in e-mail communication than in face-to-face talk.

However, there seem to be no fixed, standard e-mail writing rules for users to observe, especially since e-mail is a hybrid discourse inheriting features of both written and spoken language. On one hand, e-mail users may feel liberated from the restriction of traditional letter writing rules; on the other, they may struggle to produce an appropriate e-mail to meet the recipient's standards. Though the appropriateness of language use in e-mail may differ from person to person, it is generally determined by those who have more power, like any other communication medium. As Fairclough (1995) points out, 'appropriateness is an "ideological" category, which is linked to particular partisan positions within a politics of language' (p. 234). That is, appropriateness is ideologically situated in different sociocultural contexts and those who have less power need to observe standards of a dominant sociocultural group. This critical perspective on language use implies that e-mail users do not always have freedom in writing when they are in a position of lower power; instead, they have to follow the standards of appropriateness set by those who are on the dominant side in order to communicate successfully.

For nonnative speakers, writing status-unequal e-mails can pose an even greater challenge because they need to have sophisticated pragmatic competence in the second language (L2) and critical language awareness of how discourse shapes and is shaped by power relations, identity, and ideologies established in the target culture. Due to their limited linguistic ability and unfamiliarity with the norms and values of the target culture, confusions or problems can occur in their L2 communication, including e-mail communication. Shetzer and Warschauer's (2000) discussion of electronic literacy placed strong emphasis on the importance of L2 learners' pragmatic competence for computer-mediated communication, such as the ability to perform speech acts and use appropriate communication strategies in the online environment, yet they did not address how L2 learners develop such pragmatic competence for producing electronic discourse. The development of pragmatic competence and critical language awareness in using the e-mail medium, which I would like to term as 'e-mail literacy', is a pressing issue in the digital era and needs to receive greater attention in second language research and education.

To gain a deeper understanding of how an L2 learner develops e-mail literacy, I conducted a longitudinal case study of a Taiwanese graduate student's e-mail practice in English during her studies at a U.S. university for two and a half years. This case study particularly focused on a type of status-unequal e-mail practice in the academic context: the student's e-mail communication with professors. Using a critical discourse analysis approach (Fairclough, 1995), this study aimed to uncover the complexity of an L2 learner's developing e-mail practice and to explore sociocognitive and sociopsychological factors affecting her language use via this medium in relation to power relations, identity construction, and culture-specific ideologies.

Appendix 2

Conclusions from published articles

Chik, A. (2014). Digital gaming and language learning: Autonomy and community. *Language Learning & Technology*, *18*(2), 85–100.

Conclusion

This exploratory study examined how gamers practice autonomy within community by managing their gameplay both as leisure and learning practices in five dimensions: location, formality, pedagogy, locus of control, and trajectory. The study also identified autonomy as one of the keys to facilitate L2 learning through L2 gaming. Autonomy can be exercised differently in different dimensions, and findings indicate the affordances are not only limited to in-game interactions with game texts and with other gamers. The extended online gaming communities provide support in both L1 and L2 through paratexts and language learning advice. However, given that the present study is a small-scale exploratory study, there are certain limitations: the gamer-participants were university students and were gamers who have achieved a high level of L2 proficiency, so their practices may reflect a certain bias towards L2 learning. Also, these gamers grew up in the late 1990s, a period when Chinese games were almost non-existent, whereas there are more Chinese-language online games available now. The online discussants cited in this study are self-selected groups of gamers who are keen on L2 gaming, and sharing their L2 gaming and learning experience; there are other groups that advocate and support gaming in L1.

Notwithstanding the limitations, findings from the present study may have some important research and pedagogical implications. First, for some gamers, organizing L2 gaming practices is a learning process, thus further research on exploring the organization of L2 gaming practices over time and space will be informative. When language use is an integral part of gaming, the trajectory of L2 gaming practices can well reflect the gamer's L2 learning trajectory. A better understanding of the trajectory can inform the gap between L2 learning in school and in out-of-class contexts. Second, this study suggests that game-related paratexts in both L1 and L2 form the funds of knowledge (Moll et al., 1992) for many L2 gamers. At present, we are beginning to understand the complexity and creativity of game-related paratexts (Thorne et al., 2012), but we have yet to know more about the connection between the consumption and production of L1 and L2 paratexts. It will be especially fruitful to better understand the fluidity of the consumption of these, and how similarly or differently gamers use these paratexts. Finally, when COTS games are assumed to be only entertaining, many gamers have found ways to transform them into learning resources. A major implication is that teachers and researchers should provide structures and guidance for young L2 learners on how to use L2 games to learn autonomously. In this way, students can be made aware that they have the ability to turn their preferred leisure activities into learning practices, and learn how to seek help from online communities. As we know more about these processes, we will gain more in-depth understandings of autonomy and communities in L2 gaming.

Lee, L. (2011). Blogging: Promoting learner autonomy and intercultural competence through study abroad. *Language Learning & Technology*, *15*(3), 87–109.

Conclusion

The blog project examined how students engaged in cognitive, metacognitive, social and affective dimensions of autonomous online learning. The project for the development of ICC presented both promises and challenges for the study abroad students. Overall, students found that blogging supported self-directed learning, as they individually and socially constructed meanings to develop their intercultural knowledge and skills. According to the post-survey findings, blogging promoted learner autonomy through self-regulation and self-management. In addition, students maintained that using blogs gave them a sense of belonging, as they collaboratively shared and exchanged cultural perspectives. However, a few students experienced difficulty in putting their ideas in order and suggested that the instructor should take a more active role in assisting students during the execution of the project. Furthermore, the results reveal that lack of access to the Internet at the host institution and family contributed to a limited level of participation. Consequently, some students were frustrated by not being able to participate actively in the blog discussions. The findings corroborated those reported in previous studies of CMC indicating that the accessibility of networking is essential for network-based learning and influences students' motivation to connect and interact with others (Lee, 2004; Ware, 2005).

Critical reflection as one of the major aspects of self-directing learning was manifested through collaborative interaction. Similar to Abrams's (2005) and Lee's (2009a) CMC findings, expert scaffolding played a facilitative role in cultivating critical thinking. The results of the study show that L1 partners went beyond offering cultural information and explanation of students' understandings. Their questions challenged students to think further about the cross-cultural issues. As a result, students strove for more in-depth discussions. However, some students did not find peer comments stimulating enough to generate further discussion. The analysis of selected blog entries for cognitive presence affirms that students mostly exchanged cultural information rather than challenging others' viewpoints by asking pertinent questions, as concluded in the recent CMC study of Liaw & Bunn-Le Master (2010). Despite the fact that all phases of cognitive presence were found in the blog entries, the exploration and integration occurred more frequently than the triggering and the resolution. According to Arnold and Ducate (2006), '*individual* resolutions were often based on *collaborative* integrations' (p. 57). Thus, teachers should make students aware of all four stages of sociocognitive processes and encourage them to actively engage in online exchange in order to take full advantage of their shared virtual space. Moreover, the findings suggest that topic selection (e.g., controversial issues vs. current events) and language proficiency (e.g., L1 vs. L2) may have affected the degree of interaction and quality of cognitive engagement. The option of using L1 should be considered to allow less proficient learners to fully express themselves.

In closing, this study contributes to the field of using digital technology for intercultural learning and its impact on learner autonomy, although the results reported from this study cannot be generalized to other settings. Without a doubt, the combination of CMC via blogging and FTF through interviews with L1s offered promising benefits to study abroad students, as they individually and collaboratively participated in blog activities. The findings show that the students' perceptions toward blogging have offered valuable insights into our understanding of its effectiveness for self-directed learning. Blogs as a mediated tool for intercultural learning outside of class have the potential to create a stimulating online learning community that is conducive to collaborative learning and reflective thinking. In addition, the use of free and teacher-assigned tasks contributes to the success of a blog project. The study concludes that well-designed tasks, effective metacognitive strategies, and cognitive skills are essential to maximize the potential of blogs for stimulating learner autonomy and intercultural communication.

Chen, C.E. (2006). The development of e-mail literacy: From writing to peers to writing to authority figures. *Language Learning & Technology*, *10*(2), 35–55.

Conclusion

This longitudinal case study allows us to see how a second language learner used e-mail for interpersonal communication and developed her e-mail literacy in the target language environment, particularly in communicating with authority figures in the academic context. Of particular interest in this case is how Ling made changes in her institutional e-mail practice in relation to her developing understanding of the e-mail medium, changing performance of student identity, evolving knowledge of appropriate student–professor interaction, and realization of culture-specific politeness. Three important points in addressing the development of e-mail literacy can be concluded from this study.

First, Ling's case illustrates that an L2 learner's frequent use of e-mail to communicate with peers does not indicate that she is able to use the medium appropriately and effectively for institutional status-unequal communication. Although Ling demonstrated her ability to shift between formal/epistolary and informal/conversational styles in her e-mails depending on power relations and familiarity levels with her addressees, her language use in student-to-professor e-mails was not without problems. A number of pragmatic problems were found particularly in Ling's early e-mails sent to professors, such as unclear, delayed purpose statements with many irrelevant details, requests framed from a student-oriented perspective and with a strong help-needed tone, failure to demonstrate status-appropriate politeness, and ineffective use of reasons or explanations as supportive moves.

Second, this study reveals that the development of L2 learners' language use in composing status-unequal e-mails is neither an easy nor a simple process. In Ling's e-mail practice, *we* see her constantly struggling with language use in order to achieve her communicative purpose while demonstrating politeness as well. The difficulty arose from the fact that there were no models for her to imitate and no explicit rules to follow either. She could not completely imitate the way her professors wrote e-mails to her due to the power asymmetry and neither could she imitate the way native speaker students wrote e-mails to their professors since she had no opportunity to read those e-mails. Moreover, she was unable to find out what part of her e-mails was problematic or inappropriate because her e-mail interlocutors did not tell her. Thus, she established her own rules in writing these status-unequal e-mails by either guessing what might be appropriate or observing how native speakers interacted in other types of communication practice.

Third, this study demonstrates that appropriateness is not a one-dimensional notion in status-unequal e-mail communication. It consists of an interplay of three factors: language appropriateness, culture (including institutional culture and target language culture) appropriateness, and medium appropriateness. As revealed in this case, to perform appropriately in e-mail communication with professors, Ling would need to know how students are expected to act in the academic institutional context, how politeness is realized in the target culture, and how the e-mail medium is used for institutional communication.

Such critical language awareness along with pragmatic competence is imperative for L2 learners to develop their e-mail literacy. *I* advocate that L2 learners be taught explicitly in the L2 classroom how to communicate appropriately with higher-ups via e-mail, due to the fact that those appropriateness rules are usually hidden and difficult to acquire. They need to learn how power, identity, and culture-specific ideology are constantly intertwined with communication practice and how they can use appropriate discourse forms and strategies to shape and reflect their power relations and situated identities in various sociocultural contexts.

Appendix 3

Creating transitions in your writing

You want to . . .

1 *tell the reader what the structure of your argument will be*:

to begin with, first of all, first(ly), second(ly), afterwards, subsequently, finally

2 *make the order of your information explicit*:

after, before, then, once, next, last, at last, at length, first, second, at first, formerly, another, finally, soon, meanwhile, at the same time, later, to begin with, afterwards, subsequently, previously, in the meantime, immediately, eventually, concurrently, simultaneously

3 *indicate purpose*:

in order to, with a view to, for this purpose, to this end, with this in mind, with this purpose in mind

4 *give an example*:

for instance, for example, namely, to illustrate, in other words, in particular, specifically, such as

5 *give additional information*:

in other words, moreover, furthermore, in addition (to), additionally, on the one hand . . . on the other hand, more to the point, besides, too, also, again, both . . . and, another, equally important, lastly, finally, next, likewise, similarly, in fact, not only . . . but also, as well as

6 *provide additional detail*:

specifically, especially, in particular, in this sense, namely

7 *show something is similar to what you have said before*:

similarly, likewise, analogously, relatedly

8 *provide information that negates what you have said before*:

on the contrary, conversely, contrary to, in contrast

9 *make a concession*:

although, though, even though, in spite of, despite, at any rate, at least, still, even though, granted that, while it may be true that, while

10 *contrast X with Y*:

on the contrary, contrarily, notwithstanding, but, however, nevertheless, in spite of, in contrast, yet, on the one hand . . . on the other hand, rather, or, nor, conversely, at the same time, while this may be true

11 *provide reasons against something*:

yet, however, nevertheless

12 *emphasize what you are saying*:

above all, indeed, of course, certainly, surely, in fact, really, again, besides, also, furthermore, in addition, most importantly

13 *generalize*:

usually, ordinarily, frequently, generally, in most cases, broadly speaking, in general terms

Antonyms: rarely, occasionally, on occasion, seldom, an exception to this is, although less common

14 *provide a summary or conclusion that logically follows what you have just said*:

to sum up, thus, consequently, as a consequence, hence, with the result that, accordingly, for this reason, therefore, so, because, since, due to, as a result, in other words, then, in short, in conclusion, in brief

Appendix 4

Reporting verbs

When you cite an author or report on findings from previous research, you will often use a reporting verb (integral citation). The exception to this is if you simply enclose the author's name and the year of publication in brackets after the sentence you paraphrase or quote (non-integral citation). There are a great variety of reporting verbs and you should try to vary your choice of verb in your work. Choosing an appropriate verb needs some care, however, as the meaning or connotation conveyed by reporting verbs can vary greatly. Below is a list of verbs grouped according to general meaning. Some of the verbs listed here are used infrequently because they express a very specific meaning. The list is only a guideline, however, as the context in which the verb is used usually determines its meaning. It is a good idea to start noticing the reporting verbs used in the academic texts you read. Consult a good dictionary before using verbs you are less familiar with.

You want to . . .

- *report information neutrally*:

  say, report, state, articulate, indicate, remind, identify, point out, add, believe, maintain, hold, establish

- *explain something*:

  explain, describe, justify, explicate, elucidate, clarify

- *say something indirectly*:

  imply, hint at, allude to, insinuate

- *suggest something*:

  suggest, propose, recommend, counsel, urge, appeal to, push for, press for, demand

- *express an opinion*:

  opine, consider, advise, advocate, put forward, argue, judge, observe, insist, espouse, conclude

- *indicate agreement:*

  agree with, affirm, concur, support, corroborate, confirm, demonstrate, show

- *indicate disagreement:*

  disagree, question, dispute, doubt, oppose, contradict, differ, challenge, query, object to, deny, undermine

- *indicate some uncertainty:*

  allege, assert, claim, postulate, contend

Appendix 5

Citing your sources

In-text citations using APA style

When you cite an author in your text, you:

1 cite the last name only;
2 give the year of publication in brackets;
3 for a quote (and sometimes also for a paraphrase), give the page number (use 'p.' or 'pp.'); if you put the page number after the date, sometimes you will see a colon ':' instead of 'p.'.

Look at how Chen (2006, pp. 36, 37) has cited the source for ideas and information she has incorporated into her work from other authors. The cited author may appear at the beginning of the sentence with a reporting verb, or at the end of the passage in brackets. In the former case, focus is on the author and the choice of verb; in the latter case, the primary focus is on the idea:

> Biesenbach-Lucas and Weasenforth (2000) found that L2 students used fewer modal constructions and hedged expressions in their e-mails than did U.S. students; instead, their e-mails often contained inappropriate pleading for help from the professor.

> A number of studies compared how L2 learners' e-mail discourse differed from L2 oral discourse (Chapman, 1997; Warschauer, 1996) or differed from L2 offline written texts (Biesenbach-Lucas & Weasenforth, 2001).

Citing a block of material

If your quote is long (according to APA guidelines, more than 40 words), you need to begin the passage on a separate line, indented from your own text. In this case, you do not have to use quotation marks but you must still cite the source. The citation in brackets should follow the quoted passage, and is often positioned on a separate line to the right.

Citing more than one author

If you need to cite more than one author, arrange the names in alphabetical order and use a semi-colon to separate them. If the work has more than one author, use '&' or 'and' between the two surnames ('&' is only used when the citation appears within brackets). In the following example from Chen (2006, p. 37), two authors have multiple publications; the years are arranged chronologically and, in the case of Zhang, letters ('a' and 'b') are used to distinguish works published the same year:

> These findings are consistent with studies on Chinese speakers' oral and written requests (Kirkpatrick, 1991, 1993; Nash, 1983; Zhang, 1995a, 1995b), which indicates that Chinese-speaking students probably transfer the request strategies that they normally use in Chinese to the English request e-mails written to professors.

Citing indirect sources

Often you will learn about a useful idea or an example that the author of your article (or book) attributes to someone else. For example, if you read Chen's (2006) article, you will learn about certain ideas attributed to N.S. Baron, who published some relatively early work on the use of e-mail communication. Namely, Chen (2006, p. 35) writes:

> research has shown that people in the workplace tend to feel uneasy writing e-mails to those perceived as higher in status when initiating communication, suggesting new ideas, making requests, and expressing disagreement or criticism (Baron, 1998, . . .).

Chances are you don't have access to Baron's work. If you want to attribute this idea to Baron, should you acknowledge that you didn't actually read the original text? The correct approach is to signal that you learnt about an idea (or research findings) attributed to Baron in Chen's work by using the following formulation:

> Previous findings (for instance, Baron, 1998, in Chen, 2006, p. 35) have indicated that . . .

Citing texts with no author

If the text you wish to cite has no author, use the name of the organization or institution in place of the author's name. The first time you use the name of the organization, provide an acronym e.g 'the Ministry of Education (MoE)'; you can then continue to cite this institution using the acronym.

Citing Internet sources in your text

Information taken from Internet can be difficult to cite in your text. Often there is no obvious author, no year and no page. If there is no author, use the name of the institution (if this information is not taken from an institution, it may well not be an appropriate academic source). If there is no year of publication, you can put 'n.d.' in place of the year; this means 'no date'. Some PDF documents you download may have page number, but with other documents there will be none.

Citing personal communications

If you talked to or emailed someone you consider to be an authority who gave you important information for your project that you cannot find in a published text (either because this is an idea or a view of this person, or because only this person has this information), you need to cite this person. You do this by writing '(personal communication)' after the person's name or position title (in case the person prefers to remain anonymous). You do not put this name in your list of references as this is not something that readers will be able to search for:

> The principal of the school, Mr Said AlBadri (personal communication, 12 December 2012) maintains that. . . .

Compiling your List of References

At the end of your project, you need to write a list of all the works you cite in your project (do not include anything you do not cite). The list should be arranged alphabetically (according to the authors' surnames); do not number the list. How to cite a journal article, book and Internet site is quite different.

Exercise A5.1

Compiling references

Look at the following examples (a–g) and answer the questions (1–7) below:

a Piller, I. (2002). Passing for a native speaker: Identity and success in second language learning. *Journal of Sociolinguistics* 6(2), 179–206.

b Derwing, T. & Rossiter, M. (2003). The effect of pronunciation instruction on the accuracy, fluency and complexity of L2 accented speech. *Applied Language Learning 13*(1), 1–17.

c Roberts, C., Davies, E. & Jupp, T. (1992). *Language and discrimination*. London: Longman.

d Chik, A. (2012). Digital gameplay for autonomous foreign language learning: Gamers' and language teachers' perspectives. In H. Reinders (Ed.), *Digital games in language learning and teaching* (pp. 95–114). London: Palgrave Macmillan.

e Republic of Turkey Ministry of Education. (n.d.). *National Education Statistics 2012–2013*. Retrieved 12 January 2014, from www.meb.gov.tr/english/minister.html.

f Morley, J. (n.d.). *Academic Phrasebank*. Retrieved 11 June 2011, from www.phrasebank.manchester.ac.uk.

g Brown, P. & Levinson, S. (1987). *Politeness: Some universals in language usage*. Cambridge: Cambridge University Press.

1 Which examples are journal articles?
2 Which one is a journal article with two authors?
3 Which are books?
4 Which one is a chapter in a book?
5 In which order do you write the following: the place of publication and the name of the publishing company?
6 How is citing a website different from a published work?
7 If this were your List of References, in which order would you put these seven publications?

Answer key to the exercises

This answer key does not include the Discussion tasks, as different answers are possible for these.

Chapter 2

2.1, 2.2, 2.3

Different answers are possible.

Chapter 3

3.1

Different answers are possible.

3.2

Example 1: The student doesn't end the email appropriately. The reason she gives for changing the topic is not very convincing and she doesn't suggest an alternative topic.
Example 2: The student doesn't end the email appropriately and doesn't provide a name.
Example 3: The student doesn't end the email appropriately and doesn't provide a name. The student doesn't state what he/she would like the supervisor to do with the Introduction attached.
Example 4: It would be more appropriate to request a meeting with the supervisor for this matter.
Example 5: It is generally not appropriate for the student to give the supervisor deadlines. The student could use one of the phrases suggested in this chapter.
Example 6: The implication seems to be that the student sent the work with a previous email. It would be helpful if the student mentioned when it was sent, as an indirect reminder to the supervisor of how much time has passed.

Example 7: It would save time if the student included the original email below this latest one. Abbreviations typical in text messages should be avoided. More attention to orthographic conventions is recommended.

3.3

Different answers are possible. The phrases suggested in this chapter can be used (with variations).

3.4

Different answers are possible. The main point of this exercise is to identify the different topics the student addresses and the main questions the student has for the supervisor. The different topics should preferably be organized in different paragraphs and the questions should be formulated as questions rather than as doubts or hints.

The different topics are: the new topic; the proposed method of data collection; the student's initial hypothesis; the student's plan for conducting the study; the student's motivation for choosing this topic.

The questions asked by the student are: Should I use instructors from one department for my study or can I use instructors from different departments? Do you know of any published study on questions used in the classroom by Turkish teachers in Turkish? Should I interview the instructors about the question types they use?

3.5

[1] Louisa appears to be slightly more formal than Lisa.
[2a] Examples 5 and 6 are likely to be considered appropriate by supervisors who prefer more formality.
[2b] Example 4 might be considered acceptable by supervisors who are comfortable with less formality.
[2c] Example 3 is likely to be considered inappropriate by both groups.

Chapter 4

4.1

Different answers are possible.

4.2

[1] Examples (c), (d) and (f) are open-access academic journals that might be useful for your study. Example (d) is a particularly respected journal in the field. Examples (a), (b) and (e) are not suitable academic sources and should

not be used. Example (e) looks like it might be an online academic journal, but contributions do not undergo a systematic peer review procedure and therefore do not fulfil the minimum academic standards required of literature for your research project.
[2] The URL extension '.com' signals a private or commercial website. Information from such sites is less likely to be of an academic nature. This is not always the case, however. Example (c), the *Reading Matrix Journal*, is an open-access, peer-reviewed journal that may be a useful resource for research topics investigating reading-related issues. Tip 4.4 provides more information on assessing websites.

4.3

Different answers are possible. In general, Wikipedia can be useful to check our understanding of things such as terms, the date of an event, someone's birthplace etc. Questions of this nature tend to be more factual and objective, and less prone to individual interpretations. The website should not be considered an authority, however. A widely acknowledged problem with Wikipedia is that there is insufficient control on the quality of the information that appears on the site. This is especially true when a topic or a phenomenon may be analysed or interpreted from different perspectives.

4.4

The answers to this exercise depend on the library collection at your university.

Zoltan Dörnyei is particularly well known for his publications on motivation in language learning.

4.5

[1a] As the title suggests, this journal publishes work related to the teaching and learning of English as a second language around the world.
Different answers are possible for the remaining questions.

Chapter 5

5.1

Different answers are possible.

5.2

Answers are provided for the Abstract from Chik's (2014) study.
'The relationship between digital game play and second language (L2) learning is a particularly tricky issue in East Asia.' [*Motivation for the study*.]

'Though there is an emerging presence of Chinese online games, many more young people are playing the English- or Japanese-language versions of the most popular commercial off-the-shelf (COTS) video games. In other words, most Chinese gamers are playing L2 digital games in their leisure time.' [*Background information relevant to the study.*]
'Informed by research on out-of-class L2 learning . . .' [*Reference to a theory or an approach used in the study.*]
'. . . this paper discusses findings from an exploratory study investigating L2 gaming and learning practices in young people's everyday lives.' [*The research question(s) or topic.*]
'Drawing on rich data from gaming sessions, stimulated recall, focus group discussion, individual interviews and online discussion forums . . .' [*Information about how the author did the study.*]
'. . . this paper argues that gamers exercise autonomy by managing their gameplay both as leisure and learning practices in different dimensions (location, formality, locus of control, pedagogy and trajectory). At the same time, gameplay-as-learning practices are supported by wider communities of digital gamers who take on roles as language teachers and advisers.' [*An indication of the findings.*]
'The paper discusses the research and pedagogical implications for L2 gaming and learning.' [*An indication of the study's, implications and recommendations.*]

5.3

You might have noted down something like this: 'less appropriate use of email for communication with profs'; 'transfer from L1 context'.

5.4

[1] In each case, the final noun is the nucleus of the phrase.
[2] 'interaction through e-mail'; 'strategies to make requests'.
[3] 'e-mail interaction'; 'U.S. professors'; 'request strategies'; 'request e-mails'; 'request acts'; 'lexico-syntactic mitigating forms'; 'Chinese students'; 'pre-request support moves'; 'lexico-syntactic modifications'; 'Chinese-speaking students'.

Chapter 6

6.1

[1] The meaning of words such as 'regularly', 'sometimes' and 'often' is very vague. Also, the difference between statements such as 'I sometimes attend class' and 'I am often absent' is unclear.
[2] It is unclear what courses are referred to. Does this include school, or all years of university study, or only a specific semester?
[3] There is an assumption that the teacher does these things; it may be that the teacher does something else instead. Also, it assumes that the student can identify

a cause-and-effect relationship between an action (giving study notes) and an outcome (higher grades), when in fact none may exist.

6.2

Suggested order (variations are possible): 1, 3, 2, 4, 6, 5.

6.3

[1] Zeki would need both to observe a lecture and record it. His observation sheet should ideally capture things that he cannot perceive from a recording, such as whether the lecturer is addressing the class or one student, translating a word or phrase written on the board or responding to something happening in the classroom.

If he is unable to record the lecture, the observation sheet could contain different categories of actions that occur during the class. These can be coded (e.g. A1: greet students; A2: mention the topic of the class; A3: mention where to find the reading material for the class etc.). Using codes can make it easier to take observation notes and to analyse the data later. Zeki should record which language is used for these actions and instances when the two languages are combined.
[2] Different answers are possible.

6.4

Topics (3) and (4) would be suitable. They don't require that participants read or write anything and they lend themselves to a discussion on different viewpoints and experiences. In the case of Topic (4), a focus-group discussion could usefully be combined with observations of the administrative assistants' actual practice in their work environment and an examination of their written texts. The other topic would require observations of actual practice (examples 1, 2 and 6) or interviews (examples 2 and perhaps 6). Topic (5) would be unsuitable as some people would not wish to publicly acknowledge communication problems they may experience. Alternative approaches such as observations combined with questionnaire or interview data would be more appropriate.

Chapter 7

7.1

[1]

background	Many of the most popular commercial off-the-shelf (COTS) games played in China, Hong Kong and Taiwan are developed and published by Japanese and American game developers.
definition	COTS games are 'designed purely for fun and entertainment rather than for learning' (Whitton, 2010, p. 199). These games are first released in Japanese- or English-language versions, and bilingual Chinese versions

	are often released at a much later date, if at all. In these regions, English is taught as a compulsory subject in schools,
relevance of study	while Japanese is popular as a language for informal learning, but not widely taught in schools. Chinese-speaking East Asia, then, presents an interesting context to study digital gaming and second language (L2) learning because gamers frequently use an L2 to play digital games outside the classroom. While gamers are playing L2 games, many are also using L2 gameplay for L2 learning. Some are playing and learning autonomously, while some are seeking support
reference	from communities (Chik, 2012). This paper seeks to
research question	understand the ways gamers practice autonomy within community by managing their gameplay both as leisure and as learning practices in different dimensions (location, formality, locus of control, formality, and trajectory).

[2] Chik begins with a broad focus (background on COTS games and language learning in China) and then narrows the focus as she introduces the research question.
[3] Likely topics the author will discuss include: learner communities; learner autonomy; digital games; learning practices. Variations on this are possible.
[4] The answers depend on the Introduction read.

7.2

[1a] Lee organizes this section of the Literature Review around different theoretical approaches.
[1b] Lee uses mostly parenthetical citations. The three exceptions to this are 'Lee [2009b] . . . demonstrated . . .', 'Carney (2007) argues . . .' and 'Byram's (1997) ICC model . . . appears . . .'.
[2a] Chen took a chronological approach to the organization of this section of the Literature Review.
[2b] Chen uses two reporting verbs ('found' and 'pointed out') and one reference to a study ('the earliest study on . . . by Hartford and Bardovi-Harlig (1996)').
[3] Chen establishes the uniqueness of her study across multiple sentences beginning from 'However, there are several limitations in these studies'.

7.3

[1a] Paragraph 1 introduces the case study approach; Paragraph 2 explains the selection of participants; Paragraph 3 explains the role of participant-researchers in this study.
[1b] Hong Kong.
[1c] Data were compiled through language learning histories (LLHs), a focus-group discussion, blogs, recorded live gaming sessions, stimulated recall sessions, and archived collections of discussion threads.

[1d] The participants were ten Year 1 Chinese-speaking undergraduates at an English-medium Hong Kong university.
[1e] This information appears in the second paragraph. Chik sent out a call to all Year 1 students. She interviewed 50 gamers who used games for L2 learning. Of these, she selected the ten most articulate students who were regular gamers.
[1f] None is mentioned.
[1g] The passive voice is used in the second paragraph as we can assume that Chik is the subject. The activities detailed in the third paragraph were undertaken by the participant-researchers and the active voice allows their identity to be mentioned explicitly, thereby clearly delineating their contribution.
[1h] This does not appear in the text. We can assume it is because this type of data collection is more effectively and efficiently undertaken by people with an intimate knowledge of the gaming scene. Also, a Year 1 student may provide richer responses when interviewed by a peer than by a university professor and non-gamer (the author).
[2] Various answers are possible here. The objective of this task is to focus attention on the fairly formulaic language used to describe procedures, and the predictable use of the passive voice and the simple past tense.

7.4

Different answers are possible.

7.5

	It depends on the class. If the teacher takes attendance
Reason	then maybe I attend more classes. But if he doesn't then
Reason	sometimes I don't go. It depends on whether I like the
	class. Sometimes I am too tired to go to classes all day, so
Alternative activity	I go to one and then I go back to the hostel. I don't think
	you have to attend all the classes to pass the course. Even
	I know some students who always attend and then they
Reason	failed the course. I guess I attend more classes if my friend
	is in the same course because then it isn't so boring for
Peer influence	me. But sometimes my friend tells me let's not go, and
	then we both don't go to class. Also, sometimes I don't
Reason	understand what the teacher's talking about in the class so
	I don't want to go. (ST05)

7.6

[1] Example A simply relays the same information that is displayed on the graph. Example B succeeds in in synthesizing the main findings. It also indicates where results are not clear. This paragraph is more effective.

7.7

The suggested answers are not exhaustive. The text contains additional examples of most items.
[a] 'This study confirms that the consumption and production of paratexts was common within the online Chinese gaming communities.'
[b] 'L2 gamers learned an L2 from gaming through textual and social interaction in community . . .'
[c] 'Gee and Hayes (2011) found that gamers also transferred literacy and life skills learned from gaming to their formal learning . . .'
[d] 'This may help explain how Swedish gamers . . .'
[e] 'by situating L2 gaming in the East Asian social and economic contexts . . .'
[f] 'it was not quite clear what could be learned beyond L2 vocabulary.'
[g] 'this personal preference is an underexplored area in gaming study.'

7.8

[1a] The study explores 'how gamers practice autonomy within community by managing their gameplay both as leisure and learning practices in five dimensions: location, formality, pedagogy, locus of control, and trajectory'.
[1b] The main findings mentioned here are: 'autonomy as one of the keys to facilitate L2 learning through L2 gaming'; and 'affordances are not only limited to in-game interactions with game texts and with other gamers. The extended online gaming communities provide support in both L1 and L2 through paratexts and language learning advice.'
[1c] The second paragraph contains a number of clearly labelled implications.
[1d] Limitations are outlined in the first paragraph. It was a small-scale study, participants already had a high level of L2 proficiency, games in their L1 were not available during their youth, and the participants were self-selected and therefore were not necessarily representative of the gaming population.
[2] Different answers are possible.
[3] Different answers are possible.

Chapter 8

8.1

[1a] Q; [1b] Q; [1c] P; [1d] S; [1e] Q; [1f] P, S; [1g] S, Q, P; [1h] None; [1i] All of them; [1j] None; [1k] Quotes always include the page number. A paraphrase may include the page number if the author considers it important to provide the exact place where the idea was originally expressed. This might be particularly so when paraphrasing a very specific idea or when including specific facts (e.g., numerical data) in the paraphrase that you borrowed from the author's work. This helps the reader locate the original idea if he/she decides to consult the source text. [1l] S, P (usually, although the writer may choose to give the page number in a paraphrase for the aforementioned reason); [1m] Quotes typically use reporting verbs, but you may also include one in paraphrases or summaries.

[2] Answers will vary. Typically quotes, summaries and paraphrases are used for all these functions. Although [i] would be inappropriate, inexperienced writers in particular often make this mistake.
[3a] P or S; [3b] Q; [3c] Q (this is not really an appropriate use of a quote, although novice writers in particular may use quotes for this reason); [3d] Q; [3e] Q; [3f] P, S; [3g] S.

8.2

[1] Preferences will likely differ. Note that only [a] and [c] paraphrase the final part of the sentence ('either in physical proximity or in virtual gameworlds').
[2] Preferences will likely differ. Note that only [b] and [c] include the idea of 'intentional learning' from the source text; [a] and [d] only mention incidental learning or learning opportunities.

8.3

Paragraph 1: Different answers are possible. One suggestion: 'Recent research findings have revealed that the reading and production of written texts related to games provides L2 learning opportunities.'
Paragraph 2: Different answers are possible. One suggestion: 'Such texts provide evidence of the gamers' inventiveness and linguistic resourcefulness in their L2, when communicating with their online gaming peers.'

8.4

Answers will vary for these three questions.

8.5

Incorrect: 'Tongue, Moon & Brumfit (1991): "Games are activities that children naturally and universally engage in."' *Correction*: Do not use the symbol '&' in your text; this only occurs in parenthetical citations. The page number is needed. A comma would be used after the authors' names in place of a colon if the quotation begins with a lower case letter (e.g. 'Tongue, Moon and Brumfit (1991), "[g]ames . . .)
Incorrect: 'Bedson, et al.' *Correction*: Delete the comma after 'Bedson'. The year of publication is needed after the author's name, not at the end of the quotation.
Incorrect: 'According to Bedson, et al. say . . .' *Correction*: Delete the comma after 'Bedson'. The year of publication is needed. Do not use a reporting verb together with 'according to'.
Incorrect: 'For Hadfield (1999), there are two kinds of games. "The first kind . . .' *Correction*: A colon is needed rather than a full stop after 'games'. The closing quotation mark is missing. It is unclear where the quotation ends. If the quotation includes the two sentences, the student should consider paraphrasing the idea. This quotation is very long and the exact phrasing of the idea does not appear to

be significant. If a quotation longer than 40 words is needed, it should appear separate from the main text, as an indented block quote on a new line. Finally, the page number is needed.
Incorrect: '. . . student's learning experience will be heightened". (Kiryk 2010)'
Correction: The full stop should be placed after the author citation, not before. The page number is needed.

8.6

Different answers are possible here.

8.7

[1]–[3] Incorporating information from another author's work without citing the source is plagiarism.
[4] It should be clear from your author citation exactly what information is borrowed from the source you have cited. In this example, Zareen has only signalled part of the borrowed text was taken from this source. If the initial part of the text constitutes an idea or a particular formulation that can be attributed to the author she consulted, it needs to be cited. Not doing so constitutes plagiarism.
[5] This is a quotation but Zakia did not insert quotation marks or a page number. Incorrect referencing of one's sources constitutes plagiarism.
[6] Incorporating information from another author's work without citing the source is plagiarism.
[7] Although this is not an original idea that Zeina has paraphrased, she should still cite the work in which the idea was discussed. If her paraphrase is close to the original, she should definitely cite the source.

8.8

Example 1: Plagiarism. The text is a mixture of paraphrasing and copying. There is no attempt to use correct referencing conventions.
Example 2: Plagiarism. The text is a mixture of paraphrasing and copying. There is no attempt to use correct referencing conventions.
Example 3: Plagiarism. All three paraphrased sentences originate from Chen. This is not clear from the author citation. Only the surname is required. The year of publication is missing.
Example 4: Do not include the title of the author's work in your text. The reader can find it in your List of References. Only the surname is required. The year of publication is missing.
Example 5: This example includes information attributed to Chen that does not appear in the original text. The paragraph from Chen does not discuss students' experience of writing formal texts in English.
Example 6: This is an appropriate paraphrase with correct use of referencing.

8.9

Suggested answers:
Terminology: 'commercial off-the-shelf games', 'digital gaming', 'second language (L2) learning', 'gameplay', 'location', 'formality', 'locus of control', 'trajectory'.
Formal academic words: 'presents', 'autonomously', 'seeking support', 'dimensions'.

8.10

The following are the original sentences in Lee (2011, p. 91). Alternative answers will also be appropriate.
[1] 'The project involved the students from the U.S. who participated in two study abroad programs at the University of Granada in Spain.'
[2] 'To provide students with increased opportunities to explore the target culture and interact with L1s outside of class, the researchers worked closely to design the project for intercultural learning.'
[3] 'The project consisted of three major blog tasks outlined in the syllabus, which were worth 60% of the course work.'
[4] 'Blog technology was used to foster critical reflection on cross-cultural issues, whereas FTF interviews offered real-time intercultural dialogue with L1s.'

8.11

Different answers are possible in addition to the original text provided.

8.12

As some examples may serve more than one function, alternative answers may be possible in some cases.
[1] Help organize the text: 6, 10, 13, 20.
[2] Explain experimental procedure: 4.
[3] Personalize claims: 1, 2, 8, 14, 19.
[4] Show the writer's familiarity with the field through self-citation: 7.
[5] Underscore the importance of the writer's work through self-promotion: 7.
[6] Introduce the research question(s): 9, 11, 15, 18.
[7] Make public acknowledgements: 3, 5.
[8] Clarify the use of terminology: 12, 16, 17.

8.13

[1] a; [2] b, d; [3] b, d; [4] k, f, i (or) e.
Suggested answers for the paragraph in Exercise 8.9: [1] a; [2] c, f; [3] d/b; [4] d/j; [5] b, f; [6] e; [7] m; [8] d, f; [9] e, f; [10] i; [11] l, f.

8.14

The letters refer to the examples in Example 8.1.
[1] Gives a general description of the phenomenon: A, D, E, F, G.
[2] Gives a more general term for the phenomenon: B, F.
[3] Describes what the phenomenon does or what we use it for: C, F, G.
[4] Gives examples of what the phenomenon is: B, C, D, H.
[5] Gives examples of what the phenomenon is not (usually the antonym): (no example).
[6] Explains why the phenomenon occurs: (no example).
[7] Identifies or categorizes sub-types of the phenomenon: C, H.
[8] Gives a reason for the name: (no example).
[9] Differentiates this phenomenon from another related phenomenon: C, H.

8.15

Answers to these two questions will vary.

8.16

[1] 'such as'; [2] '(wikis, blogs, podcastings), for example'; [3] 'such as'; [4] 'such as'; [5] 'For example'; [6] 'illustrate'; [7] 'such as'; [8] 'The following is an example of'; [9] 'including'; [10] 'see, for example'; [11] 'illustrates'; [12] 'such as'; [13] 'e.g.'; [14] 'for example'.

8.17

Answers to these two questions will vary.

8.18

Answers to these two questions will vary.

Chapter 9

9.1

[1] Instructors usually have a number of students under their supervision at any one time, in addition to other academic duties. It is the student's responsibility to remain in fairly regular contact and to undertake any work by the deadlines agreed upon.
[2] Answers to this question will vary.

9.2

Different answers are possible.

Appendix 5

A5.1

[1] Examples (a) and (b) are journal articles.
[2] Example (b) has two authors.
[3] Examples (c) and (g) are books.
[4] Example (d) is a chapter in a book.
[5] The place should appear before the name of the publishing company.
[6] The website doesn't usually have a year of publication or place of publication. The date the site was accessed is often required, however. Instead of an author, the name of the institution or, if none is given, the title of the website appears. Provide the full URL of the website in your list of references.
[7] Always put your references in alphabetical order. In this case: g, d, b, f, a, e, c.

References

Biber, D. & Gray, B. (2010). Challenging stereotypes about academic writing: Complexity, elaboration, explicitness. *Journal of English for Academic Purposes*, 9, 2–20.

Biber, D. & Gray, B. (2011). Grammatical change in the noun phrase: The influence of written language use. *English Language and Linguistics*, *15*(2), 223–50.

Biber, D., Johansson, S., Leech, G., Conrad, S. & Finegan, E. (1999). *Longman grammar of spoken and written English.* Harlow: Pearson Education.

Biesenbach-Lucas, S. (2007). Students writing emails to faculty: An examination of e-politeness among native and non-native speakers of English. *Language Learning and Technology*, *11*(2), 59–81.

Bolton, K., Nelson, G. & Hung, J. (2002). A corpus-based study of connectors in student writing: Research from the International Corpus of English in Hong Kong (ICE-HK). *International Journal of Corpus Linguistics*, *7*(2), 165–82.

Bowles, M.A. (2010). *The think-aloud controversy in second language research.* New York: Routledge.

Bunton, D. (2002). Generic moves in Ph.D. thesis introductions. In J. Flowerdew (Ed.), *Academic discourse* (pp. 57–75). London: Longman.

Carter, S. (2012). English as an additional language (EAL) viva voce: The EAL doctoral oral examination experience. *Assessment & Evaluation in Higher Education*, *37*(3), 273–84.

Charles, M. (2011). Adverbials of result: Phraseology and functions in the problem–solution pattern. *Journal of English for Academic Purposes*, *10*, 47–60.

Chen, C.E. (2006). The development of e-mail literacy: From writing to peers to writing to authority figures. *Language Learning & Technology*, *10*(2), 35–55.

Chik, A. (2014). Digital gaming and language learning: Autonomy and community. *Language Learning & Technology*, *18*(2), 85–100.

Cortes, V. (2013). *The purpose of this study is to*: Connecting lexical bundles and moves in research article introductions. *Journal of English for Academic Purposes*, *12*, 33–43.

Davies, M. (2008–). *Corpus of Contemporary American English: 450 million words, 1990–present.* Available online at http://corpus.byu.edu/coca/. Accessed on 3 February 2014.

Economidou-Kogetsidis, M. (2011). 'Please answer me as soon as possible': Pragmatic failure in non-native speakers' e-mail requests to faculty. *Journal of Pragmatics*, *43*(13), 3193–215.

Fakhri, A. (2004). Rhetorical properties of Arabic research article introductions. *Journal of Pragmatics*, *36*(4), 1119–38.

Gu, Y. (2014). To code or not to code: Dilemmas in analysing think-aloud protocols in learning strategies research. *System*, *43*, 74–81.

Harwood, N. (2005a). What do we want EAP teaching materials for? *Journal of English for Academic Purposes*, *4*(2), 149–61.

Harwood, N. (2005b). 'Nowhere has anyone attempted . . . In this article I aim to do just that': A corpus-based study of self-promotional I and we in academic writing across four disciplines. *Journal of Pragmatics*, *37*(8), 1207–31.

Harwood, N. (2009). An interview-based study of the functions of citations in academic writing across two disciplines. *Journal of Pragmatics*, *41*(3), 497–518.

Howard, R.M. (1995). Plagiarisms, authorships, and the academic death penalty. *College English*, *57*(7), 788–805.

Hyland, K. (1998). Boosting, hedging and the negotiation of academic knowledge. *TEXT*, *18*(3), 349–82.

Hyland, K. (2000). Hedges, boosters and lexical invisibility: Noticing modifiers in academic texts. *Language Awareness*, 9(4), 179–97.

Hyland, K. (2002a). Options of identity in academic writing. *ELT Journal*, *56*(4), 351–8.

Hyland, K. (2002b). Authority and invisibility: Authorial identity in academic writing. *Journal of Pragmatics*, *34*(8), 1091–112.

Kaktiņš, L. (2014). Appraising plagiarism policies of Australian universities. *Text & Talk*, *34*(2), 117–41.

Koro-Ljungberg, M., Douglas, E., McNeill, N., Therriault, D. & Malcolm, Z. (2012). Reconceptualising and de-centering think-aloud methodology in qualitative research. *Qualitative Research*, *13*(6), 735–53.

Kwan, B.S.C. (2008). The nexus of reading, writing and researching in the doctoral undertaking of humanities and social sciences: Implications for literature reviewing. *English for Specific Purposes*, *27*(1), 42–56.

Kwan, B.S.C. (2009). Reading in preparation for writing a PhD thesis: Case studies of experiences. *Journal of English for Academic Purposes*, 8(3), 180–91.

Lee, L. (2011). Blogging: Promoting learner autonomy and intercultural competence through study abroad. *Language Learning & Technology*, *15*(3), 87–109.

Loi, C.K. (2010). Research article introductions in Chinese and English: A comparative genre-based study. *Journal of English for Academic Purposes*, 9(4), 267–79.

Mohamed-Sayidina, A. (2010). Transfer of L1 cohesive devices and transition words into L2 academic texts: The case of Arab students. *RELC Journal*, *41*(3), 253–66.

Morley, J. (n.d.). *Academic Phrasebank*. The University of Manchester. Available online at www.phrasebank.manchester.ac.uk/. Accessed on 10 January 2014.

Park, C. (2003). Levelling the playing field: Towards best practice in the doctoral viva. *Higher Education Review*, *36*(1), 47–67.

Parkinson, J. & Musgrave, J. (2014). Development of noun phrase complexity in the writing of English for Academic Purposes students. *Journal of English for Academic Purposes*, *14*, 48–59.

Peacock, M. (2011). The structure of the methods section in research articles across eight disciplines. *The Asian ESP Journal*, *7*(2), 97–124.

Pecorari, D. (2003). Good and original: Plagiarism and patchwriting in academic second-language writing. *Journal of Second Language Writing*, *12*(4), 317–45.

Pecorari, D. & Petrić, B. (2014). Plagiarism in second-language writing. *Language Teaching*, *47*(3), 269–302.

Petrić, B. (2007). Rhetorical functions of citations in high- and low-rated Master's theses. *Journal of English for Academic Purposes*, 6(3), 238–53.

Richards, K. (2003). *Qualitative inquiry in TESOL*. Basingstoke: Palgrave Macmillan.

Roulston, K. (2011). Interview 'problems' as topics for analysis. *Applied Linguistics*, *32*(1), 77–94.

Ruiying, Y. & Allison, D. (2003). Research articles in applied linguistics: Moving from results to conclusions. *English for Specific Purposes*, *22*(4), 365–85.

Soler-Monreal, C., Carbonell-Olivares, M. & Gil-Salom, L. (2011). A contrastive study of the rhetorical organisation of English and Spanish PhD thesis introductions. *English for Specific Purposes*, *30*(1), 4–17.

Stephens, K.K., Houser, M.L. & Cowan, R.L. (2009). R U able to meat me?: The impact of students' overly casual email messages to instructors. *Communication Education*, 58(3), 303–26.

Swales, J.M. [1981] (2011). *Aspects of article introductions*. Michigan Classics Edition. Ann Arbour, MI: University of Michigan Press.

Swales, J.M. (1990). *Genre analysis: English in academic and research settings*. Cambridge: Cambridge University Press.

Wellington, J. (2010). Supporting students' preparation for the viva: Their pre-conceptions and the implications for practice. *Teaching in Higher Education*, *15*(1), 71–84.

Yeo, S. & Chien, R. (2007). Evaluation of a process and proforma for making consistent decisions about the seriousness of plagiarism incidents. *Quality in Higher Education*, *13*(2), 187–204.

Index